THE STORY OF THE WAR IN LA VENDÉE
and
THE LITTLE CHOUANNERIE

THE ABBE BERNIER BLESSES THE ARMS OF THE VENDEANS.

THE STORY
of
THE WAR IN LA VENDÉE
and
THE LITTLE CHOUANNERIE

By
GEORGE J. HILL, M.A.

[The march of the Peasants on Laval.]

ST AIDAN PRESS, LLC
Morning View, Kentucky

The Story of the War in La Vendée and the Little Chouannerie.

First published in 1856 by Burns and Lambert, of London, and D. & J. Sadlier & Co., of New York, Boston and Montreal.

Typesetting, layout and cover design copyright 2023 St. Aidan Press, LLC.

Cover image is *Henri de la Rochejaquelein au combat de Cholet*, painted in 1899 by Paul Emile Boutigny and now in the Musée d'Art et d'Histoire, Cholet, France.

All rights reserved.

ISBN-13: 978-1-962503-01-3
ISBN-10: 1-962503-01-1

For more information, contact:
www.staidanpress.com
staidanpress@gmail.com

We have made no intentional change from the original text except to correct mistakes in spelling and punctuation.

Preface

IT IS COMMONLY ARGUED by writers on the French Revolution that the state of the Church, as well as of the nation in general, must have been exceedingly corrupt, and that both clergy and people were equally destitute of religious belief and of moral principle, or so total a disruption of all the bonds of society could never have taken place, attended as it was with circumstances of unprecedented confusion and horror; and they point to the fact of priests and religious, and even bishops, openly apostatising from Christianity, and abandoning themselves to all the infamous license of the times, and the atrocious crimes perpetrated by a people so lately, in profession at least, Catholic.

That society was radically and irretrievably corrupt, especially in high places, and that many of the clergy, and in particular those about the court, were deeply infected with the taint of infidelity, is unhappily too true. But such writers seem utterly to overlook a fact equally patent and remarkable, that hundreds of ecclesiastics not merely retained and avowed their religious belief, in spite of persecution and contempt, but *shed their blood* for the faith; enduring the grossest insults and the most agonising torments, not only with meekness and resignation, but with a touching piety, and a sweet and tender charity towards their murderers, such as make their constancy and fortitude differ in kind from any thing which mere natural heroism, however exalted, has at any time exhibited; while thousands risked their lives and abandoned all things for conscience sake. If a few traitors and apostates—for few they were in comparison with those who stood firm in the hour of trial, and nobly suffered all that a diabolical malice could inflict, rather than abate one tittle of their obedience to the Divine law;—if this wretched minority are to be taken as a proof of the inroads that vice and infidelity had made upon the Church of France, how triumphant is the demonstration afforded by her numerous martyrs and confessors that she was yet sound and pure at heart!

And as respects the people at large: "To judge of a whole nation," says Mr. Belaney in his *Massacre at the Carmes*, "by the conduct or manners of its populace in its capital and larger cities in times of great excitement, would lead to as false and unjust, as well as ungenerous conclusions, in respect to that nation, as it would to judge of an individual only by what he did when under the effects of *delirium tremens* or intoxication." "The populace," as he elsewhere observes, "required to be deceived, as well as bribed, into the commission of acts which cause us to shudder when we look back on them, even at a distance of sixty years." An execrable faction, devoid of every principle of morality and every feeling of humanity, had usurped the power of the state; and while overawing the better portion of the nation by wholesale proscription and slaughter, drove the masses of the people to enact, in a frenzy of terror and fury, excesses which, left to themselves and in their sober senses, they would never have had the heart to perpetrate. That under the seething surface of vice and impiety which covered the land, there lay hid all the while, even in the worst days of the Revolution, fathomless depths of sanctity and devotion beyond the ken of the godless world, the annals of the times sufficiently testify; and that, even when the nation had passed through its fiery conflict, and a generation to whom religion was an effete superstition, and priests but tyrants and impostors, appeared upon the scene, there still remained, not only among the country populations, but among the inhabitants of the towns, a vast amount of supernatural belief, which waited only for an occasion to manifest itself, one circumstance alone would prove:—the demonstrations, not of sympathy and affection merely, but of religious veneration, with which Pius VII. was every where received on his entrance into France, a prisoner, in the year 1809; multitudes crowding round the carriage in which he was seated, and begging his benediction on their knees as he passed along.

But if the clergy of France contributed its noble army of martyrs at Paris, Lyons, Nantes, her peasantry of Brittany and La Vendée sent forth an heroic band of veritable soldiers of the cross, as admirable and as worthy of being held in everlasting honour as their enemies are deserving of the universal reprobation of mankind. Brave, generous, honourable, merciful, and pure—in the heat of the fight resolute and undaunted as veteran soldiers, and in the hour of victory as tender-hearted as children—what a contrast do these "brigands," as their opponents called them, present to the self-styled "patriots" of the republican forces! Sensual, treacherous, bloodthirsty, breathing only hatred and revenge, exhibiting a cruelty and a ferocity truly satanic, their delight seemed to be only in massacre and rapine, and in the commission of the most hideous crimes. Catholic France may well be proud of her heroes of La Vendée. What but simple, supernatural faith could have produced such an army of patriot crusaders, and inspired a system of warfare so truly Christian!

For it is not possible to separate the religion and devotion of the Vendean peasants from their natural virtues and martial qualities. As they fought primarily for their Church, and only secondarily and, as it may be said, accidentally, for their king, so first and before all things they were Catholics:—to their heart's core they were what the pseudo-philosophers of the day would call "superstitious and bigoted;" as much so as the priests who walked calmly forward to meet their assassins with their breviaries in their hands, and the names of Jesus and Mary on their lips. These men, so intrepid, so cool and yet so daring, so generous and so noble-minded, recited their rosaries on their way to the battle-field, and threw themselves on their knees before the image of the Crucified as they charged down upon the bayonets of the foe. Abstract from the Vendean his faith, and he is no longer the same man: that faith not only inspired his actions, it made him what he was.

As to the conduct and results of the war, it is unnecessary to anticipate here remarks that are made in the course of the narrative. In spite of some signal and palpable blunders, no candid mind, which considers the disadvantages under which they laboured, will withhold from both generals and subordinates a very high meed of praise, not only for their courage, which was undoubted, but for their strategic skill and address. Unhappily, as the contest proceeded, and their first chosen leaders perished in battle, serious evils began to show themselves; fatal jealousies were engendered, dissensions broke out amongst the new commanders, cruelties were perpetrated which rivalled in barbarity the enormities by which they were provoked, unjustifiable severities were adopted even against members of their own body, and the whole *morale* of the army notably degenerated. Such were but the inevitable consequences of long-continued warfare, and that of so embittered a character, the subversion of all established order, and the absence of any legitimate head. And yet to the end sufficient of the old spirit remained to excite the fears and even to elicit the admiration of their foes. Despite the terrible reverses encountered in the field, and the general disorganisation which ensued, their bravery and tenacity had made themselves so effectually felt, that the Vendean insurgents succeeded finally in obtaining an honourable peace. But their greatest glory consisted in the fact, that the Catholic religion never ceased to be openly professed in La Vendée; nor did they consent to lay down their arms until liberty of worship was guaranteed to them, and their priests were recognised and protected by the laws.

Hence the moral effects of this war it is hardly possible to overrate. Not only did it prove that France never could be one and indivisible, never could be at peace with herself till religion was re-established; not only did the valour and enthusiasm which were evoked insure respect to the religion which was able to produce such sensible effects,—but the multitudes whom terror had silenced and isolated, the weak, the timid, the despondent, and even they in whom the light of faith was well-nigh quenched, felt the influence of a struggle in which they took no part; it awoke and sustained a secret sympathy in their breasts, and kept them in a state of continual readiness to welcome back, even with acclamations, the religion for which they had neither the courage nor the will to suffer or to contend.

What, therefore, may not the France of this day owe to La Vendée? How much of the religious revival which now fills Catholic Christendom with admiration and joy may be due to that contest, so obstinately and so fruitlessly maintained, as some may think, in that little corner of the West? And this in two ways: first, as has been intimated, by keeping the lamps burning in her sanctuaries when elsewhere they had been extinguished and the very altars themselves overthrown, and leaving them as beacons to announce to all failing and faltering hearts that an Incarnate God still had worshippers, and Peter loyal subjects, among a rebellious and apostate people; and secondly, and principally, by willingly offering that sacrifice which God never fails to accept and to requite—the sacrifice of the heart's-blood of the best and purest of her children. That blood, like the blood of the martyr-priests, has never ceased to cry out, not for vengeance, but for mercy and for blessings—the richest and the choicest, because spiritual and heavenly—on the land that poured it out as though it had been the blood of brute cattle that die unpitied in the shambles, or rather of the wild beasts of the forest whom it was a necessity to exterminate. Certain it is that nowhere has religion, so trodden down and all but exterminated as it was, had so speedy and so astonishing a resurrection as in once infidel France; and to what can this be more probably attributed, than to that spirit of immolation which animated alike the priests of the Carmes and the peasants of La Vendée? If the butcheries of Tyburn are one day to yield, as we may piously hope, a fruitful harvest of souls to the Church in our land, what might England long ere this have become, had more of her sons bled and died with the gallant Nortons around the banner of the Five Precious Wounds, and the gibbets stood tenfold thicker between Newcastle and Wetherby?

The strength and reality of the principles for which La Vendée contended, and the ardour with which the flame there enkindled burned on despite the indifference and secularity which weighed upon the land, may be estimated by the enthusiasm excited in the breasts of the young students of Vannes, and the bravery and fortitude displayed in their defence. Singular phenomenon! that some hundreds of boys should turn soldiers in sober earnest, all because the great emperor bullied the Pope, changed their Catechism, and gave them Charlemagne for their patron instead of St. Catharine and St. Nicholas; but no ambiguous omen of bright and glorious days to France, that, in what with many would have passed for a mere piece of state-policy, with which they had no concern, these school-boys and seminarists should feel to the quick that a great principle was at stake, for which they were bound, as with all their hearts they were willing, to fight and to die.

The scholars of Vannes—as many as survive—have now passed the prime of their life; but during the forty years that have gone by, what services have they not rendered, by their labours, their writings, their courageous examples, to the Church, to literature, to society! And whence had they derived their first inspirations, but from those annals of the old Chouannerie which as boys it was their delight to collect, and from those bearded men, with their bronzed countenances and thoughtful brows, who had returned to renew the studies of their youth, only that they might complete, as ministers of peace, at the altar the warfare they had begun on the battle-field? True patriots, whose *patria* is not of this world;

though accidentally and from circumstances associated with monarchy, their Catholicism was subservient to no form of government, albeit respectful and friendly to all; upholding obedience to constituted authority as the ordinance of God, it looked, above all things, to maintaining intact the liberties of the Church and the independence of the spiritual power. To such men and such principles France owes every thing; and on France at this moment hang the destinies of the world.

The story of La Vendée and of the Little Chouannerie is gathered from the various extant sources; but in the case of the latter, which is drawn principally from M. Rio's own narrative, an endeavour has been made to assign to that gentleman the position which rightfully belonged to him, but which his modesty and humility prevented him from assuming.

The reader will find a most striking description of the old "Chouans" and the "Little Vendée" among M. Souvestre's *Tales and Sketches of Brittany and La Vendée*, published in Constable's *Miscellany of Foreign Literature*. The incidents, which were taken by the author from the mouth of one of Jean's brothers-in-arms, are related in a style as graphic and touching as it is simple and unadorned.

The conflict in La Vendée had its counterpart in Flanders. M. Hendrik Conscience, in his spirited historical tale of *Veva*, has described with much dramatic power the sufferings of the people, and their determined, but disastrous, and, as it turned out, fatally ineffectual resistance to the revolutionary forces, and (in the worst sense) revolutionary principles of France. The work in question has just been translated into English. Although fictitious in form, it adheres faithfully to the facts of history: the notes to the original Flemish show, by extracts from the accounts, proclamations, &c., which appeared in the Antwerp newspapers of the time, that the

Preface

gatherings, skirmishes, and principal events therein depicted, down to the great battle with which the story closes, actually occurred as represented. A few resolute and courageous men, while the masses of their countrymen "looked on in dumb terror" at the destruction of all they held dear and venerable, kept up a continual harassing warfare against the invader, until they were either individually taken and shot, or mowed down in hundreds by the musketry, or hewed and hacked to pieces by the merciless sabres of the French soldiery. But though crushed, and to all outward seeming annihilated, that insurrection against the most intolerable of all despotisms, the tyranny of an impious liberalism, and in defence of altar and hearth, faith and liberty, had, as in La Vendée, a most powerful moral effect at the time, and exerted doubtless, both in the natural and in the supernatural order, influences the operation of which we have still before our eyes. For we may well consider the present prosperous condition of Belgium, the freedom, both political and religious, which she enjoys, and the simple piety of her people, to be at once the result and the reward of the spirit displayed, and the sufferings endured, in that truly patriotic struggle.

E. H. T.

Contents

La Vendée

CHAPTER   PAGE

I. State of popular feeling in the west at the commencement of the French Revolution—Indignation at the oath imposed on the clergy—Outbreaks in various parts of Brittany, Anjou, and La Vendée—Carnage at Bressuire—Lull before the storm 1

II. Levy ordered by the Convention—Commencement of the insurrection—Jacques Cathelineau, Castle of Jallais, Chemillé, Forêt at Chanzeau—Stofflet—Chollet, Vihiers, Marie Jeanne—Bonchamps—D'Elbée—Bas Poitou, Massacres at Machecoul under Souchu—Charette—Joly, unsuccessful attack on Sables d'Olonne—Brittany—Check at Nantes—Advice of Canclaux to the Convention, and pacification of Brittany 7

III. Boundaries of La Vendée—The plain—The marais—The bocage—Telegraphic system of the insurgents—Their tactics—Organisation—The women; anecdote of Jeanne Robin—The priests—Universality of the insurrectional spirit—Alleged cruelty of the peasants—Charge of forged miracles 22

IV. Renewal of hostilities—Defeat of the Blues at Chemillé—Henri de Larochejacquelein—Henri beats Quetineau at Aubiers, who retires on Thouars—Lescure—Siege of Thouars—Gallantry of Lescure—Forbearance of the besiegers—*Soi-disant* Bishop of Agra—Success at Châtaigneraie—Defeat at Fontenay; siege and capture of that town. 35

V. Supreme council of administration: the Abbé Bernier, Father Jagault, Abbé Brin—Proclamation of the Catholic army—Fresh exertions of the Convention—Victories of Vihiers, Doué, and Montreuil—Siege of Saumur—Quetineau—Cathelineau elected commander-in-chief—Forestier—D'Autichamp, Piron, Talmont—The army march into Angers, and determine to lay siege to Nantes 47

VI. Successes of Charette in Bas Poitou—Union of Charette with Cathelineau—Siege of Nantes—Death of Cathelineau—Westermann in the Bocage, his defeat at Châtillon—D'Elbée elected commander-in-chief—Reverses at Pont Charron and Luçon—Victory over Santerre at Chantonnay—Horrible designs of the republicans—Poisonings *en masse*—Mission from the English Government 59

VII. The army of Mayence in Bas Poitou—Erigny, Doué, Thouars—Rout of Santerre at Coron—Duhoux beats his uncle at Barré Bridge—Victory over the Mayence army at Torfou—Beysser surprised at Montaigu—Charette routs Mieskowski at St. Fulgent—Repulse of Bonchamps—Dissensions of the Vendean chiefs—Disgrace of the republican generals, and appointment of L'Echelle—Overtures of the Mayence men to the Catholic army—Lescure beaten at Moulins—Sack of Châtillon—The republicans concentrate their forces on Chollet—Check at La Tremblaye, where Lescure is wounded—Battle of Chollet—D'Elbée and Bonchamps retreat on St. Florent—Banks of the Loire—Death of Bonchamps 68

VIII. Passage of the Loire—Lechelle reports the defeat of the insurgents and the devastation of La Vendée—Successes at Chateau Gontier and Laval—The Little Vendée—Larochejacquelein chosen commander-in-chief—Victory of Laval—Reverses of the republicans, and new organisation of the Catholic army—Last moments of Lescure—English emissaries—Unsuccessful attack on Granville—Alleged treason of Talmont, Bernier, and others—Imposture of the *soi-disant* Bishop of Agra detected—Return of the Catholic army—Affairs of Pontorson and Dol—Bravery of Talmont and the curé of St. Marie de Rhé—State of the army on the road to Angers 83

IX. Siege of Angers and defeat of the army—Retreat on Baugé—Occupation of Mans—Defeat and massacre of Mans—Larochejacquelein and Stofflet fly before Westermann—Final annihilation of the whole army at Savenay—Atrocities of the republicans—Reflections on the expedition beyond the Loire—Charette's successes in Bas Poitou—Successful stratagem of Joly at Quatre-Chemins—Charette named commander-in-chief—His interview with Larochejacquelein—Recapture of Noirmoutiers—Execution of D'Elbée . . . 99

X. The reign of terror under Carrier at Nantes—The infernal columns . . 119

XI. Death of Henri de Larochejacquelein—Stofflet elected to the chief command of the grand army—Successes of Charette—His guerilla warfare—Death of Haxo—Turreau receives one month to finish the insurrection—Confederation of Charette, Stofflet, and Marigny—Death of Marigny and Joly—Partial cessation of hostilities—Tinténiac appears again in La Vendée—Pacific change in the attitude of the Republic—Renewed successes of Charette—Bernier civil commissary-general—Pacification of La Jaunais—The secret articles—Triumphal entry of Charette into Nantes—Stofflet ratifies the pacification 153

XII. The Chouannerie—History of Jean Chouan—He joins the Vendean army at Laval at the head of the Little Vendée—Tactics of the Chouans—Measures of the Convention—Puisaye's system—His departure for England—Pacification during his absence—Family of Jean Chouan—Jambe d'Argent—M. Jacques—False Chouans—Anecdote of Madame Huneau 173

XIII. Puisaye in England—The royal agency at Paris—Renewal of hostilities in Brittany and in La Vendée—Aide-de-camp of the Count d'Artois in Bas Poitou—Quiberon. 199

XIV. Georges Cadoudal—Puisaye after Quiberon—Frotté in Normandy—Fresh dissensions between Charette and Stofflet—The Count d'Artois at the Ile-Dieu—His vacillation—Dispositions on both sides towards peace—Death of Stofflet—Last combat, capture, trial, and death of Charette—Submission of Brittany in 1796—After three years' dubious peace the Chouannerie breaks forth again—Bonaparte becomes first consul, and treats with Bernier—His vigorous measures, and their success. 215

XV. Intrigues in Paris—Fouché—Moreau—Conspiracy of Pichegru, Moreau, and Cadoudal—Death of Cadoudal—The infernal machine—The Concordat—The Little Church—The Abbé Bernier Bishop of Orleans—Royalism in the west under the Empire—Rejoicings at the Restoration—Ingratitude of the Bourbons—Insurrection in 1815—Crafty conduct of Fouché—Death of Louis de Larochejacquelein—Defeat at La Roche Servière—Pacification after the battle of Waterloo. 232

XVI. Insensibility of the Bourbons to the services of La Vendée—Charles X. appeals again to the loyalty of the West—The Duchess de Berri in La Vendée—Brave conduct of the peasants at the Chateau of Penissière-de-la-Cour—Death of the son of Jacques Cathelineau and of Mademoiselle de Roberie—Departure of the Duchess de Berri—Cause of her failure—The end 246

The Little Chouannerie

I. The College of Vannes 254

II. Insubordination of the scholars—They arm, and join the insurgents. . 263

III. Battles of St. Anne's, Redon, and Muzillac—Debarcation of arms and defeat at Auray—Victory at Plescop 277

IV. Pacification—Triumphant entry into Vannes—The Cross of the Legion of Honour awarded to the most worthy 309

LA VENDÉE

Chapter I

State of popular feeling in the west at the commencement of the French Revolution—Indignation at the oath imposed on the clergy—Outbreaks in various parts of Brittany, Anjou, and La Vendée—Carnage at Bressuire—Lull before the storm.

THE PEASANTRY of the western provinces of France, afterwards so famous for their heroic struggles in defence of their religion, viewed the rise of the revolution with indifference. There was little in the first measures of the reformers to excite their fears or seduce their affections. Neither the Church nor the throne appeared to be in danger, nor had they any interest in the reform of abuses of which they had no experience.

The rising party were then moderate in their proposals. Nothing had occurred to indicate a design to subvert the existing order of things; and with all their loyalty, the peasants were not so conservative as to take alarm at the attempt to set bounds to the royal prerogative. They had preserved more of liberty than the rest of France, which may account for the fact that the recoil from the despotism of the Bourbons was more violent in other provinces. While no direct blow had been aimed at the king or the clergy, they were not averse to the movement. Far-seeing men might and did

Chapter I

prophesy the inevitable effects of that spirit of insubordination and unbelief which was abroad; but the poor inhabitants of La Vendée and Brittany, far away from the theatre of action, went about their daily labour undisturbed by prognostications which they never heard, or heard incredulous. They knew that a great change was going on; but its principles and probable results they did not perceive, and did not care to investigate.

On the other hand, the abuses of society were unknown in that remote region. The arguments, therefore, of the revolutionary party had little weight on their unsophisticated minds. Towards the two classes against which the spirit of the age was directed they had only kindly thoughts. Their priests were poor and devoted; their nobility, scarcely richer than the clergy, were equally attached to the people, who had therefore no desire to reform the manners of the one, or to curtail the privileges of the other. Indeed, so entirely was the bulk of the population on the side of their local superiors, that the question may arise whether hostility to the revolution might not have been expected from that cause alone. But, as has been observed, they had no idea at first of its real character; and the parish-priests and rural nobles were themselves not unwilling to see the overgrown wealth and privileges of their more courtly brethren somewhat diminished; so that any dislike which the peasantry might have conceived towards a change which, so far as themselves were concerned, was uncalled for, was corrected by the sympathy displayed for its objects by the parties personally interested in opposing it.

Upon the whole, therefore, it may be said that the people watched the progress of events with indifference. But this remark does not apply to the more important towns and boroughs of the west; for there the partisans of order were in a minority from the first, and the convocation of the states-general, and every other step in the revolution, were hailed with enthusiasm: these places subsequently became the head-quarters of the republican troops, and the main objects of the insurgents' attacks. Nor does it apply to the Protestants, who, with instinctive sagacity, attached themselves at once to a party which promised to overthrow the Church.

After a time, the gentlemen of the west began to detect the tendency of those measures to which they had at first been favourable. They soon perceived that not the privileges of individuals, but the very existence of the class, the integrity of their order itself was in danger; and various conspiracies were formed in defence of the throne and the aristocracy. These associations were purely political, and failed therefore to obtain the co-operation of the peasants. In consequence, indeed, of the dissatisfaction of their superiors, a growing inquietude spread among the lower orders, but none of them joined the confederated nobles. A decisive blow at their religious rights was needed to rouse the peasants to a general revolt.

And at length the blow came. On the 24th August 1790, the unfortunate Louis XVI. gave his royal assent to the law on the civil constitution of the clergy, by which the Church of France, from being Catholic, was turned into a mere national establishment. By this law, every priest and bishop holding office had to take an oath by which he declared that he derived his jurisdiction from the state. The spark of insurrection was instantly lit in the west, although more than two years passed away before it burst into a flame; during which time a vast conspiracy of the nobles under Rouerie, which greatly alarmed the revolutionary party, rose, flared, and went out, without attracting the sympathies of the people generally. But still that attack on the liberties of the Church laid the foundation of the civil war which for seven years distracted the country. All classes at once protested against the insult which was offered to their religion. As a body, the clergy refused to take the oath; and the municipal authorities gave in their resignation, rather than concur in the deposition of their own priests, or hold intercourse with those appointed by government. Some municipalities declared in writing that the oath sought to be imposed upon the ministers of God

Chapter I

was at once contrary to reason, to faith, and to common sense, and refused to enforce it. Appeals were made to Rome. In many communes persons could not be found to keep the civil records; the service of the national guards was abandoned; government placards and proclamations were openly torn down and defaced; and the very peasants, poor as they were, preferred to keep, and even lose, the produce of their fields, to carrying it for sale into towns where religion was oppressed in the person of its ministers. The intruding priests were in some places openly insulted; in all they were treated with contempt. It is said that the new curé of Echaubroignes was compelled to quit the parish without having even obtained fire to light his tapers. At Plouguerneau the constitutional priest could be installed only by the aid of six hundred men and four pieces of artillery. Every where the attachment of the peasants to their old pastors was so strong, that the churches served by intruders were deserted; while men, women, and children went to hear Mass in any retired spot on the moor, or in any lone hovel which the banished curé could discover for the purpose. And when the government attempted to procure flocks for the new clergy by military force, not a few encounters were the consequence; which elicited sparks of the same bravery which was afterwards to defy the armies of the Republic. Two anecdotes of the kind have been recorded. A labourer of Bas Poitou, armed only with a fork, made an obstinate resistance to a party of gendarmes who attempted to coerce him. "Yield," cried the officer. "First yield me my God," he replied; and instantly fell, pierced with twenty-two wounds. A Breton peasant suffered his hand to be consumed, rather than consent to burn his Catechism. "Well done!" cried his wife; "it is for the good God, and He will reward thee."

These indications of the popular spirit were sufficient to make the revolutionary party perceive the probable results of hasty and intemperate proceedings. Even before the passing of the law on the civil constitution of the clergy, they had instinctively felt that

Indignation at the oath—Outbreaks in various parts

the religious character of the west would put many obstacles in the way of their designs; and as the movement advanced, the more prudent members would have preferred to proceed warily and stealthily along the path of innovation. But the current which they had set flowing was already beyond control; violence and intimidation were the order of the day. So far from adopting conciliatory measures, fresh orders were issued against the nonjuring priests said to be in hiding in the country; and military aid was put in requisition with unrelenting severity, to enforce the penalties incurred by the faithful clergy who were still in possession of their benefices.

It was in Morbihan, a department of Brittany, that the greatest animosity was shown against the Church; and there the peasantry began to meditate an armed opposition, when as yet the Vendeans had conceived only the resolution to suffer martyrdom for their faith. An insurrectional movement broke out on the 7th February 1791, in the parish of Sarzeau, near Vannes. The Bishop of Vannes, although not personally maltreated, had been impeded in the discharge of his episcopal duties; and the peasants assembled in some force in his defence. Twice they were repulsed by the garrison with great loss. Demonstrations less grave as to their consequences, but in themselves as significant, took place at the same moment in various parts of Brittany; and the local partisans of the constitutional worship, exasperated beyond measure at these acts of insubordination, enforced the penal laws with the greater severity. Presently the insurrection spread into La Vendée. Here and there, in Anjou, in Maine and Loire, in Poitou, and elsewhere, risings were reported; and from St. Malo to Luçon the west appeared one great volcano. At length news arrived of the catastrophe of the 10th August, the storming of the Tuileries and imprisonment of the king. Soon afterwards the law of the 16th of the same month was promulgated, ordaining the general deportation of the Catholic priesthood. And now the whole of the west was in commotion: daily encounters took place between the military and the people, with more or less

Chapter I

of bloodshed; and at Bressuire a body of seven thousand men, the largest that had yet assembled, was defeated with terrible carnage. Many prisoners were taken, who were massacred in cold blood. Suddenly the country assumed a peaceful attitude. There ensued a period of repose. The peasants seemed to be insensible to any acts of aggression—the measures of the revolutionists passed without notice. On the 21st September 1792, the Republic was proclaimed; and La Vendée heard it, and gave no sign of opposition. On the 21st January 1793, Louis XVI. ascended the scaffold; and the news was received with the most profound silence. The Republic believed that La Vendée had been terrified into submission; it was, in truth, making ready for battle.

Chapter II

Levy ordered by the Convention—Commencement of the Insurrection—Jacques Cathelineau, Castle of Jallais, Chemillé, Forêt at Chanzeau—Stofflet—Chollet, Vihiers, Marie Jeanne—Bonchamps—D'Elbée—Bas Poitou, Massacres at Machecoul under Souchu—Charette—Joly, unsuccessful attack on Sables d'Olonne—Brittany—Check at Nantes—Advice of Canclaux to the Convention, and pacification of Brittany.

THIS OMINOUS SILENCE was broken by an act of the Convention. The Republic, menaced from within and from without, had need of soldiers. An extraordinary levy of three hundred thousand men was ordered to take place immediately. The authorities were quite aware of the indignation which this decree would excite in the west, but the peasants were supposed to be intimidated. La Vendée and Brittany had just been reported quiet, and the recruiting sergeants were sent into those provinces confident of success.

But they met with universal opposition. A general rising took place over the whole country; although, as each parish acted independently, the several revolts were easily quelled. But at two spots, at some distance from each other, at St. Florent in Anjou, on the banks of the Loire, and at Challons in Bas Poitou, the movement became at once important. From them sprang two great bodies of insurgents, acting at first independently of each other, and achieving separate successes.

At St. Florent a cannon, which had been placed to overawe the district, was fired upon a body of young men, who, under a peasant of the name of Forêt, had assembled, irritated at the attitude of the

Chapter II

enemy, but without any definite intention of attacking the gendarmes. As soon as the cannon was fired, this small party rushed upon the soldiers and put them to flight. It was the 10th March 1793. The insurgents marched into the town, seized the public chest, and distributed its contents, burned the papers of the district, and dispersed, astounded and alarmed at their own exploit. Nevertheless that shot was the commencement of the war.

There dwelt at Pin-en-Manges, a village near St. Florent, a peasant named Jacques Cathelineau, a hawker of woollen goods. To this man five of the insurgents repaired, to inform him of what had taken place. They found him surrounded by his wife and five children, peacefully bruising his corn. He listened with intense emotion; and knowing that the authorities would exact a terrible vengeance for their defeat, he resolved to put himself at the head of his countrymen and oppose force by force.

"The republicans will seize them and put them to death:" that was his first thought. "They must be saved at any cost:" that was his second. And lifting his eyes towards heaven, as if to seek there counsel and assistance, he instantly took his resolution, and quitting his labour reached down his arms.

"What are you going to do?" said his wife.

"Save these young men," he replied.

"But you and your family will be lost. It is not your business; keep out of it."

"We should not the less be lost if I did. The country is going to be crushed to pieces by the Republic. We must rise, and begin the war."

"Begin the war!" cried his wretched wife, now terrified more than ever. "And who will be with you to make war?"

"God," he answered sternly. "God will be with us;" and with these parting words he left the house. He then assembled the villagers, and in a few impassioned words exhorted them to take up arms.

Cathelineau was thirty-five years of age, and known throughout the canton for his generous devotion to his country and his religion. His saintly and austere life, his firm and resolute but most gentle spirit, together with the wisdom of his counsels, which had been long held in great respect, ensured him the concurrence and support of the peasants; and when he appealed to their patriotism, he could count with certainty on their ready obedience. Twenty-six volunteers immediately answered to the summons. At the head of this little troop he advanced to Poitevinière, where he caused the tocsin to be rung; and he had soon more than a hundred men under his orders. With these he marched against the Castle of Jallais, which was defended by a detachment of national guards, a few soldiers, and a six-pounder. The royalists were armed only with clubs, scythes, and a few bad fowling-pieces; but before starting they had all received absolution. Each man carried his rosary, and recited it as he marched; and they went secure of victory, and not afraid to die. As they proceeded recruits poured in; and by the time they reached Jallais, Cathelineau's troop was three thousand strong. Rousseau, who commanded the republicans, fired on the assailants as soon as they appeared; but without effect. They immediately rushed up the height, and after a brief struggle took the castle. This first success supplied the royalists with arms, ammunition, and a piece of artillery, which, in their enthusiasm, they christened the "Missionary." Without pausing, Cathelineau marched on the little town of Chemillé, which was defended by two hundred men and three culverines. In less than half an hour they took it by assault. The news of this second victory spread far and wide, the tocsin rang in every parish, and the little band swelled into an army.

Meanwhile Forêt at Chanzeau had organised another company of insurgents. Known to have been the ringleader in the attack on the gendarmes at St. Florent, a party was sent to apprehend him. He waited quietly for their advance, killed the foremost man, and

THE "MISSIONARY."

fled to the church, where he rang the tocsin and summoned the inhabitants to arms. At Maulevrier a gamekeeper, called Stofflet, assembled another party; and he and Forêt marched on immediately to join Cathelineau.

Stofflet was a man of an utterly different stamp from Cathelineau, although destined to act an equally important part in the insurrection. He shared, in common with all the royalist chiefs, Cathelineau's courage, but he had not the same devoted piety. He was distinguished by his indefatigable activity, and the influence which he exercised over the peasants at times when they were most demoralised. In a rout his presence and voice were sufficient to maintain order; and his corps always surpassed the rest of the army in discipline. His colleagues fully recognised this valuable qualification, and on all occasions when it was requisite to rouse the flagging zeal of the army for any projected expedition, it was to Stofflet that the duty was confided. As an illustration of his prompt and decided character, an incident that occurred one summer during the harvest will suffice. The enemy were near; but his men wished to go and reap their corn. The curé of St. Laud delivered a long sermon to them on the duty of remaining with the army. "There is no need of so many words," cried Stofflet; "now my men," he said addressing the soldiers, "mark me! the service of the king demands your presence. I command you to stay; and I will blow out the brains of the first man who talks of going." It is needless to say that not a man left. In battle Stofflet was impetuous; carried away by his own fury, and insensible to danger, nothing could withstand him; but in the council-chamber he was easily swayed by a more vigorous mind. The Abbé Bernier acquired a complete ascendency over him in the latter part of the war. Cathelineau, on the contrary, was as cool in the field as at the council. "Have you any brandy for our lads?" Stofflet used to ask before going into action. "Let us implore the assistance of the God of armies before fighting," was Cathelineau's more noble precaution against defeat. Such was the

Chapter II

distinction between these two peasants, who rose at the same moment to head their countrymen in the same glorious cause.

By the 14th the Vendean army could boast of four thousand men; and Cathelineau, Forêt, and Stofflet thought themselves strong enough to attack Chollet, the most important town in the district. In half an hour the place was taken, and with it a quantity of ammunition and four pieces of cannon.

The local authorities at length became alive to the danger, and the national guard of Saumur were ordered out to occupy Vihiers. They were attacked on their way and defeated, with the loss of a magnificent bronze eight-pounder, which Louis XIII. had given to Cardinal Richelieu. It was said that the Blues in vain attempted to discharge this gun. The peasants, amazed at its beauty, and thinking that they distinguished on the carriage an image of the Blessed Virgin, looked upon it as their palladium. They gave it the name of Marie Jeanne, after a young girl from Chanzeau, who appeared suddenly during the battle, and continued on her knees during the whole time amid the smoke and flame. Her unexpected presence at such a moment and in such a manner struck the imagination of the peasants. They cried that it was she who had gained for them the victory, and that the beautiful cannon had refused to fire in answer to her prayers. Upon this fresh shouts of admiration rent the air. The young girl was led up to the bronze gun, and enthroned upon it; and the conquering peasants dragged her away in triumph. The news of the victory preceded them, and from all sides the population thronged to see the two Marie Jeannes. The old men uncovered as they passed, the children strewed flowers along the way, as at processions of the Blessed Sacrament, and the women took off their ribbons and tied them round the cannon; even some noble ladies, who were attracted by curiosity, found themselves constrained to do reverence to the miraculous gun. The name of Marie Jeanne is to this day popular in all Vendée. By the victory which was so gained the royalists obtained possession of Vihiers.

Chollet, Vihiers, Marie Jeanne—Bonchamps

As the insurrection gathered strength, it assumed order. Two gentlemen were now compelled to take the command, both of whom afterwards played a conspicuous part in the civil war, although they joined the peasants originally with great reluctance. The Marquis de Bonchamps was thirty-three years of age, and had already exhibited considerable military talent in India; but although a most devoted royalist, he was no advocate for an armed defence of the king's cause. He saw from the very first the terrible disasters which would follow in the train of civil war, and shrunk from the encounter. Yet this very foresight but exhibits the nobility and courage of his soul, in daring all at the call of duty. His parting words to his wife prove with what exalted sentiments he consented to take up arms: "Arm yourself with courage," he said; "redouble your patience and resignation; believe me, you will have need of them. It is useless to dissemble the truth. It is not on earth that we must look for reward,—nothing that this world can give is worthy of the purity and holiness of our cause,—we must not even pretend to human glory; and if we might, we could never find it in civil war. Our dwellings we shall see in flames, ourselves despoiled, proscribed, outraged, defamed, it may be massacred. Let us thank God for enabling us to see these things before they come to pass; so will our actions be more meritorious, so shall we enjoy beforehand that heavenly reward, the hope of which makes men courageous in danger and unconquered in defeat. Let us look above, and place our affections where we shall find a guide who cannot lead us astray, a rock which cannot be shaken, an infinite reward for a momentary labour."

The other gentleman, who joined the insurgents at the same time as Bonchamps, was D'Elbée. He was an *ancien* lieutenant of the Dauphin cavalry, but had retired from service during the revolution. His military talents were far inferior to those of Bonchamps; but by his sanctity, and his coolness in danger, he acquired unbounded influence over the peasants. He was afterwards made

Chapter II

commander-in-chief of the Vendean army, and he filled the post with firmness during a period of terrible disaster. Cathelineau resigned the command to him on his joining the camp, believing that an old soldier was fitter to take the lead than an inexperienced peasant. But in this the hawker's modesty deceived him. The rules of war were inapplicable to the peasants' mode of fighting, and Cathelineau proved a better general than D'Elbée.

D'Elbée was not more prepossessed in favour of the insurrection, nor less blind to the inevitable ruin which it would entail on the persons and property of all who should take part in it, than Bonchamps. "My children," he said to his tenants, when they pressed him to put himself at their head, "you know I have never deceived you; and I shall not deceive you now in this most important matter. The revolution is a fact: it will not, it cannot be undone. It will devour all that is good in France; and our efforts at best can be but feeble against a power which strengthens every day. I am ready to die for God and my king; but I will not command men who are not worthy of being martyrs. Go back for this night to your cottages; reflect that an act of yours may set them on fire, and ruin your families; and weigh well what I have said to you. Tomorrow morning come back again, if God inspires you with courage to die; and then I will go with you."

The next morning a still greater crowd thronged the avenue to his chateau at Beaupreau; and D'Elbée became their chief.

These facts are sufficient to show the feelings with which the Vendean gentlemen entered the arena of civil strife. Yet the republicans charged these men, and such as these, with the selfish object of exciting the peasants to revolt for the restitution of their own privileges.

Bonchamps and D'Elbée had scarcely joined, when Easter summoned the insurgents to other duties than those of fighting; and they dispersed to their several homes. The army vanished as rapidly as it had assembled; and a republican corps from Angers traversed

D'Elbée—Bas Poitou, Massacres at Machecoul

the country which had been the scene of these brilliant successes, without perceiving the vestige of an enemy.

In Bas Poitou the insurrection had also commenced. A hairdresser, named Gaston, at Challons, slew the gendarme who was sent to apprehend him, dressed himself in his uniform, and marched through several parishes raising the inhabitants. He was killed the next day; but the peasantry continued in arms. In other districts of the same department many bodies of insurgents were in course of organisation; but we need only particularise the rising in a town some leagues to the north of Challons, called Machecoul, which is remarkable for the excesses with which it was disgraced. The peasants of the neighbouring parishes attacked the place, and put the garrison to the sword; even women and children, drunk with blood, joined in the slaughter, and a committee was formed, under a man of the name of Souchu, to judge the prisoners. Forty-four were condemned to death, and were executed the following day. This was but the beginning of outrages. Souchu sent through all the neighbouring country, and ruthlessly destroyed the republican soldiers. Nor was this enough: he seized a number of prisoners, and tying them together by a cord round their necks, which in bitter irony he called their rosary, he shot them in parties; and after each volley bayoneted those who survived. Nor did he even stop here: he buried men, and, it is said, even women alive. This butchery lasted twelve days without interruption, during which time the number of victims exceeded five hundred.

The republicans took care to charge the whole insurrection in La Vendée with the massacre of Machecoul. It is true that Souchu found imitators in other places; but all excesses were immediately stopped as soon as the movement took shape and came under the control of regular leaders. They were, even at first, quite the exception to the general practice of the royalists, who were accustomed, after each success, to rush to the churches and return thanks to God for their victory. With the republicans, on the contrary,

Chapter II

cruelty was the rule, and forbearance the exception. Unable to overcome the peasants by fair fighting, they deliberately resorted to the most barbarous and bloody measures.

Souchu was superseded in the command by a gentleman from the neighbourhood of Nantes, whose name will ever be identified with this glorious struggle. François-Athenase Charette was at this time thirty years of age. He had early entered the navy, and was lieutenant of his ship when the revolution broke out; but he resigned his command rather than take the oath to the constitution. On the 10th August 1792 he took part in the defence of the Tuileries, and escaped the fury of the populace by raising aloft the mutilated limb of a Swiss guard as a trophy, and so passed through the mob. He returned to Poitou; but was soon arrested as a suspected person, and consigned to Nantes Castle. He contrived, however, to make friends with the authorities, and obtained his liberation. His character was totally different from that of the other chiefs of Anjou and Haut Poitou; they were all of religious, some even of saintly habits. Charette, on the contrary, was a man of not very rigid morals, but he was inspired with the most dauntless courage, the most indefatigable energy, and a military genius. He seemed to lead two lives—a life of sensual enjoyment, and a life of martyrdom and glory. He could, without effort, turn from the one to the other. Today he supports with all the endurance of a stoic danger and privation, famine and fatigue—tomorrow he will abandon himself to luxury and ease, and will busy himself on the smallest details of his dress. Long after the cause had been abandoned in other parts of Vendée he continued to maintain a desperate struggle in the inaccessible marshes of Poitou; and so great was the terror with which he had inspired the Republic, that when attended only by a few followers, they offered him a bribe of a million of francs to abandon the contest. He refused their overtures with disdain; and yet the camp of this heroic warrior was the scene of rioting and excess. His exterior had little in it that was imposing at first sight;

but when he spoke there was a flash beneath his dark overhanging eyelids which commanded obedience—which told of an iron will and a loftiness of soul; and there were few men that durst contend with Charette to the face, though he was not without rivals throughout his career. He acceded to the clamorous request of the peasants, to put himself at their head, with great reluctance; but when he yielded, he gave them to know what sort of a leader they had chosen. He said, that since they would have it so, he would command them; but that they must make up their minds to obey, for he should punish severely. On their arrival at Machecoul, he repaired to the church, and swore on the Evangelists to perish with his arms in his hands rather than abandon his party; and the same oath he exacted from all his followers.

Charette had from the first energetically protested against the massacres of Souchu; and now that he had authority to stop them, he commenced by giving orders for the liberation of all the women who were lying in the prisons of Machecoul. The priests, who had not ceased to preach the duty of mercy, seconded his efforts for the suppression of cruelty. But Souchu had still much influence, and cried out for more executions; and Charette was more than once compelled, sword in hand, himself to mount guard before the door of the castle to prevent the massacre of the prisoners. The strife between the two leaders lasted several weeks, when Souchu put an end to it in a manner worthy of himself. The republican general Beysser appeared on the 22d April before Machecoul. Seized with terror, Souchu drew up a proscription-list, with the names of all the royalist chiefs, and Charette at the head; and putting on a tricolour cockade, he ran to meet the Blues, crying *Vive la Nation!* But his cowardice did not save him: he was cut down with a hatchet. His death put a stop to the committee, and freed Charette of a troublesome enemy.

The better to establish his authority, Charette had need of some victory of importance. On the 29th March he made an attack on

Chapter II

Pornic, which was taken and given up to pillage. This success, inasmuch as it gave the insurgents three pieces of cannon, ammunition of every kind, and a large quantity of muskets, filled them with enthusiasm for their new chief.

His power was, however, at that time very limited. It scarcely extended over twenty parishes round Machecoul and Challons. Other parts of Bas Poitou obeyed different chiefs, who were all independent of him and of each other. The most noted of these was Joly, an old surgeon, who had raised the canton of Aizenay, and had formed, with the aid of two of his sons, the division afterwards called the Army of the Sands. The feast of Easter, which had arrested the Angevins in the full tide of success, was chosen by Joly for some very important conflicts with the Blues. He attacked the town of Sables d'Olonne, situated on the sea-shore, and a great magazine of the Blues. On the 24th March he made his first unsuccessful attack; on the 27th he returned to the assault, and engaged in a fusillade which lasted till dark. On the 29th he was reinforced; but the besieged were also strengthened by a portion of the garrison of La Rochelle. After a little skirmishing, the insurgents established in the neighbouring villages a battery to throw red-hot balls. It was not, certainly, very successful; however, the garrison, alarmed at the possible result, made a sally, and a furious battle took place in the open country, which lasted six hours. Neither side were successful; and at night-fall the Blues returned to the town, and Joly, who had lost a considerable part of his troops, and had fired away all his ammunition, slowly retired. The attempt, although imprudent and unsuccessful, was practically of great value to the Vendean cause, as proving that the royalists were not easily discouraged and could endure a reverse.

While the army under Bonchamps, D'Elbée, and Cathelineau, called the grand army, and that under Charette and others, called the central army, were manœuvering on the left bank of the Loire, the insurrection also propagated itself in Brittany. Jean Chouan, of whom we shall hear more in the sequel, Puisaye, and others, were active in opposing the Republic; and at Rochefort, Laval, La Rochebernard, and elsewhere, the Bretons exhibited the greatest courage. Nantes itself narrowly escaped being taken and sacked by the insurgents. The details of that affair are interesting, as illustrating the manner in which the insurgents won their victories and came by their defeats. They attained their successes by headlong daring; and if their enthusiasm was checked, the chances of victory were always against them. Napoleon used to say, that in war the moral was to the physical as three to one. If he had been referring to La Vendée, he would have rather estimated the proportion at ten to one. The peasants were frequently successful when there was not a musket between five of them,—witness Cathelineau's first victories; and they were often defeated when they had ammunition in abundance,—witness the siege of Nantes.

Nantes was threatened on the left bank by Charette, and his coadjutor in Bas Poitou. But its chief danger lay on the right bank, from a body of twenty thousand men who had been assembled by two Bretons named Richard-Duplessis and Morin-Premion. A chief being wanted for this large force, the choice fell on an old lieutenant-colonel called Gaudin-Laberillais. Anxious to avoid bloodshed, Laberillais endeavoured to make terms with the republicans. He demanded liberty of worship, the free return of all nonjuring priests to their churches, the abolition of the militia, and other concessions which the authorities of the town had not the power, if they had had the will, to grant. In reply, they demanded five days' delay, not to consider the matter, but to gain time. Duplessis, transported with fury, insisted on immediate hostilities, and charged Laberillais with treason. But the peasants, influenced by the pacific bearing of their general, declared that they would wait the five days. That delay was fatal. The army which would have attacked Nantes with enthusiasm on the 14th March, was on the 19th dispersed with some rounds of artillery.

Chapter II

This check, however, did not affect the general course of the insurrection in Brittany. It proceeded, if not with the same great results as in La Vendée, certainly with equal spirit. The Convention were not slow to perceive the danger arising from the disaffection of two important provinces, and despatched a commission to report upon the state of the insurgent population. Meanwhile a stormy debate was held as to the proper measures to be adopted, one party clamouring for vengeance, the other advocating a lenient policy. The discussion was closed by a letter from Canclaux, one of the republican generals on the spot. He wrote: "The game can no longer be kept up. It is now but the second week of March, and more than two hundred thousand men have risen in Brittany. This rebellion is due to several causes; but all may be referred to two principles—religion and royalty. On the other side of the Loire the same motives actuate another population, but La Vendée is the most threatening: there pitched battles have been fought, and generals defeated, and many able officers have appeared to head the insurrection. The gage which the rebels have cast down, the Republic is bound in honour to take up; but it cannot wage war with external foes, and with all its own provinces also; and happily Brittany as yet has had no successes. My advice is, therefore,—march only on La Vendée, and pacify the Bretons by acceding to their demands. Withdraw the levy from them, permit their priests to return, and cut off all communication between the two provinces. Silence the one with kindness, in order that you may suppress the other by force."

This plan, which the delegates of the Convention had the wisdom to adopt, completely succeeded. As soon as the Breton priests perceived that they could practise their religion in peace, they recommended their flocks to remain tranquil; and the peasants, seeing their priests in safety, and themselves no longer subject to conscription, returned to their labours. However, the enemies of the revolution were not all to be deceived by this stratagem, and

Advice of Canclaux, and pacification of Brittany.

Brittany continued still in a state of excitement. But the Republic were enabled to concentrate their entire force upon La Vendée, and so arrest the ruin which a combination of the insurgent populations would infallibly have brought upon them.

Chapter III

Boundaries of La Vendée—The plain—The marais—The bocage—Telegraphic system of the insurgents—Their tactics—Organisation—The women; anecdote of Jeanne Robin—The priests—Universality of the insurrectional spirit—Alleged cruelty of the peasants—Charge of forged miracles.

IN PURSUANCE of the decree, that energetic measures should be taken for the suppression of the insurrection in La Vendée, four detachments were ordered at once to the west, to operate on four distinct points. But this order was only partially obeyed. The danger was too great on the frontier to allow of very large bodies of men being withdrawn; and an army on the left bank of the Loire was all that could be spared by the Convention. These troops were intrusted to the command of Berruyer, who at once commenced operations with vigour. Nor were the royalist leaders inactive. The Easter recess had not been thrown away in idleness; and they were prepared to take the field at the beginning of April with thirty thousand men. But before we enter upon the history of this campaign, it will be necessary to give some details of the nature of the country, and the mode of fighting in favour with the insurgents.

La Vendée properly speaking, that is to say, the department of La Vendée, forms but a small part of the extensive district which was the scene of this glorious contest, and which generally goes by that name. From the very first the insurgents were called Vendeans, whether of Anjou, Poitou, or Maine and Loire,—all, in fact, south of the Loire. La Vendée, then, in this its widest acceptation as a *nomme de guerre*, consists of four departments—Lower Loire,

Boundaries—The plain—The marais—The bocage

Maine and Loire, Vendée, and the two Sèvres. A glance at the map will show its limits. It is bounded on the north by the Loire, from its mouth to the Ponts-de-Cé, about four miles from Angers; on the east by a line drawn through Doué, Thouars, and Parthenay, to Niort; on the south by the road from Niort to the sands passing through Fontenay, Luçon, and Talmont; on the west by the sea from the sands to Paimbœuf. This vast tract, comprising an area of eight hundred square leagues, is divided into three parts—the bocage, the marais, and the plain.

The inhabitants of the plain, being chiefly Protestants, never made common cause with the insurgents, although their land was more than once occupied by the Vendean army. By sympathy they adhered to the revolutionary party, and fought on that side; but they were little to be feared, on account of their cowardice in battle. The plain skirts the bocage.

The marais extends from St. Hilairie-de-Rie to the Isle of Bouin. It is a wild country, and to the stranger almost impassable, from the immense number of dykes with which the industry of the people has intersected it. These dykes are often as much as twenty-five feet wide, and are always full of water. They wind round fields bordered with trees; and access to the miserable mud hovels in which the people live is along a narrow path shelving down on each side to a canal. The marshman traverses his country by means of a long pole called a *ningle*, with which he leaps over the dykes; and those which are too wide to be crossed in this manner he passes in flat-bottomed punts. With these simple instruments he became a very difficult foe to overcome; for as soon as he found himself pressed, he leaped into his *niole*,—so he called his rude boat,—and in a few minutes appeared again in the rear of his assailants. The marais could put under arms about fifteen hundred men, which formed a division of Charette's army.

But the strength of the Vendean party lay in the bocage, or cover, a name originally applied to but a small portion of the insurgent territory, but afterwards to some districts of Poitou, Anjou,

Chapter III

and Nantes, whence the insurrection derived its greatest strength and obtained its most glorious successes. It is formed of hill and dale; the hills low, and the valleys narrow. There is scarcely a considerable elevation throughout the country. As its name indicates, it is very woody; not on account of any large forests, but of the dense brushwood with which it is covered. The fields are small and innumerable, and divided by thick quickset hedges. A number of brooks traverse it in all directions, and there are a few lakes here and there. The waste lands are covered with broom and furze. The roads, almost all dug between two hedges, and in many instances as much as twelve or fourteen feet deep, are just wide enough for a cart pass; and the branches of the spreading trees intertwine overhead. To the traveller on a sunny day no road could be more charming, but to an invading enemy none could be more dangerous. Many of these wild roads are also river-courses; all are extremely rough, and the rock frequently breaks through in the most awkward forms. Where there is no rock, the wheels of the ox-cart stick fast in thick yellow clay. Along such roads, three or four leagues is a good day's journey. Above the cutting, and behind the ridges, there runs a narrow footpath called *la voyette*, which gave the insurgents a vast superiority over the invading army. Along it they could march expeditiously, or lurk in ambush, while the enemy floundered on in the deep rugged road beneath, exposed to the cross-fire of an unseen and ubiquitous assailant. The whole country is thus one network of deep trenches, presenting greater obstacles to the passage of an army than even the crags and precipices of the Alps. With great labour and skill other armies are compelled to throw up field-works and entrenchments, behind which they take shelter; and if they are driven from these, they are no longer protected from the attacks of the enemy. The Vendeans found ready to their hand such ditches and embankments as no engineer could construct,—the work of centuries, the combined result of generations of labourers, all united together by the roots and branches of old trees.

The bocage—Telegraphic system of the insurgents

In such a country as this, it is not surprising that the ablest generals of the Republic should have met with defeat. The most ordinary military evolutions were impossible; and cavalry and artillery, except in sieges, and in one or two more open districts, were almost useless. To this must be added the difficulty of obtaining a knowledge of the field of battle. Without a single elevated chain, without a large river, or an extended plain, the bocage formed one vast labyrinth, in which it is said that even the peasant who wandered a few miles from his own home, if unacquainted with the landmarks, was liable to lose his way. And even from the few points, such as Pouzanges, La Châtaigneraie, and the Hill of Larks, from which an extensive prospect was to be obtained, nothing was to be seen but one vast sea of foliage, dotted here and there with corn-fields. Farms and *châteaux*, villages and towns, were all lost in the maze; and except perhaps some church-tower, or some mansion more pretentious than its fellows, not a sign of human habitation could be observed. To the natives of the country this labyrinth was not without its clue. A tall tree, a windmill, an open space served them as landmarks where the stranger wandered hopelessly; and, with untaught ingenuity, they organised a telegraphic system by which all the natural difficulties of the ground were overcome. On light portable ladders, placed against the branches of the loftiest trees, watchmen posted themselves at regular intervals within earshot of each other. As soon as any one discovered the line of the enemy's march, he blew on his shepherd's horn certain notes agreed upon beforehand; and in a short time the news was transmitted along the whole line to the insurgents' head-quarters. The sails of the windmills also, arranged in particular positions, were made telegraphic signals. The Hill of Larks, above Les Hertiers, from which the view extends over the two valleys of the Loire and the Sèvre, is consecrated in the memory of the Vendean peasant by the good service which it rendered by its many windmills. But the republicans had no such organs of intelligence. They could communicate with each

Chapter III

other only by means of couriers; and these continually lost their way, or fell into the hands of the insurgents. Indeed, the various republican corps were almost completely isolated from each other; whence arose misunderstanding, disunion, and want of confidence. These peculiarities in the country were alone sufficient to repel an invader, though the peasants had abstained from insurrection: and they explain the policy, though they do not palliate the iniquity, of the republican government, in laying waste the insurgent territory with fire and sword. After a few months' fighting, the Convention discovered that nothing could be done against a country where every bush might shelter a rifleman, and not a road was free from danger; and they determined to waste and destroy every village and every wood, to burn the very heather, and exterminate the enemy whom they could not overcome. How terribly this order was executed, with what bloodshed and ruin, with how much of savage cruelty to the very women and children, are matters of history. There is not a more fearful page in the annals of the revolution.

The peasants, unacquainted with any rules of warfare, adopted instinctively the mode of fighting best suited to their country and their absence of discipline. They marched in irregular columns, three or four abreast; and a few officers, well mounted, preceded the army to reconnoitre the position. As soon as the enemy appeared in sight, they returned to the main body, and each chief traversed his company, crying, "Forward, my lads! the Blues! the Blues!" At this signal, the men hid themselves behind the hedges, and even climbed the trees above the road; and as soon as the republican columns were fairly involved in the snare, they commenced a sharp fire upon them from all sides at once, and then rushed upon the enemy with loud cries, disordered as they were by the suddenness of the attack. Their chief efforts were directed against the artillery, which they often succeeded in capturing by the very simplicity of their plan. A party of powerful volunteers, especially picked for the service, rushed upon the battery, armed with clubs hardened in the fire. The Blues, perceiving the charge, fired upon their assailants, who suddenly threw themselves upon their faces as they observed the match-fire flashing at the touch-hole, in which position they continued till they heard the balls whizzing over their heads, when they jumped up, and before there had been time to load again, leaped into the battery, knocked down the astonished artillerymen, and captured the guns. This manœuvre, common as it became, never failed to stupefy the republicans.

Thanks to their knowledge of the country, the Vendeans generally contrived to avoid the consequences of defeat. As soon as they saw they were beaten, they dispersed on all sides, crying "Long live the king," all the same; and were soon safely concealed in some obscure retreat. It was impossible to follow them across hedges, ditches, and thickets; nor was there any longer an army to pursue. It was dispersed in every direction. Not so with the enemy: a republican column beaten was a column destroyed; the runaways lost themselves in the labyrinths of the bocage, and fell in detached groups into the hands of the insurgents. And in all engagements, the Blues were certain to lose a great number of men without any corresponding loss to the Vendeans; for they were compelled to fire at random at unseen foes, who were excellent marksmen and could take deliberate aim. Living in a country stocked with game of all sorts, the Vendeans were devoted to hunting. They were sportsmen from the cradle; every child was familiar with the use of the gun. The insurgent army, therefore, was really a vast regiment of sharpshooters, who were enabled, by their constant practice of their weapon, to pour in a most destructive fire on the enemy from their hiding-places.

On entering battle most of the peasants made the sign of the cross. They used to march with their rosary beads in their hands, and recite them as they went along. In the evenings, on halting for the night, the whole camp often joined in the same devotion. Before any great engagement, they heard Mass; and on capturing any town or village, they repaired to the churches. They were frequently

Chapter III

known to kneel down on the field of battle itself, beneath a hot fire and in the very moment of success, on passing a wayside cross. Throughout the long and disastrous war with which their country was ravaged, the restoration of the Catholic faith was their one object; nor did they make peace till it had been attained. The very existence, therefore, of the Vendean army was a standing protest against the infidel spirit of the revolution.

The organisation of the Vendean army was as simple as its tactics; but it was not the less complete. Each parish named its captain, and marched to battle under his orders. All who were capable of bearing arms were expected to volunteer; and the coward or the sluggard would have been scouted by his very children. The parochial captain obeyed the chief of the canton, who, in his turn, submitted to the general. Thus a natural network existed for the transmission of orders, by which a summons to assemble at any particular spot could be communicated to a whole district instantaneously; and a very short time sufficed to collect the insurgents in considerable force. Under two conditions the Vendeans were always ready to fight. They must know the general object of the projected expedition,—information which might be safely communicated to a body of twenty or thirty thousand men, and was never divulged to the enemy; and the chiefs must occupy the first ranks. Theirs was that primitive state of society in which personal prowess, and valour, and muscular strength, are indispensable requisites in a leader; and it was owing to their superiority in these qualities that first Cathelineau and then D'Elbée were chosen to the supreme command; both of them able men, but far inferior to Bonchamps in military genius. In battle every thing depended on the commander. The Vendean peasant, so courageous and so calm even to the extreme of temerity, was, on the other hand, easily discouraged. If the officers appeared irresolute or disconcerted, the whole army gave way. Many a victory was snatched from the very grasp of the insurgents by a wound of their leader. Whenever, therefore, there appeared a chief in whom the peasants could place confidence, and they knew the object of the expedition, hosts of volunteers joyfully repaired to the rendezvous. But after the battle they dispersed as hastily. Seldom could they be kept under arms for more than a few days together; and hence the impossibility of undertaking any great enterprise. The safety of Paris itself might have been compromised had the Vendean peasantry been otherwise constituted. As it was, they could achieve great successes, but they could seldom follow them up; and the victorious general had often to lament the gradual melting away of his army just as the concentration of his force was most required.

At the commencement of the war none of the royalists wore uniform; nor was there any distinguishing mark for the chiefs. But Larochejacquelein having appeared at one of the battles at Fontenay with red handkerchiefs of Chollet manufacture round his head, neck, and waist, which drew down upon him specially the fire of the republicans, the other officers adopted the same costume, that none of them might be more exposed than the others. But it was a device rather than a uniform. The men of the Haute Vendée wore their usual dress,—that is to say, a short grey vest tied with blue, a waistcoat of white wool or coarse calico, a flat broad-brimmed hat, for which a woollen cap was frequently substituted, breeches and gaiters, or short striped trousers. In Bas Poitou the vest was of a brown colour. The great badge of the Vendean was the rosary hanging from his neck or from a button, and the scapular placed upon his breast. A few, both officers and soldiers, wore, by way of cockade, knots of white ribbons, or oak sprigs.

The Vendean army had no waggons, no reserve, no baggage. Each volunteer carried his own victuals. The following were the terms of a summons to the scene of action: "In the holy name of God, on the king's behalf, this parish is invited to send as many men as possible to such a place, on such a day, at such an hour. They must take provisions with them." That was enough. The peasant forthwith left his labour, shouldered his musket, took ammunition

Chapter III

and a little bread, embraced his family, and presented himself at the appointed time and place. Besides what the peasants brought themselves, the generals exerted themselves to obtain supplies of all sorts. Through whatever village the volunteers passed, the inhabitants thrust upon them all the bread they had: nor had the army any lack of food so long as they remained on their own side of the Loire; and their wants were very few. The republicans contrasted this generous devotion of the insurgents with the selfish love of plunder and licentious excess that alone animated the self-styled "patriots" in the Vendean war.

As the Vendean army had no baggage or reserve, so they had no camp-followers, sutlers, or hangers-on. It was said, in the journals of the day, that both women and priests figured among the combatants; but this is totally false. The presence of women was absolutely prohibited, even for purposes of cooking. However, there were a few, ten at the most, who fought in disguise as men. This breach of the law was either unknown to the authorities, or excused by some peculiar circumstances. One young girl, known as the *Angevin* (in the masculine) and enrolled in Bonchamps' cavalry, performed prodigies of valour. She fought to avenge her father's death. Another, Jeanne Robin, served in Lescure's division. One day she went to him, and said: "My general, I am a girl; Madame de Lescure knows it, and she knows also that there is nothing to my discredit. Tomorrow is the battle; give me a pair of shoes, and you shall see me fight." The next day Lescure found her in the front rank. She cried out, "My general, you shall not pass me; I will always be nearer the Blues than you." She was slain. But these are exceptional cases. The part which the women played was confined to providing their husbands and brothers with food in their own villages, and praying for success upon their arms.

The priests were constantly upon the field of battle; but not to fight. If any of them carried pistols, it was only in self-defence; they never used their arms except in the last necessity, and to protect

The women—The priests—Universality of insurrectional spirit

themselves from the fury of the Blues, who entertained a special hatred against the clergy. Many bodies of priests were doubtless found among the slain; but they had been killed in the discharge of their sacred duties—while administering the Sacraments to the dying and binding up the wounded. The peasants would have ceased to respect their clergy if they had seen them fighting by their side. The generals had to imprison M. de Soulier, who concealed his quality of subdeacon in order to join the army.

Both in Brittany and in La Vendée the spirit of insurrection was shared by persons of every sex and age. The sufferings of Madame Lescure, afterwards Madame de Larochejacquelein, are familiar to every reader of history. The heroism displayed by women during the fearful massacres of Nantes, and the horrors of the Infernal Columns, was not surpassed by the most brilliant acts of the greatest general; and even little children dared to encounter death in the cause of religion. A child scarcely twelve years of age was stopped by a patrol, as he was conveying a basket of food to a priest in his concealment. "Where are you going with that basket?" asked the soldiers. The little fellow trembled and stammered. "Tell us the truth, young brigand," said one of them, "or I will shoot you." The unhappy child paused a moment, hesitating between his conscience and his fear of death; then making the sign of the cross, he answered: "Kill me, do what you like to my body; but I call our Lady to witness that I will not say another word to you." The national guards threatened him, put their bayonets to his throat, but all in vain, they could not extort a word. Touched with his heroism, they let him go. But a poor girl, a few years older, was not so fortunate. Marie Papin, for that was her name, was surprised by the soldiers as she was carrying some bread to a couple of royalists in the furze. They seized her, and beat her, but she would not speak, lest she should tell an untruth; and when they threatened her with death, she simply made the sign of the cross, and without a word to them fell on her knees and began the prayers for the dying. In

Chapter III

that attitude she was killed. These are not peculiar cases: striking, indeed, they are, but the whole population, from the youngest child to the aged peasant, exhibited the same enthusiasm. In Brittany, after the dispersion of the ill-fated expedition across the Loire, when death was certain to follow any act of mercy shown to the Vendeans if discovered, the most generous hospitality was shown to the hunted patriots. In defiance of the threats of the republicans, and the terrible examples of their vengeance daily before their eyes, the Bretons extended to the unhappy remnant of the grand army whatever assistance was in their power; concealing them from their pursuers, facilitating their escape, and providing them with food and clothing.

The Vendeans have been accused of the greatest barbarities. At the close of the war the charge is, to a certain extent, just; but although nothing can excuse the crime of putting prisoners of war to death, it may be said, in extenuation, that from the very beginning the insurgents were averse to acts of violence; and that they were guilty of them only after long experience of far greater atrocities from their foes, and frequent proofs of the vanity of trusting the word of republicans who fell into their power, not again to bear arms against the Catholic cause. It must be remembered, that as the insurgents had no fortresses or public buildings, they had no means of confining their prisoners; and revolting from the sin of putting them to death, it was long their practice to extort from them a promise not to serve again in La Vendée; then, after half-shaving their heads, in order that they might be recognised for some time, they set them free. But none of the republicans kept their word; and therefore it was that the insurgents afterwards in some cases executed those who were taken in battle. These executions were rendered necessary, in a certain sense, by the nature of the war, and differ, not only in degree, but in kind, from the horrible massacres which the Blues perpetrated, and which have not even the poor excuse of that necessity to palliate them. In the

Alleged cruelty—Charge of forged miracles

very greatest extremity to which the Vendeans were reduced, they performed acts of mercy towards their enemies conceived in the highest Christian spirit. On the contrary, the republican system, from first to last, was one of barbarity and bloodshed, unrelieved by the slightest humanity, until after the fall of Robespierre; when the Directory, beginning to perceive the futility of a violent policy, attempted to conciliate the insurgents by an opposite course.

The world was never able to unravel the mystery of "inexplicable Vendée;" steadily blind to the real spring whence flowed that noble obstinacy, that patient suffering, that heroism, which defied armies, and devoted life and property and family to the defence of a prostrate cause, each party sought to explain the enigma in a different way. According to the royal family, the peasants were actuated by loyalty to the throne. By radicals, the insurrection was attributed to the nobles, who had stirred up their peasantry to fight for the rights of the aristocracy: while infidels maintained that the priests were the real culprits, and that they had worked on the superstitious fears of the people by false miracles. This was a favourite mode of explaining away the difficulty. Thus Turreau writes word that "reports of miracles were rife in Vendée. Here the Virgin had appeared in person to consecrate a temporary altar in a wood; there the Son of God had Himself descended from heaven to assist at a benediction of flags; in a third place angels had been seen with wings and rays complete, laden with promises of victory to the champions of the altar and the throne." They little knew the inhabitants of the Bocage, who thought them likely to attach credence, without proof, to prodigies such as these. What was more miraculous than any of these wonders was the courage of the Vendeans. But one fact, placed beyond all suspicion of forgery by a host of contemporary witnesses, may have given rise to the charge. The old men, ancients as they are called in the Bocage, had not forgotten the words of the blessed Father Grignon de Montfort, founder of the missionaries of St. Laurent-sur-Sèvre, as he was preaching

Chapter III

his last mission at Bressuire. More than half a century had elapsed since that moment, and yet the prediction of the holy father had been preserved along with the hymns of which he was the author. It was well known in every hamlet. Standing at the foot of a Calvary, the saint exclaimed, "Brethren, one day God, for the punishment of sinners, will send into all this region a horrible war. Blood shall be shed; men shall be slain; the whole country shall be ravaged. These things will come to pass when my cross is covered with moss."

Gradually the lichen crept over the stone; the people knew and remembered the warning of what should be when its growth was complete. In 1793 the cross was covered, and the prediction was fulfilled. The war came—a bloody and destructive war; it passed away, and is now matter of history. Some of its principal details will be found in the following pages.

Chapter IV

Renewal of hostilities—Defeat of the Blues at Chemillé—Henri de Larochejacquelein—Henri beats Quetineau at Aubiers, who retires on Thouars—Lescure—Siege of Thouars—Gallantry of Lescure—Forbearance of the besiegers—*Soi-disant* Bishop of Agra—Success at Châtaigneraie—Defeat at Fontenay; siege and capture of that town.

THE REPUBLICANS entered upon the campaign fully determined to put an end to the rebellion by the most vigorous measures. The Convention, although uneasy at the prospect of a civil war, far underrated the strength of the new enemy which had arisen to embarrass its operations; and supposed that one great battle would suffice to quell the insurrection of a horde of peasants. General Berruyer arrived at Angers, his head-quarters, on the 29th March, and posted his army in several columns; one on the left bank of the Loire at St. Florent, one in the Bas Poitou, one in the Bocage, and another under Quetineau at Bressuire, with others of minor importance. The object of these combinations was to surround the royalist army, and drive it either into the sea or into the Loire.

The Vendeans assembled to the number of thirty thousand men. Berruyer changed his head-quarters from Angers to St. Lambert on the other side of the Loire, and Cathelineau, D'Elbée, and Stofflet combined their forces at Chollet, and marched on Chemillé to encounter the republican general. After a desperate conflict, they routed him with great loss on the 11th April; but the victory was almost fatal to the Vendeans; for though it left them masters of the

Chapter IV

field, it left them also destitute of ammunition. They retired farther into the Bocage, and encamped at Tiffauges, where the safety of the army was secured by the accession of a new chief and fresh soldiers. This new chief was the heroic and chivalrous Henri de Larochejacquelein.

The peasants between Tiffauges and Châtillon, in the very centre of the Bocage, had hitherto abstained from joining the insurrection from lack of a chief, although well disposed to revolt. Some of them had left home to follow the flag of Cathelineau or of Charette; but it was reserved for Henri de Larochejacquelein to organise the general rising of that part of La Vendée. For some months he had lived retired in the chateau of Clisson, the residence of Lescure, his relation and friend, where only indistinct rumours reached him of the fighting in Anjou; for Clisson was jealously watched by the partisans of the Republic. While here he received a summons to draw for the militia. Quite determined not to obey, he still meditated no more than a passive resistance, when a young peasant inspired him with a more energetic resolution. "Is it possible, Monsieur," said he, "that you are going next Sunday to draw for the militia, when your peasants are about to fight, not to draw? Come with us; the whole country looks to you, and will obey you." No more was said; but in the middle of the night Henri started from the chateau, and riding nine leagues across country to avoid the Blues, reached the grand army, where he learned that they had just gained a great victory, but that all was lost for want of ammunition. Upon this Henri repaired to his family chateau at St. Aubin, and all the peasants instantly entreated him to put himself at their head. In less than four-and-twenty hours a numerous company was under his orders. But what soldiers to oppose regular troops! not more than two hundred had muskets; the rest were armed only with clubs, scythes, or even spades. Their ammunition consisted of sixty pounds of blasting-powder. However, they were nearly as well armed as the grand army; and they marched without hesitation on Aubiers, which the Blues had occupied since the evening before. Before setting out, Larochejacquelein addressed his army as follows:

"My friends, if my father were here, you would have confidence in him. I am only a boy: but by my courage I will show myself worthy to command you. If I advance, follow me; if I flinch, cut me down; if I fall, avenge me!"

The young orator who pronounced this gallant address was only twenty years of age. He had been trained in a military college, and had obtained a commission in the royal Polish regiment of cavalry. On the 10th of August he had formed part of the garrison of the Tuileries, and after the disaster of that day had escaped to his native country. He was reserved and modest, but without a shade of fear. His conduct during the battle was marked by the most reckless contempt of danger; after it he was as gentle as he had been brave. On taking a prisoner, he would frequently offer his antagonist the chance of a single combat. Of all the chiefs, Henri de Larochejacquelein was the most popular among the peasants. They used to call him familiarly Master Henry. He was a leader after their own heart. The noble lad, so reserved, and yet so rash, who in the field marched in the first rank, and at the council-board durst not raise his voice, could not fail to attract those brave and simple Vendeans, who fought like heroes, and obeyed like children. His highest ambition in the event of success was, that the king should give him a regiment of hussars.

The battle of Chemillé took place on the 11th April; on the 12th the Vendean army retired on Tiffauges; on the 13th Larochejacquelein beat Quetineau's division at Aubiers three thousand strong. The Vendeans, crouching behind the hedges, attacked the Blues on all sides at once. Larochejacquelein, posted in a garden with the *élite* of the volunteers, directed a most murderous fire on the enemy, and Quetineau, thinking himself entrapped, beat a retreat. Larochejacquelein instantly cried out, "See, the Blues are flying! charge!" His

Chapter IV

men charged, and the republicans were totally routed. They fled to Bressuire, leaving three pieces of cannon, twelve hundred muskets, and several barrels of powder to the victors as their spoil. The next day he joined the army at Tiffauges, and placed Cathelineau in a position to take the offensive again. In a few days the republicans were completely driven out of the Bocage. Berruyer retired to the Ponts-de-Cé, the only post on the Vendean side of the Loire which remained in his hands, and the peasants retired to their homes.

Quetineau, beaten by Larochejacquelein at Aubiers, retreated upon Bressuire; but on the 3d May, having no confidence in the ruined fortifications of that place, and hearing of the advance of a body of thirty thousand peasants who had assembled at Chollet, he retired farther, to Thouars. Bressuire, thus evacuated by the enemy, fell into the hands of the Vendeans, and thereby the insurrection gained three fresh chiefs of great importance, viz. Marigny, Donissan, and Lescure; and with Lescure an entire regiment of fighting men.

Lescure was the cousin and most intimate friend of Henri de Larochejacquelein, and rivalled him in bravery; but he joined to equal courage a more sagacious judgment. At this time he was no more than twenty-six years old, tall, well-built, and of great personal strength; but in wisdom he was of mature age. Some idea of the firmness of his principles may be gathered from the fact, that having lost his mother in childbirth, and being left entirely to the influence of a dissolute father and tutor, he had avoided all contamination, and at length succeeded in reclaiming to the paths of virtue the men who should have been the first to lead the way. His father, the Marquis de Lescure, died when he was eighteen, leaving to his son an encumbered property. The young man was advised to repudiate so embarrassed a succession; but for the honour of his father he determined to pay his debts, and he lived for many years a life of the most rigid economy and self-denial. At length he had so re-established his affairs, that he was in a position to marry his cousin, the only daughter of the Marquis de Donissan. He was in Paris on the fatal 10th August, but escaped in safety to his chateau at Clisson, along with Henri de Larochejacquelein and Bernard de Marigny, his cousins.

The men of his parish had suffered severely in the massacre at Bressuire of the preceding year; and when Larochejacquelein departed to join the insurrection, Lescure had not as yet dared to organise a rising among the peasantry, deterred by the memory of that disaster. But the departure of his friend drew down upon himself the vengeance of the republicans; and Henri had scarcely left the chateau, when Lescure and his whole family, and almost all the parish, were seized and conducted to Bressuire. In the hurried evacuation of that town he was forgotten. The Blues massacred eleven of the wretched peasants; but Lescure, by some happy accident, was overlooked, and he found himself free before the insurgents entered the place.

On his return to Clisson, he judged that the moment of insurrection had at length arrived. He instantly sent a summons through fourteen parishes; and the next day he mounted, and, with Marigny, rode out to raise the country, in order to possess himself of Bressuire on the morrow. But hardly had he started, when he met a party of horsemen at full gallop, crying *Vive le Roi!* It was Larochejacquelein on his way to the town. The two friends exchanged hasty greetings, and Lescure went on his way to beat up recruits. The peasants replied in great numbers to his appeal. A captive on the 2d of May, he found himself on the 3d at the head of a formidable body of men. He immediately joined the grand army, all the chiefs of which received him with distinction, as they did also Donissan and Marigny. The latter received the command of artillery. He was a man of forty-two years, tall and muscular, of kind and gentle manners, spirits which nothing could depress, and bravery which no danger could daunt. But his temper was bad. At the first obstacle he lost his self-command, and gave way to the impulse of the moment.

Chapter IV

Thus reinforced, the Vendean army continued its march upon Thouars. This town—built upon a height, defended on all sides by a strong wall, and almost surrounded by the Thouet, a little river with deep rocky banks—was justly considered one of the strongest military positions in Poitou and Anjou; and Quetineau, with a garrison of seven thousand men, believed it impregnable to the assault of any number of peasants. When the attack commenced at six o'clock in the morning, he had taken but little pains about its defence. The Vendeans advanced in four divisions: one, under Larochejacquelein and Lescure, was directed against Vrine, a little village commanding the Thouet; another, commanded by Bonchamps, undertook to force the passage called the Gué-aux-Riches; the third, consisting of the artillery of Donissan and Marigny, marched against the Port Saint Jean; the fourth, under Cathelineau, D'Elbée, and Stofflet, had orders to attack the Port du Bec-du-Château.

On the bridge of Vrine an obstinate conflict took place, which lasted for six hours without advantage to either side; and at length powder began to fail the Vendeans. Larochejacquelein ran to obtain a supply; and while he was gone Lescure imagined he perceived symptoms of indecision among the enemy. He seized a musket, and calling upon his men to follow him, he rushed down the hill on which he was posted amid a shower of balls. He reached the bridge unwounded, although his clothes were riddled with shot; but he found himself alone. He returned to his men, appealed to the bravest among them, and again precipitated himself upon the bridge. But the peasants admired without daring to imitate his bravery. One man alone followed him. He returned, and was about to make a third appeal, when Larochejacquelein arrived with Forêt, the mover in the original affair at St. Florent. These two accompanied Lescure in his third attempt; and now the whole division, ashamed of their backwardness, charged tumultuously down the hill and carried the bridge in a moment. This was Lescure's first battle.

About the same moment Bonchamps, with his cavalry, crossed the ford and cut to pieces the republican division which opposed his passage. Upon this Quetineau advanced his reserve, but was repulsed. In vain he attempted to maintain his ground between Vrine and Thouars; his troops, thrown into confusion, took refuge within the walls, the last obstacle now remaining to be overcome. The four Vendean divisions, animated with enthusiasm, pressed on to the assault. Donissan and Marigny battered the gates of the Pont Neuf; and Cathelineau, with the other peasant chiefs, attacked the fortress from the Saumur side. Larochejacquelein was the first to begin the escalade. Mounted on the shoulders of a peasant of the name of Tixier, one of the bravest men in the army, he reached the coping of the wall and pushed down the stones with his hand; the breach thus commenced soon became wide enough to admit the besiegers, and in a few minutes the town was won. The republicans all laid down their arms, and rendered themselves prisoners. By this victory the insurgents became possessed of four or five thousand muskets, twelve pieces of cannon, and ammunition in abundance.

The inhabitants of Thouars were notorious for their extreme revolutionary opinions, and had taken a large share in the massacres perpetrated the year before in the neighbourhood of Bressuire. The defence had been obstinately prolonged, and the victorious party had lost eight hundred men; the citizens therefore had reason to expect but little mercy from the peasants. But the Vendeans had no thought of vengeance; in the hour of triumph they were intent only on thanking God. No sooner were they masters of the town—even before their foes were well disarmed—than they hurried to the churches and threw themselves upon their knees before the altars. Both at Bressuire and Thouars they respected private property. Madame de Larochejacquelein relates a striking instance of this. She says that in the house where she lodged at Bressuire (for she had been seized at Clisson along with Lescure) there were quartered a number of soldiers, and she heard them lament that

Chapter IV

they had no tobacco. "Is there none to be had in the town?" she asked. "Plenty," they replied; "but we have no money." That these peasants should have abstained from taking what they could not buy, in a hostile town, argues a very high state of moral discipline.

The insurgents made many recruits among the republican soldiers at Thouars; and several royalists of consideration, who had been hitherto compelled to hold themselves aloof, now joined the insurrection. Some also who had been forced to enroll themselves in the national guards came over to their own flag. Among them were De-la-Ville-Beaugé, afterwards one of the best officers of La Vendée, and the *soi-disant* Bishop of Agra, Guyot-de-Folleville.

When the revolution broke out the Abbé Guyot-de-Folleville was curé of Dol in Brittany. He at first consented to take the oath, but almost immediately afterwards retracted it, and took refuge in Poitiers. Here he gave out that he had been named Bishop of Agra *in partibus*; that the Pope had constituted four vicariates apostolic for the whole of France; and that he was set over the dioceses of the west. But while he represented himself as the envoy of Pius VI. to some religious of the town, he professed revolutionary opinions to the authorities; and by them he was enrolled in the national guard of the district, and sent to the relief of Thouars. As soon as that town was taken, he presented himself to the Vendean chiefs and announced his religious title. Believing his story, they invited him to join the army; and he consented, to the immense joy of the peasants, whose enthusiasm was raised to the utmost pitch by the presence of a bishop in their ranks.

The Vendean army remained two days at Thouars, when they marched to attack Fontenay, the capital of Bas Poitou. Before leaving the town they liberated their prisoners, to the number of nearly three thousand, only shaving their heads, and exacting from them an oath not again to bear arms against the defenders of religion and the throne. At Châtaigneraie, on their way, they achieved another success against General Chalbos; but it was unhappily soiled by

Soi-disant *Bishop of Agra—Success at Châtaigneraie*

some excesses. A number of peasants pillaged the houses which had been pointed out to them as belonging to the chiefs of the republican party. After the capture of Châtaigneraie, many of them returned home; the army became considerably reduced, and on reaching Fontenay, it was found to consist of not more than from eight to ten thousand men. With these, however, it was resolved to make the attack; and on the 16th the battle took place. But it was a disastrous combat for the insurgents. Lescure and Larochejacquelein, in command of the left wing, possessed themselves of the faubourgs, and congratulated their men on another victory; but the right wing and the centre were repulsed, D'Elbée was wounded, and Cathelineau in vain attempted to rally his troops. The rout became general, and the Vendean army lost that day four hundred killed, two hundred prisoners, and sixteen pieces of cannon—including the famous Marie Jeanne—with all their carriages and ammunition.

The peasants dispersed after this defeat, and the republican general reported to the Convention the close of the insurrection. This took place on the 16th of May; on the 25th, nine days afterwards, the Vendean army attacked Fontenay a second time and took it, and more than repaired its losses. This second expedition was planned and executed by Cathelineau, who, after leaving the peasants two or three days' repose, traversed the Bocage in all directions, and roused them again to the attack. "This is nothing," said he to the insurgents; "our misfortune will be soon retrieved. In fifteen days we shall occupy Fontenay. I know the causes of our defeat, and my plan is formed for a new attack. Besides, we must not forget that we deserved to be punished for the disorders committed at La Châtaigneraie." Wherever that man appeared, confidence was restored. On the 23d May, twenty thousand insurgents assembled at Châtillon and heard mass celebrated pontifically by the Bishop of Agra. The whole army was full of the most lively enthusiasm; and in order to obtain pardon for their faults at Châtaigneraie, they marched chanting aloud the penitential psalms and religious hymns.

Chapter IV

The republicans, on their side, awaited them with impatience. They were fully prepared for the battle; with fresh troops and abundance of ammunition. The insurgents advanced in three columns, and took up their position on the very spot where they had been beaten on the 16th. Before commencing the attack they knelt down to receive a last benediction from the supposed bishop, and then advanced against the enemy with enthusiasm. Many of them were without cartouches, and asked to be supplied. "You will find some there," said Marigny, pointing to the Blues. "March!" said the other chiefs; "you must take the cannon with your staves. You must regain Marie Jeanne. She will be for the best runner." The whole army rushed forward, but they encountered a terrific fire; and the right wing, commanded by Lescure, for a moment hesitated. But their gallant chief, as at Thouars, advanced alone to cheer them on with the cry *Vive le Roi!* A republican battery replied to his cheer with a storm of grape, and he leisurely returned to his troops; his clothes were torn with shot, his spurs were carried away, but he was himself unhurt. "See, my friends," said he coolly, "the Blues do not know how to shoot." Upon this they rallied, and charged upon the foe. Suddenly, in height of the onset, they paused before a cross and fell upon their knees in prayer, although the bullets were falling among them like hail. Some of their officers would have made them rise: "Let them pray," said Lescure calmly, who was himself standing in the very thick of the fire; "they will fight none the worse for it." And the next moment they leaped up, hurled themselves upon the enemy, and drove them back like sheep. Staff in hand, Bonchamps and his men cast themselves upon the artillery, knocked down the cannoneers, and seizing the cannon, forthwith directed them upon the Blues. Larochejacquelein, at the head of a few hundred peasants mounted on cart-horses, attacked the republican cavalry, and decided the day by a charge, as well-timed as it was vigorous, upon the left wing of the enemy, where General Chalbos and several representatives of the people were standing.

"Let them pray," said Lescure; "they will fight none the worse."

Chapter IV

In a few moments the victory was complete; and the mass of the republican army precipitated itself in disorder on the road to Niort.

Bonchamps, Lescure, and Forêt were the first to enter Fontenay, and alone dived into the streets of the town, while they were still filled with soldiers. "Down with your arms!" they cried; and entire companies cast themselves upon their knees and asked for quarter. When they arrived at the *place*, the three Vendeans each took a different direction, to secure the more speedy submission of the town. Lescure ran to the prisons to release any insurgents who might be there. Bonchamps had a narrow escape from being slain. A Blue, who had just surrendered, seeing his victor alone, fired at him and wounded him dangerously in the breast. The peasants were now pouring in, and, lest the guilty man should escape, massacred all who were on the spot. But there was no other act of violence committed.

A great number of cannon were taken; but to their dismay Marie Jeanne was still missing. The republicans were as eager to keep as the Vendeans to recapture that trophy, and a detachment of infantry and mounted gendarmes had seized it, and were conveying it along the Niort road. Five-and-twenty peasants, with Forêt at their head, rushed in pursuit, overtook the escort about a league from Fontenay, and after a smart struggle defeated the guard, harnessed themselves to the carriage and dragged it back in triumph, adorned with flowers and ribbons.

The moderation of the victorious insurgents was not less at Fontenay than it had been at Thouars. And the Blues, unable to deny the fact, ascribed it to hypocrisy and craft. The victory dealt the severest blow to their cause which they had yet received; and the general, who a few days before had reported the insurrection quelled, was obliged to acknowledge that he had to do with an enemy who braved all dangers. "The defeat," he wrote to the minister of war, "was general. I do not know our loss. Many guns were abandoned, even the one which the enemy had so much regretted (Marie Jeanne), and large magazines of powder have fallen into his hands."

Chapter V

Supreme council of administration: the Abbé Bernier, Father Jagault, Abbé Brin—Proclamation of the Catholic army—Fresh exertions of the Convention—Victories of Vihiers, Doué, and Montreuil—Siege of Saumur—Quetineau—Cathelineau elected commander-in-chief—Forestier—D'Autichamp, Piron, Talmont—The army march into Angers, and determine to lay siege to Nantes.

THE FIRST STEP of the Vendean chiefs, upon the taking of Fontenay, was to appoint a supreme council of administration, under the presidency of the Bishop of Agra. Their object was to give more regularity to their proceedings, and to provide the poor peasants with clothing, who had left their daily labour for the defence of the Faith. The council was also charged with the whole military organisation of the country, and the development of its resources. It numbered among its members three other priests besides the Bishop of Agra,—the Abbé Bernier, Father Jagault, a Benedictine, and the Abbé Brin; all able men, eloquent, energetic, resolute, and entirely devoted to the cause. The so-called bishop, although the nominal president, was not equal to the part he had assumed; and the Abbé Bernier soon became the real chief. This priest was only twenty-nine years of age when the insurrection broke out, yet he had already acquired a great reputation. Although but the son of a simple peasant, and without interest, he had been made curé of St. Laud's, one of the chief churches in Angers. In 1790 he refused to take the oath to the civil constitution of the clergy, and immediately became a suspected man to the Angevin "patriots." Nor did

Chapter V

their instinct deceive them. Bernier turned out one of the most able of the Vendean leaders. Seldom have so much judgment and resolution been united to so much enthusiasm. Not only did his prudence and wisdom give him the ascendency in the council-chamber, but the very generals guided their military conduct by his advice. Yet his influence with the peasants was greater still. Gifted with extraordinary eloquence, he was indefatigable in preaching. "I have known him," says Madame de Larochejacquelein, "to speak for two hours with a force and sweetness which carried his hearers away with him. What he said was always to the point; his texts were happily chosen, and not less happily worked out. He seemed to be inspired." But his labours did not stop there. As ready to write as to speak, he it was who drew up all the most important documents which were circulated in the name of the insurrection. His zeal, too, was unbounded. He was to be seen wherever there were griefs to be consoled, or courage to be confirmed; and although, later on, traces of ambition were to be descried in his character, none such were apparent in the earlier stages of the war. He became chaplain of the grand army.

Father Jagault was also a very distinguished man. He, like the Abbé Bernier, had held office in Angers at the time of the revolution, when he was professor of theology in the Benedictine monastery of St. Nicholas. Upon his refusal to take the constitutional oath, and consequent deprivation, he retired to his own family, to wait patiently for the moment when God should call him to action. Less prompt and active than Bernier, he was scarcely less remarkable than his colleague for wisdom and eloquence. He was, however, unlike Bernier, of a very retiring disposition. Notwithstanding his success, he seldom preached, and would have been content to occupy the last and lowest place when the general voice summoned him to take a seat in the supreme council.

The Abbé Brin was curé of St. Laurent-sur-Sèvre, and united extraordinary resolution of character to the greatest charity towards the distressed. It was in his parish that the first hospital for the wounded was established. Thither also the Sisters Hospitallers of La Sagesse, who had been driven from all their houses, retired to tend, without distinction, the wounded of both sides. The Missionaries of the Holy Ghost were established in the same town, and discharged the same charitable office.

One of the first acts of the council was to put forth a proclamation addressed "To the French from the chiefs of the Catholic and royal armies." It was an appeal to national justice. After having affirmed "La Vendée victorious, and the Holy Cross of Jesus Christ and the royal standard every where triumphant over the bloody flag of anarchy," the proclamation went on to declare that La Vendée desired to "keep for ever the Holy Catholic, Apostolic, and Roman faith, and to have a king who would act as a father within, and a protector without." Then came a comparison between the conduct of the republicans, "who called themselves patriots," and that of the Vendeans, "whom they termed sanguinary brigands." It was a spirited recapitulation of all the crimes committed since the beginning of the war by the troops of the Convention. A call to union concluded the manifesto, which was dated "from Fontenay, the 27th May, in the first year of the reign of Louis XVII."

The Convention could no longer affect to treat the insurrection with indifference. After its first outbreak, they had speedily recovered their habitual confidence, and had accustomed themselves to regard the insubordination of peasants as an accident of small importance. But the capture of Fontenay dispersed this illusion. It was impossible any longer to deny that the arms of the Republic had suffered a serious reverse, and that the aspect of affairs was alarming. An official notification appeared, that the war in the west required as much attention as that on the frontier; and an appeal was made to the devotion of all true patriots. Numerous bodies of troops were directed upon La Vendée; the commune of Paris alone furnished twelve thousand men; the districts bordering on the scene of insurrection as many more; Orleans sent several

Chapter V

battalions, and reinforcements arrived at Niort from the most distant departments. At the head of these new troops new generals appeared in La Vendée; for the others had been guillotined for high treason. Among the new commanders, the most remarkable were the brewer Santerre, and Westermann, whose name will now be of frequent occurrence, and who later gloried in the surname of *"the Butcher of the Vendeans."*

The measures of the Convention were executed with the utmost rapidity—artillery and stores were despatched at once, and in five days forty thousand men arrived to occupy Saumur, Montreuil, Thouars, Doué, and Vihiers. But the Vendeans assembled in about the same force; and so great was their enthusiasm, that, in the short space of three days, they obtained three victories over the enemy, viz. at Vihiers, at Doué, and at Montreuil. The republicans lost a whole division, and all their artillery and ammunition fell into the hands of the insurgents. In the flush of triumph, the grand army tumultuously demanded to be led against Saumur.

This town, situated on the Vendean side of the Loire, a little below its confluence with the Thouet, might have been easily defended against a regular army, properly provided with a siege-train. It contained the united divisions of four generals, besides the remains of the defeated garrisons of Vihiers, Doué, and Montreuil; in all nearly sixteen thousand men, and eighty pieces of cannon. These troops were protected by the castle, which was always considered impregnable; by the Bournan heights, fortified by redoubts; and by the Thouet, a rapid river, the passage of which would be attended with the greatest difficulty. The Saumurese, in addition to these defences, had provided for their safety by cutting down every garden-hedge and copse which could favour the peculiar mode of fighting of the "brigands." And yet, in spite of all the advantages of such a position, the republicans awaited the attack with uneasiness. The two defeats of Montreuil and Doué especially had created much alarm among the inhabitants, and disorder among the soldiery. It was therefore determined to raise the courage of the faint-hearted, and intimidate the disaffected, by a patriotic ceremony. Sunday the 9th of June was chosen for the inauguration of the Bonnet Rouge at Saumur. The fête consisted chiefly in violent tirades against the *modérés* and the *aristocrats*; and would in all probability have been signalised there, as elsewhere, by wholesale massacres, if orators or audience had had time to think of any thing else but self-defence.

On Monday, the 10th, the attack commenced at three points at once, and with more disorder than usual. Lescure had the command of the left wing. He first turned the redoubts of Bournan Hill, and then marched upon Fouchard Bridge, where lay the principal strength of the republican division, that being the chief entrance into Saumur. Larochejacquelein advanced along the river against a republican corps occupying an intrenched camp in the meadows of Varin, between the Thouet and the Loire, while Cathelineau made a feint upon the castle.

Lescure's division was first engaged. He turned the redoubts, crossed the bridge, and was gaining ground, when, unhappily, he received a wound in the arm. The hurt was trifling; but the peasants, seeing him covered with blood, cried out, "We are lost! he is wounded!" and fell back. Lescure bound up his arm with a handkerchief, and shouting "It is nothing!" endeavoured to rally his broken troops. However, their confusion was extreme; and the enemy, seeing the advantage, charged with a troop of cuirassiers. This completed their disorder. For a while they maintained an unequal contest; but when they saw their balls glance off the steel cuirasses of the horsemen, they turned round and fled. At this moment M. Dommaigné galloped up at the head of the Vendean cavalry, and charged the enemy in flank. He attacked the republican colonel hand to hand, and both fell together. Dommaigné received at the same moment a sabre-cut and a grape-shot, and fell mortally wounded; but in falling he discharged his carbine at his antagonist.

Chapter V

Deprived of their chief, the Vendean horse retreat in disorder, and the cuirassiers charge their flying foes. One man only, named Loyseau, remains bravely fighting for the body of Dommaigné. He kills three cuirassiers; but, finding himself alone, he falls down, as if mortally wounded, across his dead chief. At this moment a happy accident retrieves the fortunes of the day. In the flight of the Vendeans across Fouchard Bridge, two gun-carriages were overturned: these formed a barricade across the way impassable to cavalry; and the peasants, finding themselves no longer pursued, gather courage, return to the attack, and behind the shelter of the carriages take deliberate aim at the cuirassiers. No longer aiming at the breast, they fire at the head. The Blues in their turn recoil, the Vendeans take the offensive, and Loyseau in the instant leaps up, and joins the first rank.

Cathelineau, from his elevated position on the heights near the castle, observed attentively the situation of the various corps engaged. The want of plan with which the eager peasants had rushed to the attack was now beginning to tell upon the fortunes of the day; and he saw that, if the assault was to be successful, Larochejacquelein must be assisted in his attempt on the camp in the Varin meadows. He consulted his colleagues, and himself advanced to the point of attack. The republican general Coustard equally perceived the importance of that movement, and gave the order to two battalions to march to the succour of the camp. The soldiers refused to obey him; and while they were parleying, a Vendean battery arrived to block up the passage. "Charge that battery!" cried he to his cuirassiers. "Whither do you send us, general?" demanded Colonel Weissen. "To death," replied Coustard; "the safety of the Republic demands it." The cuirassiers charged; their shock was valiantly sustained, and almost the whole troop perished. The battery, however, was carried. But it was immediately abandoned, for the infantry refused to advance; and Weissen regained his division covered with wounds and without a follower.

Meanwhile Larochejacquelein had attacked the republican camp. Leaving seven hundred men with De Baugé to guard the bridge of St. Just in front of the camp, he had gone round to force an entrance on the rear. But Donissan bringing up a reinforcement of about six hundred men, he and De Baugé attacked the position in front. They passed the ditch, broke down the wall beyond, and the post was carried. At the same time Larochejacquelein burst in on the other side. Taking off his cap, he threw it over the entrenchments, crying, "Who will go and get it for me?" and leaped in to get it for himself. A great number of his brave peasants poured in after him. The two assaults took place at the same moment, and the Vendeans had the misfortune to fire upon each other as they advanced from opposite quarters. The republicans, thus taken between a double fire, retreat in disorder into Saumur. Larochejacquelein and De Baugé, jumping on horseback, precipitate themselves upon their steps, and with three others penetrate into the streets. At the faubourgs they encounter a battalion from the castle, who, seeing the Vendeans, cast down their arms, and take refuge within its walls. Larochejacquelein and his gallant comrades continue their progress through the city, undeterred by the random shots which fly about their heads. At last they are rejoined by their soldiers, and by those of Lescure; for the town is now in the hands of the besiegers, although the redoubts of Bournan and the castle still hold out. The mass of the republican army were seen escaping by the great bridge across the Loire; but the conflict was still going on between Marigny and his artillery and the Bournan redoubts. When night came, the Vendeans ceased from firing, intending to renew the attack in the morning. But during the darkness the post was evacuated; and on the morrow the garrison of the castle, which was fourteen hundred strong, capitulated. The republican army attempted no sort of order in its flight. The runaways dispersed on all sides, spreading the alarm, and might have fallen an easy prey to the victors, if they had followed in pursuit. But full of

Chapter V

other thoughts, they ran to the churches, crying, *Vive le Roi! Vive la réligion Catholique!*—the bells rang, and the men who before the battle had resigned their lives into the hands of God, now thanked Him for giving them the victory.

By the capture of Saumur, the Vendeans became masters of the passage of the Loire, and found themselves abundantly supplied with ammunition of all sorts—eighty pieces of cannon, thousands of muskets, powder, lead, saltpetre, and equipments. The spoils were all shut up in a church, which the Blues had turned into a magazine of artillery. The next morning Larochejacquelein was seen at a neighbouring window buried in deep thought, with his eyes fixed on this church. An officer asked him what he was doing. "I am thinking," he said, "of our success; and I am lost in astonishment—it is the hand of God!" There was not a common soldier in the whole insurgent army who did not share his sentiments. The prisoners taken in the five days, in the four victories of Vihiers, Doué, Montreuil, and Saumur, amounted to eleven thousand. The loss of the Vendeans in this last affair was sixty killed and four hundred wounded. Among the prisoners who fell into their hands was the republican general Quetineau, whom the insurgents had beaten at Thouars. He was lying in the castle of Saumur for judgment. The Convention refused to believe that the troops of the nation could be defeated by peasants; and the unhappy generals who lost a battle were arraigned for treason. Lescure invited the captive to take refuge in the grand army, where, "in spite of difference of opinion, he should receive greater justice than from his own patriots." "Monsieur," replied Quetineau, "were you to set me at liberty, I should go back to my prison. I wish to be put on my trial. If I fled, I should be deemed a traitor; and I cannot endure the thought. Besides, in flying I should abandon my wife, who would certainly perish." Then he added, "Monsieur, the Austrians are masters in Flanders; you, too, are victorious; the counter revolution makes way. France will be dismembered by strangers."

Lescure answered, "That will the royalists never permit; they will shed their blood in defence of the territories of France." "Ah! when that day comes," exclaimed the republican, "I will myself serve in your ranks. I love the glory of my country: in this sense it is that I am a patriot." At that moment the cry of *Vive le Roi!* arose from the populace in the street below. Quetineau advanced to the window, and said bitterly, "Cowards! It was but the other day you accused me of having betrayed the republic; and now you yourselves, for fear, cry *Vive le Roi!* I take the Vendeans to witness that I do not join in the cry." The brave man was afterwards sent to Paris, where he was judged guilty of death, and executed. So little value did the Convention place on the few truly honourable men who fought under the republican flag! His wife, for whose sake he had declined Lescure's offer, refused to survive him; she cried *Vive le Roi!* in the presence of the judges who condemned him, and speedily followed him to the scaffold.

Lescure, who had been wounded early in the day, was seized with fever at its close, after seven hours' fighting; and was compelled to retire for his recovery to his chateau of Boulaye. But before taking his departure, he assembled the officers, and said, "Gentlemen, the insurrection has acquired too great importance, the success has been too remarkable, to permit us to leave the army any longer without a general-in-chief. As many officers are absent, the nomination can only be provisional; but I give my voice for M. Cathelineau." These words were received with applause by all, excepting only the good Cathelineau himself, who would have refused so great an honour. But the election was confirmed by all the absentees; and the peasant-leader received the supreme command.

The nomination of Cathelineau was in every respect a most judicious act. It was he, of all the chiefs, who exercised the greatest influence over the peasants; he possessed a sort of rude eloquence, which filled them with ardour, and his piety and virtues

Chapter V

won their respect. Besides, it was he who had begun the war, who had raised the country and fought the opening battle. He had a military eye, extraordinary courage, and great judgment. He was also so modest, that in electing him the other generals knew that their commander-in-chief would hearken to counsel. It was, moreover, a stroke of admirable policy to elect a peasant at a moment when a lively jealousy of the aristocracy had contributed in no small degree to the revolutionary movement; for thus the insurgents were themselves the more attached to their cause, and the patriots could no longer be roused to the contest by the cry of "equality." Equality, indeed, reigned far more in the Vendean than in the republican army; there were as many peasants as gentlemen in command. Merit was the sole qualification required; and in the council of war, words of sound wisdom were listened to with equal attention whether uttered by the owner of the chateau or by the tiller of the soil. Of this equality the case of Forestier affords a signal example,—a young man, scarcely eighteen years of age, the son of a poor shoemaker, who was elected to the command of the cavalry after the death of Dommaigné. This young peasant played a most brilliant part, not only in the army, but in the presence of princes and in foreign courts, till his death in 1808. He had the modesty, on his election, to accept the duties and refuse the title of general of cavalry.

Many recruits joined the army after the capture of Saumur; and some of the republican soldiers passed over to the side of the royalists. The staff was augmented by the accession of three fresh officers: Charles d'Autichamp, who, at the age of twenty-three, had been thought worthy of a high rank among the officers of Louis XVI.'s constitutional guard; he was placed in Bonchamps' division, whose cousin he was;—Piron, who had come from Brittany to share the glory and peril which La Vendée offered;—and the Prince de Talmont. The latter was the proprietor of vast estates in the west, and had returned from foreign service to organise the insurrection among his tenantry. Arrested before he could set the enterprise on foot, he obtained his liberation through his brother, the Abbé de la Tremoille, who bribed a member of the Convention to connive at the prince's escape. He was a man of brilliant powers, but of lax morals, and joined the army with a royalist rather than with a Catholic object.

Thus reinforced, the army evacuated Saumur; but as it was an important position, Cathelineau wished to keep possession of it, and left Larochejacquelein with a troop to garrison the town. It was, however, with great difficulty that the peasants could be kept together; so that in a few days the young chief found himself almost abandoned. Every road was now open to the grand army, and an anxious debate was held as to the next operations. The garrison of Angers, upon hearing of the fall of Saumur, panic-stricken, took flight before the insurgents appeared, abandoning their heavy artillery, provisions, and ammunition. It was necessary to turn their terror to advantage. Should they march on Tours, to obtain command of both banks of the Loire? or on Niort, and encounter Westermann, who was invading the opposite side of the Bocage? or should they penetrate into Brittany, organise the insurrection in that province, and form an army to threaten Paris (for till Paris was overcome, La Vendée, in spite of its victories, must be eventually crushed)? or should they attack Nantes, in order to ensure them the command of the whole insurgent country? These two last projects were those especially under discussion. The former was advocated by Bonchamps, who had numerous relations with Brittany, and whose divisions contained a troop of Breton soldiers. But the majority were in favour of the attack on Nantes; and it was decided to execute that movement. It was thought unsafe to attempt a distant expedition, without the command of the sea-coast and an open communication with England. Bonchamps, however, urged his plan with great vehemence; and Stofflet, who took the opposite view, and whose ardour sometimes became ungovernable,

Chapter V

challenged him to a duel. "No, monsieur," was the noble reply, "I will not accept your challenge. God and the king only have the disposal of my life; and our cause would suffer too severely were it to be deprived of yours."

The army, Catholic and royal, after occupying Angers seven or eight days, set out accordingly on the 27th June for Nantes.

Chapter VI

Successes of Charette in Bas Poitou—Union of Charette with Cathelineau—Siege of Nantes—Death of Cathelineau—Westermann in the Bocage, his defeat at Châtillon—D'Elbée elected commander-in-chief—Reverses at Pont Charron and Luçon—Victory over Santerre at Chantonnay—Horrible designs of the republicans—Poisonings *en masse*—Mission from the English Government.

WHILE THE GRAND army was achieving these glorious successes, Charette had been not less effectually manœuvering in Bas Poitou. His chief victory had been at Machecoul, a town defended by a garrison of twelve hundred men, which was taken, after a long and bloody struggle, on the 11th June. A glance at the map will be sufficient to show the importance of this post in reference to the contemplated siege of Nantes. Menaced from two sides by two victorious armies, the citizens were in the utmost alarm. "Not a moment must be lost in sending us succours of every kind," wrote General Petit Bois, who was in command, immediately after the battle of Machecoul. On the 20th, a second victory crowned the arms of the insurgents at Lalloué, and the Vendeans followed their flying foe up to the very gates of Nantes. At the same time arrived intelligence of the fall of Saumur. Four days afterwards, a summons came from the generals at Angers to the authorities of Nantes to surrender the town, to display the white flag on the walls, to deliver up the arms of the garrison, and to place in their hands the commissioners of the Convention as hostages. So great was the terror with which the inhabitants had been inspired by the advance of the insurgents, that the authorities kept this summons a profound secret; but they bravely resolved to defend the town, and Beysser, to

Chapter VI

whom the command was given, put the place into a state of siege, and affixed to the walls the following proclamation:—

"If, through treason or misfortune, Nantes should fall into the hands of our enemies, I swear that it shall become their tomb and ours; and that we will give to the world a great and terrible example of what a people can do which is inspired by the love of freedom and the hatred of tyranny."

Up to this moment Charette's army and the grand army had acted independently; there had been no sort of intercourse between them. But now Lescure, from his retirement at Boulaye, wrote to congratulate Charette on his success at Machecoul, and to request his co-operation in the attack on Nantes. The latter replied by complimenting the grand army on the capture of Saumur. Eventually a union was effected between the two armies. Cathelineau supplied Charette with ammunition and artillery, which he had in abundance; and Charette agreed to attack Nantes on the Vendean side of the Loire, while the grand army proceeded from Angers along the Breton bank.

The republican forces assembled at Nantes amounted to about twelve thousand men, half of whom were troops of the line. The insurgents were less numerous than their leaders had expected. After the capture of Saumur, many had returned to the Bocage; Lescure's division was paralysed in consequence of the absence of its leader, and Larochejacquelein was at Saumur with as many men as could be induced to mount guard. Moreover, the peasants marched without spirit. They could not understand the object of so distant an enterprise, and fell away as the army proceeded; so that on reaching Nantes, Cathelineau found himself with scarcely eight thousand men. Charette's army, however, were animated with enthusiasm. Nantes was the point from which the republican forces directed their operations against the whole country of Poitou, and they had consequently an interest in its capture. Not a man was absent on the 29th June, the day arranged for the attack.

Union of Charette with Cathelineau—Siege of Nantes

The storming commenced at two o'clock in the morning. Cathelineau and D'Elbée led the assault on the north side of the town, Bonchamps on the east; Charette, with twenty-five thousand insurgents, was on the other side of the Loire. The besiegers were repulsed with enthusiasm. The inhabitants had recovered their courage; and conscious that the proclamation of Beysser was no vain bravado, were prepared to resist to the last. So strong was public opinion within the town, that many of the friends of the insurrection, instead of attempting a diversion in their favour, ranged themselves among the republicans. Yet the attack was at first successful on all points. The Vendeans had penetrated into the faubourgs, and the Blues were beginning to yield; indeed, the victory was substantially gained, when two unhappy circumstances entirely changed the fortunes of the day. The Vendean chiefs had learned from experience that it was unwise to drive their opponents to extremities, and leave them no alternative but to conquer or die; and there was always left an outlet by which the routed columns might escape. Upon this occasion it had been determined that no attack should be made on the Vannes side, but that it should be left free for the enemy. As soon as the insurgents had found their way into the town, the enemy began to fly along that road; and if they had been allowed to continue their flight, the victory would have remained on the side of the peasants. But Talmont, misunderstanding, or in his ardour forgetting the wisdom of Cathelineau's arrangement, attacked the runaways, and drove them back into the town. The disheartened garrison, who were about to lay down their arms, took courage at this reinforcement, as they conceived it, and commenced the battle again. Cathelineau then charged at the head of his bravest men, and penetrated as far as the Place de Viarmes. The Blues fled on all sides, and the Vendeans believed themselves again the victors, when Cathelineau fell pierced through the breast with a ball. In the very moment of victory, the peasants caught up the body of their beloved chief, and rushed with him out of the

Chapter VI

town. After that moment the attack became hopeless. Charette bravely endeavoured to animate the fainting ardour of his men, and the battle was prolonged till night-fall, when all the army crossed the Loire in boats. The right side was abandoned, and the Nantesmen were left in possession of the town. It was a repulse more than a defeat, for the garrison were afraid to pursue the enemy; but it was a day of great disaster to the Vendean cause. The wound of Cathelineau, not at first judged mortal, carried him off in a few days, and the insurrection lost its most able promoter. The Saint of Anjou, as he was popularly called, died blessing God. He had fought his first battle on the 13th March, at the head of two hundred peasants armed with clubs. Four months afterwards he died commander-in-chief of the whole country, and covered with glory. Upon his death the army was dissolved in an instant. The peasants all retired to their own homes, and again the insurrection was supposed to be at an end.

While the grand army were under the walls of Nantes, several engagements had taken place in La Vendée. Westermann, at the head of a German legion, advanced into the heart of the Bocage, after making himself master of Parthenay, on the 20th June. On the 1st July he burned the town of Amaillou; he then set fire to M. Lescure's chateau at Clisson, and sent a detachment to destroy La Durbeillère, Larochejacquelein's family mansion at St. Aubin. By this time the Vendeans had recovered from their repulse at Nantes; and, indignant at the atrocities of the republican army in the very heart of their own territory, rose in great numbers and attacked the Blues at Châtillon. Lescure, who was perfectly acquainted with the country, assumed the command; and by a most able and vigorous movement, the enemy were entirely routed in little more than an hour. Two-thirds of Westermann's army were destroyed; and the peasants, in the heat of their revenge, would have massacred some hundreds of prisoners. Marigny declared he would give no quarter. Lescure, learning what was going on, came up, and put a

Death of Cathelineau—D'Elbée elected commander-in-chief

stop to these reprisals. "Go back," said Marigny, "while I kill these monsters—they have fired thy chateau." "I will rather defend them against thee," was the reply; and the men were saved.

Westermann was called to the bar of the Convention to answer for his defeat. Biron, his colleague, was also arraigned, and condemned to death. But the former was restored to his functions, in consideration, said the judge, of his *"energy and his principles of humanity!"* After the death of Cathelineau and the expulsion of the Blues from the Bocage, D'Elbée was named generalissimo of the royalist forces. The four generals of division were Bonchamps, Lescure, Donissan, and Royrand. The Prince de Talmont commanded the cavalry; for on his arrival at the camp, the modesty of Forestier had insisted upon his accepting that post; Marigny, as before, the artillery. Larochejacquelein was chosen by Lescure for his lieutenant-general, and Charette by Donissan. There were also various other leaders, with whose names it is not necessary to encumber this narrative. Three troops, consisting of about a hundred and twenty men each, were formed of deserters from the republican army—one Swiss, one German, and one French.

The election of D'Elbée to the supreme command occasioned considerable surprise, and neither the officers nor the men regarded it with satisfaction. He was certainly very inferior to Bonchamps in military genius; yet he discharged his duties, during a very disastrous period, with great energy and judgment. His accession to authority was attended with the most serious reverse which the royalists had yet sustained. The Convention, more and more enraged at the successive repulses which their generals had received, prepared to pour fresh troops into La Vendée. A division posted at Luçon, under General Tuncq, surprised, on the 25th July, Pont Charron, which was occupied by the central army of the Vendeans; Sapinaud, the officer in command, was taken prisoner and massacred, and his men were put to flight. But D'Elbée, Lescure, and

Chapter VI

Talmont, hearing of the disaster, came to the succour with a fresh division; and the Blues were driven back upon Luçon, which the insurgents at once prepared to attack. The Vendeans opened a terrible fire upon the enemy's centre; and Tuncq, dreading a general rout, ordered a retreat. The peasants, believing that the object of this movement was to turn their flank, became disordered. The Blues attacked them in this condition, and but for Prince Talmont they would have been completely destroyed. As it was, they lost fifteen hundred men and eighteen pieces of cannon. Notwithstanding this victory, Tuncq durst not penetrate farther into the Bocage.

Animated by this success, the armies of the Convention bore down upon the insurgents from every quarter. Charette maintained the struggle in Lower Vendée, sometimes beaten, but never crushed, and at times obtaining signal advantages. But the most remarkable victory was gained over Santerre, at Chantonnay, by the valour of Bonchamps. The republican general had penetrated into the Bocage, wasting the country on every side with fire and sword, destroying the very farm-houses and mills, in accordance with the orders of the Convention. The peasants poured in from all quarters to the attack; and the Blues were totally defeated, with the loss of their artillery. Santerre with difficulty escaped; and scarcely eighteen hundred men could be collected out of the immense force which had entered the insurgent country. The enemy fled in all directions, many without firing a shot; and some refused to believe themselves in safety till they were within the walls of Paris. By this victory Vendée was again quit of the presence of a hostile army.

But the struggle which La Vendée had thus long maintained served only to exasperate the revolutionary party; and they determined to commence a war of extermination against the inhabitants, that they might colonise the insurgent provinces with "true patriots." "Destroy La Vendée, and you will save the country,"— such was the advice given by Barrère on the 2d August; and it was unanimously adopted. Orders were given for the immediate

Victory over Santerre—Horrible designs of the republicans

preparation of combustible materials, to fire the woods, heaths, and copses. The forests were to be hewn down, the houses overturned, the crops cut, the flocks seized, the women and children carried off into the interior of the country, and the property of the insurgents confiscated to the Republic. In order to carry out this savage design, which was to be brought to perfection afterwards by Turreau, a vast military force was required; and the garrisons of Mayence, Valenciennes, and Condé, which had entered into an engagement not to bear arms against the allied powers, and which were justly considered the *élite* of the French army, were despatched on that service. These corps amounted to twenty-four thousand men. A *levée en masse* in the neighbouring departments was also decreed; and the various republican divisions of the two armies, of Brest under Canclaux, and of Saumur under Rossignol, were united under the former of these generals. The force thus assembled amounted to a hundred thousand regular troops, and as many more of the volunteers of the *levée en masse*; and with this overwhelming host of combatants the invasion of La Vendée was resolved on. Yet success appeared so problematical, on account of the determined valour of the insurgents, that to the aid of fire, sword, and the guillotine, was summoned the terrible instrument of poison; and horrible inventions were proposed and tried, by which a stifling vapour should be diffused over a wide extent of country, to destroy every living thing within its influence—man and beast and the very trees of the field.

It was now that the error of the insurgents in the election of their commander-in-chief began to affect the fortunes of the insurrection. Had Bonchamps been placed at the head of affairs, it is probable that all the subsequent disasters would have been averted. That wise general appears to have detected from the first the policy of the Convention in confining the war to La Vendée; and he had made more than one attempt to defeat that policy, by proposing to open communications with Brittany. Now that the enemy threatened to overwhelm them with numbers, he urged again the

Chapter VI

importance of a movement on the other side of the Loire. "Hitherto," he argued, "the enemy have encountered us, and have been beaten in detail; now they perceive their error, they are combining their forces, and they will sweep us out of our own country. Let us extend our operations, and compel them to divide their strength. Brittany has not as yet borne the brunt of the battle; yet our cause is hers, and when we are subdued she will have the same contest to maintain. It is fair that she should assist us, and she is ready to do so. Let us cross the Loire, and so relieve our own territory, double our strength, and attack the enemy in the rear." This most sagacious counsel was rejected; D'Elbée considered it too hazardous: and as some of the other generals agreed with the commander-in-chief, it was resolved to remain on the defensive in La Vendée. They prepared, therefore, to meet the dangers which were thickening around them; and the various chiefs repaired to their several districts to raise the peasantry. Bonchamps was stationed on the banks of the Loire, Larochejacquelein in Southern Anjou, Charette in Lower Vendée; and besides the four divisions mentioned above, a fifth was formed under Royrand and Sapinaud, nephew of the leader who was murdered at Pont Charron. Other arrangements were in contemplation, but the urgency of the occasion rendered it impossible to carry them out.

At this moment, there arrived from England an ambassador with the offer of supplies. The envoy was a Breton gentleman, named Tinténiac, well known to all the Vendean generals. He carried his despatches in the wadding of his pistols, and he had passed through the greatest perils in the execution of his mission. The greater part of the chiefs assembled were for rejecting overtures that would never have been made but out of enmity to their country; but Lescure replied, that they might accept from England ammunition and subsidies; and answer was returned, that if a debarcation was made at the Sands or at Paimbœuf, fifty thousand men should be ready to receive it on the appointed day; but that

Mission from the English Government

the expedition must consist chiefly of Vendean *émigrés*, and be commanded by a prince of the house of Bourbon. Tinténiac departed with this reply; but the promise was not then fulfilled by the English government. The manner in which it was subsequently performed, and its effects on the insurrection, will be related in its proper place in this narrative.

Chapter VII

The army of Mayence in Bas Poitou—Erigny, Doué, Thouars—Rout of Santerre at Coron—Duhoux beats his uncle at Barré Bridge—Victory over the Mayence army at Torfou—Beysser surprised at Montaigu—Charette routs Mieskowski at St. Fulgent—Repulse of Bonchamps—Dissensions of the Vendean chiefs—Disgrace of the republican generals, and appointment of L'Echelle—Overtures of the Mayence men to the Catholic army—Lescure beaten at Moulins—Sack of Châtillon—The republicans concentrate their forces on Chollet—Check at La Tremblaye, where Lescure is wounded—Battle of Chollet—D'Elbée and Bonchamps retreat on St. Florent—Banks of the Loire—Death of Bonchamps.

THE REPUBLICAN troops consisted of eight divisions, of which the army of Mayence was the most important. This formidable corps crossed the Loire, and in a week, after a feeble resistance, possessed itself of all the forts in Charette's country. The terrified inhabitants followed the army about in its constant flight; and Charette, dreading the demoralisation of his troops, sent messenger after messenger to Bonchamps to come to his assistance. In Anjou and Poitou the Blues were less successful. At Erigny, Bonchamps and Larochejacquelein obtained a victory, though the latter was wounded. At Doué, Stofflet was beaten by Santerre; but at Thouars, Lescure attacked twenty thousand of the National Guard, and repulsed them. In consequence of these successes, a retrograde movement was, to the astonishment of the insurgents, commenced by the invading army; and the victorious generals had liberty to go to the assistance of Charette at Tiffauges, although the danger was equally imminent in several other quarters.

Rout of Santerre—Duhoux beats his uncle

Santerre and two other generals, with twenty thousand men, had marched upon Vihiers, where there was no one to oppose them. The supreme council of La Vendée roused the country for more men, and ten thousand fresh insurgents were collected; but they possessed only three bad eight-pounders to oppose a complete park of artillery; they were, therefore, compelled to have recourse to stratagem to win the victory. Piron, who commanded them, enjoined his men to recoil at the first shock, and entice the Blues from their position on the heights into the town of Coron. Santerre fell into the snare, and allowed his army to be hemmed up in a long and narrow street. Meanwhile Piron took the heights, and the republican troops found themselves in a hole in which it was impossible to act. The defeat was total; and the battle ever after went by the name of the Rout of Santerre. It took place on the 18th September; and it gave Piron the possession of eighty pieces of cannon, sixty barrels of gunpowder, and three thousand muskets.

After the Rout of Santerre, Piron sent some of his men to the assistance of Duhoux, who commanded the Vendeans of Chemillé. His uncle, General Duhoux, commanded an important division of the republican forces, and had just entered the Bocage by the Ponts-de-Cé. The two relatives fought at the Bridge Barré, over the river Layon, when the nephew was victorious. The two wings of the insurgent army fell back, but the centre remained firm; and a peasant named Bernier, followed by a few friends, swam across the river, and attacked the rear of the Blues. General Duhoux lost his baggage, his artillery, and three thousand men; with the rest he retreated to Angers. A pleasantry of the younger Duhoux almost cost the elder his life. The Vendeans being in want of ammunition, their chief said before the battle, "Do not distress yourselves; my uncle will take care to provide some." This *bon-mot* was reported to the Convention, and the republican general was summoned before a court-martial. The battle took place a day after the Rout of

Chapter VII

Santerre. We have another victory to record of the same date: it is the grand defeat of the Mayence corps at Torfou.

Bonchamps, D'Elbée, and Lescure, having repulsed the enemy in Anjou and Poitou, were left free, as we said, to succour Charette; and with that view had marched to Tiffauges. On the 18th the chiefs met and adopted a plan of attack suggested by Bonchamps, who, ill as he was, was carried to the council-chamber, and the next morning to the field of battle. At midnight the Abbé Bernier said Mass at an altar hastily prepared, in view of the whole Vendean camp, and solemnly blessed a great white flag, embroidered with a gold cross and three *fleurs-de-lis*. Till the moment of battle every combatant remained upon his knees, and when the word was given rose secure of victory.

The advanced guard of the army of Mayence, under Kleber, had only one fear, viz. that the enemy would not stay long enough to be destroyed; and at first they appeared to carry all before them. They possessed themselves of Boussay and Torfou, and gave those places up to fire and pillage: and when Charette with his cavalry advanced, they drove him back in disorder, and not even the entreaties and threats of the women, who had taken refuge behind the army, could stop the runaways. At length Bonchamps, carried on a hurdle, and Lescure appeared with the insurgents of Anjou and Haut Poitou; and then Charette's troops rallied, and the real battle began. Kleber and his officers perceived in a moment that at length, for the first time, they were matched with the grand army, Catholic and Royal; but this only inflamed their courage, for they believed that the victory, when gained, must be decisive. The two armies rush on each other in a sort of frenzy: Charette charges the column which Kleber in person leads on; the republican general is wounded, but remains with his men, and they once more become the assailants. Bonchamps and Lescure redouble their efforts. The former, forgetting his wound, leaves his hurdle, and jumping upon a horse, charges the enemy at the head of his Angevins. The latter, stamping with excitement, cries out, "Are there not four hundred men brave enough to die with me?" "We'll follow where you lead," answer with one voice the men of Echaubroignes and the grenadiers of Poitou; and Lescure leads them into the thick of the fight. Again the enemy fall back, and at the same moment several bands of insurgents, crouching, after their manner, among the thickets and hedges, open a murderous fire upon the flank and rear of the retreating column. The Blues execute a movement for the rescue of their artillery, now seriously endangered, which throws them into irreparable disorder; and Kleber beats a retreat. The Vendeans pursue, and the Mayence men fall back, fighting as they go. Every step cost them more and more men; and at two leagues from Torfou the fight was as bloody as ever. At length they arrived at Boussay Bridge. "If the Vendeans pass this," said Kleber to Colonel Chouardin, "we shall be all cut to pieces. Stay here. You will be slain; but you will save your comrades." The brave man stayed, and he and the greater part of his troop were destroyed; but the rest of the army effected their escape.

This was one of the most bloody of all the battles in which the insurgents had been engaged. Their chiefs, considering that the Mayence men had violated their engagement to the allied forces, had forbidden the peasants to cry as usual, *Rendez vous! Grâce!* and not a single prisoner was taken on either side. The road between Torfou and Boussay was strewn with the dead.

Still the Mayence corps was not destroyed; and it being ascertained that General Beysser, who, it will be remembered, had commanded the Blues at Nantes, was about to effect a junction with Kleber, Bonchamps resolved to attack Kleber at Clisson, while Charette and Lescure undertook to surprise Beysser at Montaigu.

At three o'clock in the morning of the 21st, Beysser's scouts brought him news that the enemy was in sight. "Pooh!" said he; "the enemy will not dare to attack me. It is a reinforcement which I expect from Clisson;" and he refused to take the slightest

Chapter VII

precaution. However, before long the rattle of musketry showed that the "brigands" would dare any thing; but it was then too late to take the necessary measures. The posts, badly guarded, were carried in an instant, and the republican army was beaten without a struggle: in fact, it was almost entirely destroyed. Here, as at Torfou, no prisoners were made. Beysser, badly wounded, fell back into Nantes; the Convention immediately withdrew his command, and soon afterwards he mounted the scaffold.

Instead of following up this success, according to the plan concerted with Bonchamps, whose military eye saw the necessity of annihilating the Mayence corps, Charette insisted the next day on attacking Mieskowski's division at St. Fulgent. Lescure reluctantly consented; and while Bonchamps was counting on their co-operation against Kleber, these two leaders were withdrawing their forces in another direction. It is true that they were successful: after eight hours' fighting hand to hand, and latterly so close that both sides took their ammunition out of the same cartouch-boxes, the Vendeans were victorious, and the republicans fled, leaving all their artillery and baggage in the hands of the conquerors. But the loss of time, and the dissensions which arose out of this movement, were very injurious to the Vendean cause. Mieskowski joined Beysser at Nantes.

The same day Bonchamps, as had been arranged, attacked at Clisson the army of Mayence, eighteen thousand strong, commanded by Canclaux. The Vendean general had only seven thousand men; repulsed, he returned three times to the attack, certain of being seconded by the columns of Charette and Lescure, of whose success against Beysser he had received intelligence. He assailed the enemy again and again, now in flank, now in the rear, but he could not shake their firmness. Unsupported as he was, he was compelled to retire, with the loss of eight hundred men, burning with fury against Charette for his breach of promise; and his troops dispersed, sharing their chief's indignation. And not

Charette routs Mieskowski—Dissensions of the Vendean chiefs

without reason, for if Charette had adhered to his agreement with Bonchamps, the Mayence corps would in all probability have been destroyed, and the invasion virtually repelled.

The divisions of Santerre, Duhoux, Beysser, and Mieskowski, being thus destroyed, and the Mayence men, if not annihilated, at least repulsed, there ensued an interval of repose, during which the peasants returned to their homes, and in every parish sang *Te Deum* for their glorious victories. However, the peril was not yet passed, and the chiefs kept round them as many men as possible. The advantage gained was not very substantial. If the Republic had lost some thousands of men, and much artillery, in four defeats, La Vendée was still surrounded by enemies; yet union and energy might even then have achieved success. Unfortunately, the conduct of Charette had sown the seeds of dissension, and the insurgents began to be threatened with a double danger.

The Convention, thus unexpectedly baffled, resolved on a new plan of attack; all the generals in command were disgraced, and a new commander appointed over the entire forces. Of General Lechelle, the leader selected, Kleber has drawn no very flattering portrait. He said, "Lechelle was the most cowardly soldier, the worst officer, and the most ignorant chief ever seen. He knew nothing of the country; he could scarcely write his own name; and never once did he approach within cannon-shot." It was to make way for such a man as this that Canclaux, Dubayet, and Mieskowski were recalled.

Canclaux and Dubayet were informed of their disgrace just as they had recommenced operations with success. The Mayence corps had beaten Bonchamps on the 5th October, at St. Symphorien; and would probably have immediately entered Mortagne, if the recall of their generals had not condemned them to inaction till the arrival of the new commander-in-chief. The brave men were disgusted at this conduct of the Convention, and during the cessation of hostilities sent a deputation of eight grenadiers into the camp of the

Chapter VII

royalists, offering to join their cause for a certain regular pay and a sum of four hundred thousand francs. The council-general having no such funds at their command, and dreading besides to be entangled in some treachery, refused the proffered alliance. If they had been able to arrange a treaty with the formidable bands of Mayence, certainly the insurgents would have been more than a match for any troops which the Convention could have sent against them; and the council-general were severely blamed for not making an effort to secure such valuable assistance. But it seems doubtful how far Kleber and the other generals concurred in the offer of the deputation; and, upon the whole, the council must be judged to have acted wisely.

On the 8th of October, Lechelle joined the army, and the republicans immediately resumed the offensive. Kleber, who had been charged with the command in the interior, explained his plan of attack to the new general. Lechelle adopted, without in the least understanding, the combinations: "Yes," he replied, "your plan is quite to my mind; but it is on the field that you must show it me. We must march in full array, and with our troops in close order." Yet the nature of the Bocage had just been explained to him. The divisions of Saumur, Thouars, and Fontenay, received orders to assemble at Bressuire, in order to attack Châtillon. They did so; burning their way through the country, and deliberately stopping to destroy what the flames spared. The three divisions were under the command of Chalbos, and comprised twenty thousand men. Lescure, who had to defend Châtillon, had not more than three or four thousand under his orders, nor could he obtain reinforcements; Bonchamps and D'Elbée were occupied with the Mayence men, and Charette would not even vouchsafe a response to his urgent applications for assistance. Stofflet and Larochejacquelein, however, brought up two thousand Angevins; and these were all that could be obtained for the defence of Châtillon. Nevertheless, they took up their station on the height of Moulins, above

Lescure beaten at Moulins—Sack of Châtillon

Châtillon, and engaged the enemy with great bravery and resolution; but the attempt was hopeless.

Lescure was completely beaten, and Chalbos and Westermann occupied Châtillon. Westermann immediately set fire to the whole surrounding country: villages and farms were destroyed, and the unhappy inhabitants massacred without mercy. The commissioners of the Convention wrote to the Committee of Public Safety: "Terror every where precedes the army—fire and steel are now the only arms we use."

After this defeat, Bonchamps and D'Elbée came up and routed the Blues, with the loss of all their artillery and ammunition. Westermann left the battle in a rage, accusing his men of cowardice. They indignantly denied the charge. "Well, then," said he, "come with me, and either win back what you have lost, or die in the attempt." He picked out a hundred horsemen, set a foot-soldier behind each rider, and took the road to Châtillon at full speed, followed by the rest of his troops. It was the dead of night, and the Vendeans were lying asleep and drunk in disorder about the town. Then began such a slaughter as the insurrection had not yet seen. The Blues had no other object but to burn and to destroy; they spared neither women nor children; they laid their bloody hands on every living thing, and, not less drunk than their helpless victims, cut the throats of the wretched inhabitants, and fired the streets of the town. Except the royalist leaders, only one man preserved his senses in that awful scene: that man was Westermann, who had turned up his sleeves and taken off his coat to be the freer for the work of butchery. A few of the insurgents escaped, and Westermann pursued them as far as Temple, which he burned, and then returned to complete the destruction of Châtillon.

This massacre could scarcely affect the relative positions of the parties; but the situation was becoming every day more alarming, as three armies were advancing from different quarters to the very heart of the Bocage. The Mayence men were in possession of

Chapter VII

Mortagne; Chalbos threatened Chollet; and the division of Luçon, in spite of some feeble opposition, were able to execute the same movement. The chiefs of Anjou delayed awhile to act, counting on the assistance of Charette; who, however, persisted in a separate warfare, and was bent on an attack upon Noirmoutiers, at the other extremity of La Vendée. Under these circumstances, D'Elbée, Bonchamps, Lescure, Larochejacquelein, and Royrand concentrated their forces before Chollet.

The Vendeans had arranged to attack the Blues on their march upon Chollet; they had calculated that the battle would take place on the 14th October, and the various posts were assigned; but a delay in the enemy's advance prevented the execution of the plan. Lechelle did not appear till the next day; Lescure, warned the first of his approach, placed himself at the head of a party to make a reconnaissance, and met the Blues in the avenues of the Chateau of La Tremblaye, which lies midway between Chollet and Mortagne. He gave the word to charge, without troubling himself about the number of his foes. His brave men gallantly obeyed; but he was himself unable to join them: at the first discharge he was shot in the eye. They did not, however, see him fall, and were maintaining an obstinate struggle, not without success, against the whole body of the Blues, when the cry rose that Lescure was wounded. They at once fell back in disorder, and Lescure, whose wound appeared mortal, was carried to Beaupreau.

The insurgents at Beaupreau numbered forty thousand men, while the republican strength was about five thousand less, all of whom, however, were regular troops. Under these circumstances, several of the chiefs proposed to cross the Loire. Bonchamps had never ceased to urge a diversion in Brittany, and Talmont, with some others, forming a "Breton party," eagerly declared in favour of that movement; while D'Elbée and Larochejacquelein were for remaining in La Vendée, beaten or victorious. Without discussing the merits of these two plans, certainly it may be said that the

Check at La Tremblaye—Battle of Chollet

middle course, which was the course adopted, was the worst of all. Four thousand men, under Talmont, were withdrawn from the army, and sent to St. Florent, where there were already several Breton companies, in order to make themselves masters of the passage of the Loire. Thus the Vendean army was deprived, upon the eve of a great battle, of the assistance of four thousand of its best soldiers and a portion of its artillery; while the expedition towards Brittany was too small to be of importance, for to effect the rising of the Breton population, it should have been undertaken by the whole Vendean army.

On the 17th October, the Vendeans took the offensive, and marched on Chollet. The republicans were encamped in front of the town towards Beaupreau, and not expecting an attack, were preparing to pursue the enemy. They were not, however, off their guard, and as soon as the Vendean skirmishers appeared, put themselves in battle-array. Kleber and Bard commanded the centre, Chalbos the right, and Haxo the left wing; Müller commanded the reserve, four thousand strong; but nothing could stand the first shock of the insurgents, who advanced in three columns. Bonchamps and D'Elbée charged the right wing, which fell back; Larochejacquelein and Stofflet assailed the centre, and broke the line; upon this Kleber called up Müller with his reserve. That general obeyed; but his soldiers turned round and fled without firing a shot—terrified at the sight of peasants rushing upon them at full speed, in spite of the storm of grape and musketry with which they were enveloped. The advance-guard of the Blues also fell back, and Larochejacquelein and Stofflet possessed themselves of a park of artillery and turned it upon the enemy. Already the cry was heard of *Sauve qui peut*, and the Vendeans believed that the day was their own; but at this critical moment Haxo, throwing himself down a gorge, attacked Stofflet's column in flank, retook the artillery, and drove the insurgents back. Seeing this, Bard cried out to his troops: "Will you be less brave than the Mayence men? Do you want to be taken for

Chapter VII

cowards?" At these words the disordered column rallied, and at the same moment the republican cavalry charged,—thus the peasants lost the advantage they had gained. Still neither side was victorious; and the combatants were so involved in one dense *mêlée*, that their leaders could no longer issue their orders. It was a hand-to-hand fight, rather than a battle. Suddenly a few shouts were heard in the rear of the Vendeans for a "retreat on the Loire." A panic began to spread among the peasants: the bravest hearts gave way to the general discouragement, and defeat became certain. In vain the chiefs strove to restore their fainting courage; the battle was lost—the insurgents were broken in heart. However, D'Elbée, Bonchamps, and Larochejacquelein could not make up their minds to quit the field; and assembling three or four hundred men well known for their personal heroism, they rushed on the victorious Blues, crying "Death to the republicans!" At their first charge, they penetrated into the very midst of the enemy's ranks; but the mass of their army durst not follow, and their heroism served merely to render the defeat more bloody, and the disaster more irretrievable. D'Elbée and Bonchamps fell nearly at the same time. The little band was hemmed in by the Blues; escape was impossible; and night came on, to add its horrors to the scene of carnage. No one any longer fought to conquer, but to slay; and of those three or four hundred men, all must have been cut to pieces, but that Piron and Lyrot came up with a fresh division, not to retrieve the battle, but to save the fallen chiefs. Bonchamps and D'Elbée were taken to Beaupreau, where Lescure was lying wounded, and the wounds of all three were declared mortal. Before pursuing the flying army, the republicans returned to Chollet, and committed terrible outrages at that place; after which, Westermann, followed by a small division, came upon the rear-guard of the Vendeans during the night, and massacred the whole. The remains of the defeated army hurried away to St. Florent, where they joined their four thousand comrades, under Talmont, and prepared immediately to cross the Loire.

Banks of the Loire—Death of Bonchamps

Thither flocked also a vast crowd of terror-stricken women and children; more than eighty thousand persons swelled the train of the discomfited insurgents. It is impossible to describe that scene of misery; nothing was to be heard on all sides but weeping, and lamentation, and cries of distress. One thought for the future alone seemed to possess the crowd—how to escape from their burning country. A score of crazy boats ferried over a large number; others crossed on horseback; and some swam the broad and rapid river;—all were pressing and hurrying towards the other side. Presently Bonchamps and Lescure were borne in, dying, upon their litters, to increase the general despair and confusion. Loud and deep were the cries of vengeance heard on all sides, and the peasants looked round for some object on which to wreak their fury. It chanced that in the church of St. Florent there were shut up five thousand republican prisoners, and the chiefs were deliberating in Lescure's chamber what to do with these men, as they could not take them any further. It was proposed to shoot them all. Lescure cried, "Horrible!" but his voice was not heard. The thirst for vengeance was so great, that the majority of the council entertained the idea; but no one would give the order. The peasants, however, were too eager to need the word of command; and crying, "Let us slay the Blues!" they pointed the cannon against the church. Bonchamps, lying wounded on his bed of death, was apprised of what was going forward; calling his officers, he conjured them to save the republicans. "My friend," he said to Autichamps, "it is the last order I shall ever give you; tell me it shall be obeyed." Forthwith the beating of a drum announced a proclamation, and there was silence in the camp. Autichamps repeated the words of Bonchamps, and immediately was heard, on all sides, "Quarter! quarter! it is Bonchamps' order;" and the republicans were all saved. What general ever received so noble a tribute of love and respect? If the situation of the army be remembered, and the sufferings, by pillage, fire, and sword, which these very prisoners had inflicted upon them, it is impossible

Chapter VII

not to admire their self-command in thus abstaining from an act of vengeance as sweet as it was terrible.

Bonchamps was right,—it was the last order he ever gave: he died that very day, fortified by all the rites of Holy Church. He expired full of hope and joy, to the edification of the whole army, who had never more admired his heroic courage during his saintly life than in his now happy death. The Blues were as rejoiced at this event as his countrymen were afflicted: "The death of Bonchamps," they said, "is a victory in itself." But they took care not to publish the act of mercy with which it was crowned: "Free men accept their life from slaves! That is against the spirit of the revolution. We must consign to oblivion this unfortunate occurrence. Mention it not in the Convention. Brigands have no time to write journals. Let it be forgotten, like so many other things." Is it matter of surprise that ingratitude like this should have at length exhausted the patience and forbearance of the peasants? The men who, at the beginning of the war, had shown so godlike a spirit, afterwards wreaked a terrible vengeance on their bloody persecutors.

The ashes of Bonchamps repose on the scene which witnessed his last act of mercy; and St. Florent glories in the possession of his tomb. It is surmounted by a statue of the dying general. His own words form the best epitome of his character, the distinguishing virtue of which was charity, and are engraved on the monument:

"Grace aux Prisonniers. Bonchamps l'ordonne."

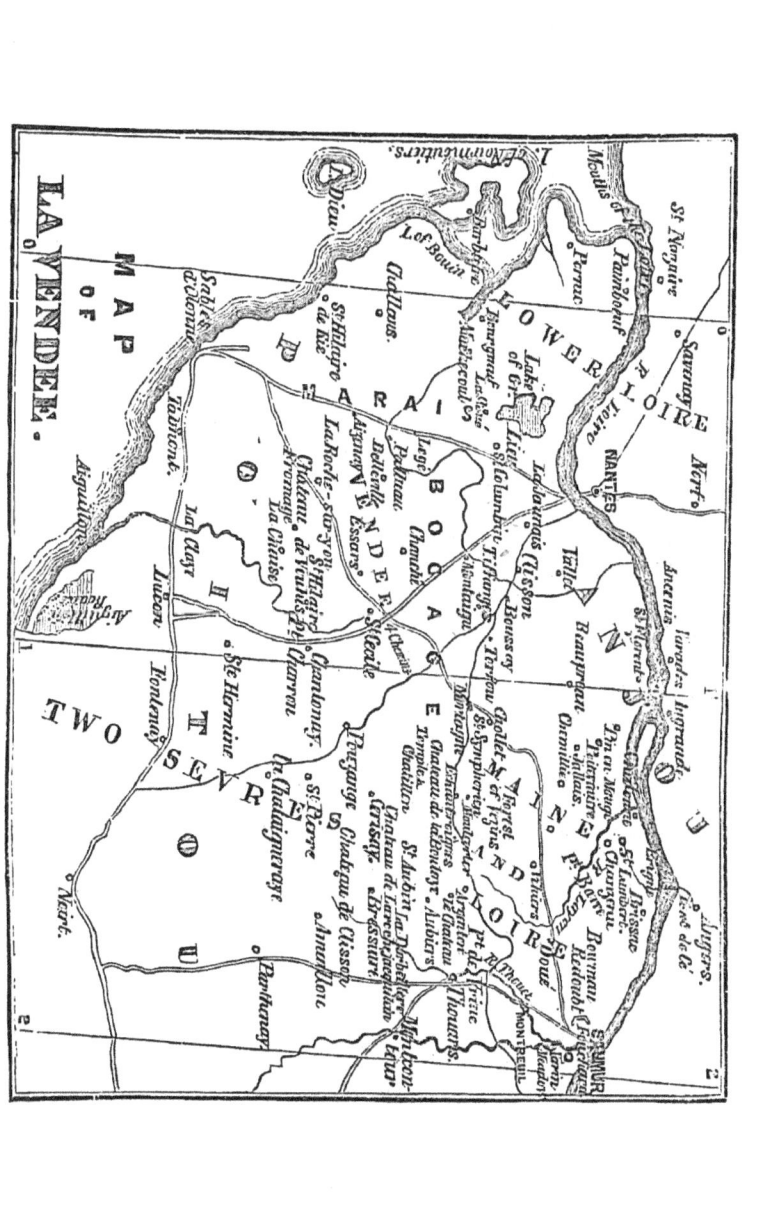

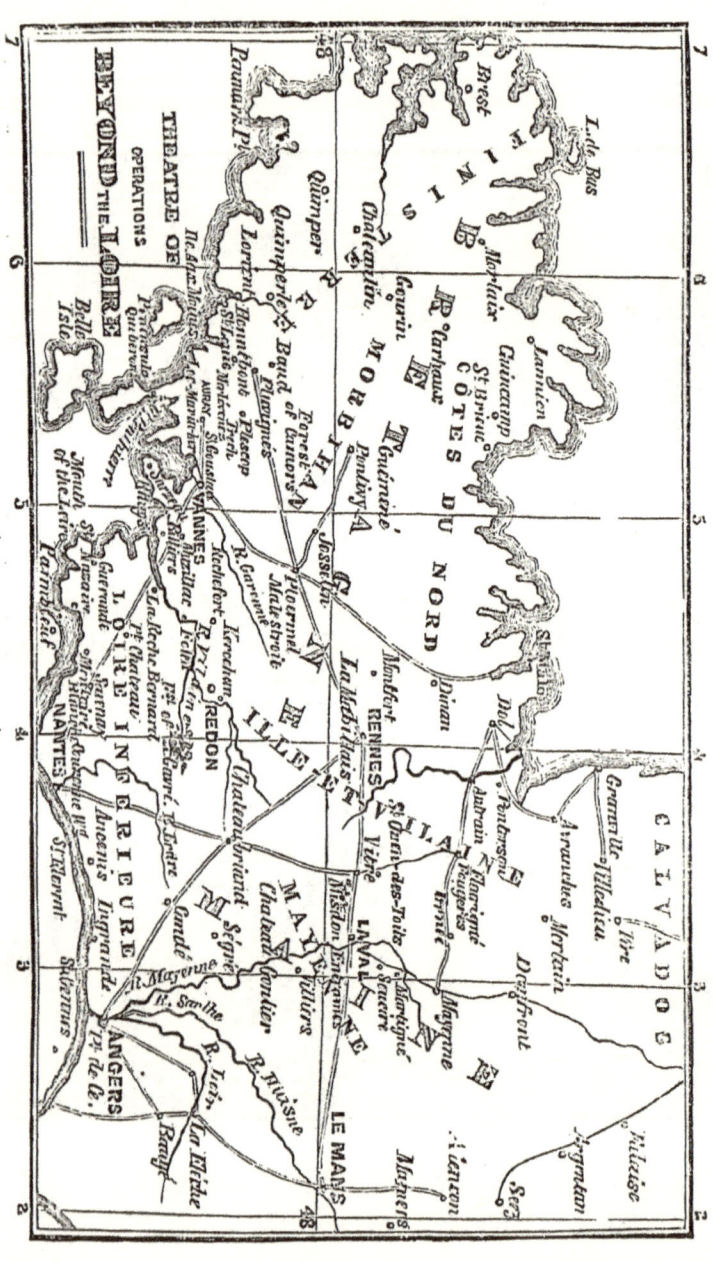

(See page 83 et seq.)

Chapter VIII

Passage of the Loire—Lechelle reports the defeat of the insurgents and the devastation of La Vendée—Successes at Chateau Gontier and Laval—The Little Vendée—Larochejacquelein chosen commander-in-chief—Victory of Laval—Reverses of the republicans, and new organisation of the Catholic army—Last moments of Lescure—English emissaries—Unsuccessful attack on Granville—Alleged treason of Talmont, Bernier, and others—Imposture of the *soi-disant* Bishop of Agra detected—Return of the Catholic army—Affairs of Pontorson and Dol—Bravery of Talmont and the curé of St. Marie de Rhé—State of the army on the road to Angers.

HOWEVER ADVISABLE might have been the passage of the Loire in the hour of victory, it was now a measure of very questionable policy; still, if Bonchamps had been alive, it might have been successful. From his knowledge of the country, and his influence over the inhabitants, it is probable that a general insurrection might have been organised throughout Brittany; but by the death of that commander the army found itself without a head in the midst of a population devoted indeed to the cause of the Church and of the throne, but untried, and of which the resources were wholly unknown. Larochejacquelein and Lescure, never favourable to the evacuation of La Vendée, were now more opposed to it than ever, and urged upon the panic-stricken peasants the advantage of staying in their own country. Lescure indeed, not having many days to live, declared that he would never cross the Loire. But the unhappy Vendeans saw behind them nothing but smoking homes—in front were blooming fields and a sympathising people; and they insisted on being led over the river. When he found that he could not stop

Chapter VIII

their fatal impetuosity, Lescure caused himself to be ferried across, determined to share to the last, as he could not avert, the disasters of his countrymen.

It was again reported to the Convention, by their commissioners, that the insurrection was at an end. "The National Convention," they said, "decreed that the war was to be terminated before the end of October; and it may be said, today, that it no longer exists in La Vendée. A profound silence reigns throughout the country lately occupied by the enemy. For miles neither man nor human habitation is to be seen. We have left behind us only cinders and heaps of corpses." Lechelle announced officially, that "La Vendée, reeking with blood, strewn with corpses, and given up for the greatest part to flames, afforded a signal example of national justice." In return for their services, the Convention publicly declared that the "brave soldiers were covered with glory, and that their country was satisfied." Other armies have been guilty of the like excesses, but the deliberate cruelty with which the republicans gloried over their deeds recalls the career of that "Scourge of God," who made it his boast that the very grass could not grow beneath the hoofs of his horse.

The passage of the Loire was but the signal for fresh atrocities. Lechelle laid down a plan of campaign in very few words: "Follow the brigands without intermission, and do not lose sight of them for a moment." The whole army of the Blues, with the exception of a corps of observation left in La Vendée, crossed at the Ponts de Cé and at Ancenis, and followed in hot pursuit, having first massacred a number of the wounded and sick whom the insurgents had left behind them. The Vendeans passed on rapidly, defeating the republican garrison of Chateau Gontier, where, in revenge for the massacre of their sick, they shot their prisoners; they then passed on to Laval, and were again victorious. There, however, they showed themselves still capable of mercy. A number of runaways had taken refuge in the house of one Madame de Montfranc, a republican lady. At her entreaties they were spared by the victorious Vendeans;

and, incredible to say, this intervention cost Madame de Montfranc her life;—the success of her intercession was taken for proof of a guilty understanding with the brigands.

Notwithstanding these two battles, the Vendeans were two days in advance of their pursuers; and some of the chiefs advised the penetrating farther into Brittany. But hitherto only six thousand peasants, who received the *sobriquet* of the Little Vendée, had joined the army, although the tocsin had been sounded in every parish; and it appeared essential to the spread of the insurrection that they should at once obtain a victory. It was resolved, therefore, to chance a battle; and with that view they halted at Laval. Larochejacquelein was chosen commander-in-chief.

Westermann, whose ferocious thirst for blood we have already noticed, followed on the track of the Vendeans with the pertinacity of a sleuthhound, and was far in advance of the main body, when, at three leagues' distance from Laval, he was attacked by the enemy, whom he supposed to be retiring before him. The combat lasted two hours, and resulted in the repulse of the republicans. In the darkness of the night, so great was the confusion, that Autichamps, mounted on a chest to serve out the cartridges, gave them indiscriminately to Blues and Vendeans. This, however, was but the commencement of the battle: in the morning the main body arrived, and found the Vendeans drawn up in order of battle on the heights of Entrames. There was the greatest ardour on both sides; the Blues hoped that day to put an end to a contest so full of danger, and so barren of glory, while the insurgents knew that on a grand victory depended all their hopes of safety, and the success of the expedition. To animate his men, Lescure, wounded as he was, had himself supported at a window, from which he could harangue the army. Larochejacquelein also addressed a stirring proclamation to his soldiers.

The republican army advanced in single line, the Mayence corps forming the van; Marigny, who had charge of the artillery, permitted them to approach within cannon-shot, and then received them

Chapter VIII

with a storm of grape. Still they came on steadily; but the Vendeans put forward a cloud of skirmishers, and they fell back in disorder upon the main army. The confusion spread through the ranks; but Kleber and Westermann rallied their forces, and at Entrames the action became general. It lasted some time, without advantage to either side. The Vendeans were much distressed by a small battery which the Blues had posted in a commanding position, and which kept up a galling fire upon their lines. Stofflet, seeing that the fate of the day depended upon silencing the battery, despatched a party of picked men on that service; after a smart struggle, they effected their purpose, and the Blues, deprived of that support, began to retire. But for the Mayence men the battle would have been already decided in favour of the insurgents; that redoubtable corps, however, advanced again and again to the charge, as with indomitable courage they were again and again repulsed; and if Lechelle had now brought up his reserve, the day would have ended in the defeat of the Vendeans. But he held back his second division, and began to beat a retreat: neither at Cholet nor at Laval would he venture under fire. This movement caused the stoutest hearts to lose courage; and the soldiers of Kleber, who had been hitherto fighting bravely, gave way and presently fled in disorder. The rout became total; and the arrival of General Bloss with new troops only served to increase the confusion. However, Bloss determined to make one effort to retrieve the day; and with a handful of chasseurs he cast himself upon the bridge of Chateau Gontier, and undertook to defend it. He was recommended by a brother officer to retire. "No," he said; "I cannot survive the disgrace of such a day;" and soon afterwards he fell mortally wounded. Victory redoubled the ardour of the insurgents; and the Blues, as they retreated, were attacked in rear and on both flanks. The Mayence corps were driven into the river Mayenne, and many of them were drowned; one whole battalion laid down their arms and begged for quarter, but the Vendeans, mindful how former acts of mercy had been repaid, shot them all

Victory of Laval—Reverses of the republicans

pitilessly. The remains of the republican army took refuge behind the walls of Chateau Gontier, where they thought themselves secure. "What! my friends," exclaimed Larochejacquelein; "are the conquerors to sleep outside, and the vanquished inside the town? We have not finished yet!" The peasants accordingly rushed to the attack, and speedily possessed themselves of Chateau Gontier. Still the battle was not finished, though it had already lasted thirteen hours. About midnight the Blues again took the offensive; but the Vendeans, though at first surprised by the suddenness of the attack, soon repulsed their assailants, and the enemy retired in the greater disorder for their last effort. Kleber thus describes the condition of their army after this "horrible rout," numbering now but seven thousand men, out of the thirty thousand who had gone into battle. "The soldiers were drenched to the skin, without tents, without straw, without shoes, without breeches, some without any clothing at all—up to their knees in mud, shivering with cold, and without a single cooking utensil; the flags surrounded by twenty, thirty, at the most fifty men to make up the several battalions." With such troops nothing was to be done but to beat a retreat upon Angers. When Lechelle, who had never been seen during the battle, showed himself to the soldiers, he was greeted with cries of *"A bas Lechelle! Vive Dubayet! Vive Kleber!* They shall give us Dubayet again." The commissioners of the Convention could not but acknowledge this demand to be just; and they recommended the general-in-chief to retire, "for the benefit of his health." Lechelle went to Nantes, and there destroyed himself with poison. Rossignol was afterwards appointed to the command-in-chief of the forces in Brittany.

That very day Berrere had announced to the Convention the extinction of the war in La Vendée; and while their army was undergoing its most complete defeat, the people of Paris were celebrating its victory with dances and festivity. The consternation may, therefore, be more readily conceived than described, when the news arrived of the battle of Laval; at the same time other

Chapter VIII

columns were defeated, and one republican general, Lenoir, wrote word that "six horsemen had put to flight twelve hundred men;" that "desertion was going on so rapidly, that of those twelve hundred only five hundred remained with him after three hours, and that before the end of the day he expected to find himself alone." The Convention hereupon decreed, in order to intimidate those suspected of "moderatism" in Brittany, that "every town which should harbour the brigands, or fail to repulse them, should be considered in rebellion and destroyed accordingly, and the property of the inhabitants confiscated to the republic." Measures were also immediately taken to prevent the return of the Vendeans into La Vendée. These were, unhappily, successful. Larochejacquelein would have recrossed the Loire immediately after the victory, but he was only commander-in-chief in action; the peasants were under no sort of control, and instead of retracing their steps, they immediately evacuated Chateau Gontier, and returned to Laval, where they endeavoured to fortify themselves. The period of rest which ensued they employed in reducing their bands to some order: hitherto they had marched in one confused crowd of men, women, and children,—all distinction of company or division had been lost on the Brittany side of the Loire; but now they attempted to organise their forces. On a general census they found that they could muster forty thousand fighting men of all arms; the number of women, children, old men, and sick, was about the same; their artillery was about fifty-five pieces of every calibre; and their cavalry from ten to twelve thousand strong.

During the battle of Laval, Lescure, whose wound detained him in the town, received a letter addressed to the general of the royal army, in which it was intimated that fifty thousand men were ready to rise in the neighbourhood of Rennes, provided the army would take that direction. This letter was the work of Puisaye, of whom we shall hear more in the sequel; but it appeared unworthy of credence to the Vendean generals: an army of such magnitude could scarcely, as they thought, be invisible, or afraid of acting independently; and they returned for answer, that if the fifty thousand men would show themselves, they should be immediately supported. It was an unhappy answer. The army was in existence, and Puisaye, dissatisfied with the reply of the Vendeans, sought a personal interview with them; but they had left Laval before he could reach them, and the opportunity was lost. It appears incredible, that after passing the Loire, in order to raise the Bretons, they should have refused an offer of fifty thousand men without inquiry; but from first to last, this unhappy expedition was conducted with equal folly and obstinacy.

The battle of Laval took place on the 26th October 1793; on the 2d November, the insurgent army left the town without having formed any plan of campaign. The majority of the peasants believed that their first destination was Rennes; but Stofflet, who commanded the advanced guard, of his own authority took the Fougères road, and instead of sleeping that night at Vitré, the army encamped at Mayenne. Here the supreme council held a stormy sitting. The Vendean party accused the Breton party of deceiving them, in affirming that Maine required only the presence of the army to rise *en masse*. The Breton party retorted, that the step should have been taken earlier. Neither party seem to have reflected that they had just been offered fifty thousand volunteers. However, it was necessary to decide on the line of march; and of three routes proposed,—towards Paris, Rennes, and the sea-coast,—the latter destination was selected. The Vendeans accordingly took the Dol road; on the 3d, they entered Ernée, on the 4th, Fougères. The Blues in garrison at these places made a feeble resistance, and fled in disorder into Rennes, where the republican authorities awaited an attack in undisguised terror.

It is unaccountable that the Vendean chiefs should have made no attempt upon Rennes. They knew it to be ill defended and well provisioned; they knew that the possession of Rennes would decide

Chapter VIII

the whole country in their favour, and that if it was essential to establish communications with England, they might as well advance towards the coast by that route as by Fougères. They knew also that fifty thousand men were said to be in a state of insurrection. Yet they allowed so great a prize to fall from their hands, without even making an effort to secure it. It was an apt illustration which a republican officer drew of the expedition beyond the Loire from the popular sport of the country: "La Vendée," he said, "during this campaign, is like a wounded wild-boar tearing hither and thither without object, and goring every body who falls in his way."

Instead of profiting by the terror with which their enemies were inspired, the Vendeans loitered four days at Fougères; and here it was that Lescure received his last honours. He had suffered great agony in the journey from Laval, and nothing can exceed the touching simplicity with which his wife, afterwards Madame de Larochejacquelein, describes his end. The day before leaving Laval, he said to her, "My love, open the shutters; is the day clear?" She said it was. "I have, then, a veil before my eyes," he said; "I can no longer see distinctly. I always thought my wound mortal, and I have no longer any doubt of it. Dear love, I am about to leave you; it is my sole regret, except that I have not been able to replace my king upon his throne. I leave you in the midst of a civil war, with a babe in your arms, and another in your bosom." Seeing her convulsed with grief, he added, "Yes, I grieve on your account, not on my own. I am going to heaven. I have fought for God, and I die for Him; and I trust in His mercy." His countenance was calm, he seemed already in heaven; but when he heard his wife's sobs his eyes filled with tears, "Be comforted," he said, "with the thought that I am in heaven." Unable any longer to restrain her grief, and not wishing to disturb him with the sight of it, Madame de Lescure left the room; but he sent for her again. He wished to receive the last sacraments, but the physicians gave him hopes of ultimate recovery. The next morning they set out for Mayenne, and on the road he received the sad news of the queen's death, which his wife had as yet studiously concealed from him. His agitation doubtless hastened his end. At Ernée he fell into his agony, and received absolution and extreme unction. His wife was asleep, and awoke to find her husband dying. Her state of despair may be imagined. Then came the order to march. "It was impossible," she said; "she would run the risk of falling into the hands of the Blues along with her husband." But recollecting with horror the indignities to which the body of Bonchamps had been subjected, she could not endure the thought of such a profanation, and summoned strength and courage to set out. For seven hours she was on horseback, having left the seat in the carriage with her husband to the surgeon. Her bodily agonies then compelled her to dismount and walk; but fatigue and suffering had exhausted her strength. At length she dragged herself into Fougères, and fell down opposite the first house in the town. It was occupied by some soldiers, who gave her a little wine and warmed her. She was then placed on a bed, distracted with suspense, no news having yet arrived of Lescure. Presently a friend entered, and said, in tears, taking her by the hand, "All your care now must be for your babe." By that she understood that her husband was dead. She was seized with the pains of premature labour, but by care and attention was saved. The next morning the chief leaders of the insurrection entered her chamber, weeping bitterly. Henri de Larochejacquelein rose and embraced her. "You have lost," she whispered to him, "your best friend; after me, you were dearest to him in the world." He answered, in accents of grief, "Could my life restore him to you, take it." Alas! Henri himself was shortly afterwards to die.

The body of the departed chief was buried secretly, that it might not fall into the hands of the republicans. They found upon it the marks of the hair-shirt which he had worn. His loss was deplored alike by the peasants and his fellow-leaders; and the insurrection never recovered the blow which it sustained in the deaths of Bonchamps and Lescure.

Chapter VIII

At Fougères attempts were again made to infuse some discipline into the insurgent camp; but the peasants paid little attention to the orders of any chiefs with whom they were not personally acquainted, and each parish had its own leader. At this time also arrived two emissaries from England, MM. Freslon and Bertin, both of them honourably known in Brittany, being, in fact, Breton emigrés,—with the offer of assistance, if the insurgents would possess themselves of some seaport. The council agreed to attack Granville; not that they were altogether satisfied as to the good faith of the British government, from whom the offer was said to come, but it was necessary to put some definite object before the peasants. Granville was a small fishing-town opposite the Isle of Jersey; of no great importance, but affording good facilities for the debarcation of the promised supplies. It is built upon the terrace of a rocky promontory projecting into the sea, and protected by a fort stretching along the top of the eminence.

With this object the royalist army evacuated Fougères, and possessed themselves in turn of Dol, Pontorson, and Avranches. At this last town a council of war was held, and the peasants, so far from feeling enthusiastic for the attack, clamoured to be led back to the Bocage; but the chiefs had gone too far to recede, and it was resolved to make at least one attempt. The attack commenced on the 14th November, in the evening. A party of soldiers, who had been pushed forward by the local authorities to intercept the Vendean skirmishers, was speedily forced back behind the fortifications, and the besieging army took possession of the faubourgs. A line of houses, occupied by Jews, was soon filled by Vendean sharpshooters, who opened a destructive fire from beneath that cover upon the garrison on the ramparts. Upon this the republican general in command, Lecarpentier, gave orders that the suburbs should be fired: this was accomplished, but not before Larochejacquelein and Forestier had pushed into the town, and seized on several of the advanced works. The want of heavy artillery rendered a breach in the walls impossible; the insurgents were therefore compelled to attempt the place by escalade, and, in default of proper ladders, they commenced mounting the ramparts, by sticking their bayonets into the crevices of the walls, and so climbing up. The garrison, panic-stricken at the sight of such determined bravery, were beginning to fly; and Forestier was already at the top, with a little band of heroes that was increasing every instant, when a voice was heard in the rear, "Fly, we are betrayed!" In an instant the courage of the peasants was damped, and instead of securing the victory now within their grasp, they leaped back in disorder. Still the fight continued; and the garrison, recovering their courage, commenced throwing red-hot balls from the battery on the hill, regardless of the conflagration which was now spreading from the faubourgs into the town itself. The next morning Larochejacquelein and Stofflet planned a fresh assault on the side of the sands at low water; but two vessels in the harbour commanded that approach, and opened a hot fire on the assailants. The Vendeans had expected that the morning's light would reveal to them the English fleet, and were discouraged at seeing no signs of the promised succour. Disheartened with their double repulse, and cursing the faithlessness of the English, in reliance on whose word they had risked the attempt, they slowly retired, after a combat of thirty hours, and with a loss of eighteen hundred men.

This check destroyed the prestige of their previous successes, and rendered hopeless the prospect of any general rising of the Breton population. Moreover, the army became mutinous; the authority of Larochejacquelein was disregarded, and there was no longer a Cathelineau or a Bonchamps to command their obedience. To increase the confusion, and to a certain extent to justify the insubordination, four of the chiefs laid themselves open at this juncture to severe animadversion. The Prince de Talmont, the Abbé Bernier, and two others left the army, and were reported to be meditating an escape into England. Stofflet, who had more

Chapter VIII

influence over the peasants than Larochejacquelein, succeeded in calming the multitude, and then galloped off to the accused leaders, and placed them all under arrest. The prince, and those who accompanied him, protested that they had no thought of deserting the insurrection; they had chartered their boat with the sole view of hastening the arrival of the English convoy, and enabling certain of the women to join their husbands in Jersey. This, no doubt, was true as regards Talmont and Bernier; the army restored to them its confidence, and by a natural reaction became more submissive. Still the retrograde movement had commenced, and the peasants now turned their back upon the sea, and their face towards the Loire. They took the road to Pontorson, abandoning, with reckless haste, a number of women and wounded in the hospitals of Avranches, where they were all massacred by order of a commissioner of the Convention.

Another circumstance occurred at this time to damp the ardour of the peasants. The imposture of the *soi-disant* Bishop of Agra transpired. St. Hilaire, an emigré, who had joined the army after the disaster at Cholet, was the bearer of a brief from the Pope addressed to the generals of the Catholic army, in which his Holiness stated that no bishop existed under that title; that he had never thought of conferring the quality of vicar-apostolic on the man who had assumed it, and that it was their duty to give no countenance to the impostor, all whose acts were sacrilegious and null. For fear of scandal, the Vendean generals abstained from giving publicity to this letter; but Guyot-de-Folleville, conscious of the detection of his imposture, acted upon it by abstaining from every episcopal act. The peasants in consequence suspected the truth, and the ardour with which they had at first received him into their ranks, now produced a corresponding dejection.

On their return, the insurgents found the country, which they had just traversed as conquerors, in possession of the enemy, and they had to contest every inch of the way, first at Pontorson,

Alleged treason—Return of the Catholic army

afterwards at Dol. At Pontorson they routed the Blues, after five hours of desperate resistance. Here Forêt received his death-wound: no quarter was given on either side; the struggle was for life and death. Yet the battle of Pontorson is remarkable for at least one gleam of mercy. The wounded republicans, mingled with the wounded of the Catholic army, united with the latter in imploring the aids and consolations of religion; and the priests passed the night in administering the last rites of the Church alike to those who had died in the cause of God, and to those who had so lately fought in the ranks of His foes.

After this victory the insurgents marched into Dol, and here a yet more bloody battle ensued. For the armies of Kleber, Westermann, and Marceaux, after reforming at Angers, now appeared on the field, all furious to wipe off the stain of their defeat at Laval. The unhappy peasants were in a sad condition to meet these fresh troops: without shoes, or linen, or clothes, anxious for the safety of their wives and little ones, exhausted with fatigue, and dying of hunger. Yet they were animated by the burning desire to find their way back to the Bocage, and this bore the appearance of enthusiasm; so that, notwithstanding their distress, the majority of the republican generals would have preferred to a pitched battle the more sure method of fortifying the several passages across the Loire, and thus hemming the insurgents in on all sides, and driving them into the sea. But Westermann was too eager for blood to endure this slow process, and precipitated a collision at Dol. The battle commenced towards midnight. Thanks to Larochejacquelein's activity, the Catholic forces were all under arms; for Westermann had counted on surprising them, and there would have then ensued the same dark scene of slaughter in which he had exulted at Châtillon. But it was a terrible night, nevertheless; the cries of the soldiers, the roll of the drums, the gleam of the shells bursting over the town, the noise of the musketry and artillery, together with the smoke and smell of powder in the midst of the thick darkness,—these were the tokens

Chapter VIII

of a death-struggle on which the very existence of the Vendeans depended. At length, so devoted was the courage of the insurgents, the Blues were repulsed, and Forestier with the cavalry pursued the flying columns of Westermann's army, while Larochejacquelein drove back the advanced guard on Pontorson. The main street of Dol branches off into two roads; one leading to Pontorson, the other to Antrain. The Vendeans were divided into two columns, in order to guard these two approaches to the town; Larochejacquelein and Forestier in command of one, Talmont and Stofflet at the head of the other. When the brave Henri returned to Dol with shouts of victory, he found the other division of his army hotly engaged with the enemy, and giving way in all directions; even Stofflet had fled from the field, and so terrified were the poor peasants, enfeebled with famine and distracted with their sufferings, that they ran away, trampling on the wounded, and deaf to the screams of their wives and children. However, the chiefs attempted to rally the fugitives; D'Autichamps harangued, and Marigny sabred them; some of the women, among whom were the noble widow of Bonchamps and Madame de Lescure's mother, rushed into the midst of the battle and exhorted the soldiers to do their duty. The priests, too, exhibited extraordinary energy. The curé of St. Marie-de-Rhé, posted on a mound of earth, raised aloft a large crucifix, and cried to the peasants, "Will you be guilty of the infamy of abandoning your wives and children to the knives of the Blues? Return and fight; it is the only way of saving them. Will you abandon your general in the midst of the foes? Come, my children, I will march at your head with the crucifix. Kneel down, mount you who will follow me, and receive absolution; if you die, you will go to heaven; but the poltroons who betray God and their families will be massacred by the Blues, and their souls will go to perdition." Two thousand men instantly fell upon their knees, and received absolution; then leaping up, they cried, *Vive le Roi! Nous allons en Paradis!* and rushed to the rescue of Larochejacquelein. That intrepid young chief fought

Bravery of Talmont and the curé of St. Marie de Rhé

with the courage of a lion while there was a man to stand by his side; and when all had fled, disdaining to turn his back, he crossed his arms upon his breast, and stood calmly facing a battery. While in that attitude, he learned that the battle was still raging in another quarter. Talmont, with eight hundred men, chiefly belonging to Little Vendée, was fighting hand to hand with the republicans, and thus had prevented the enemy from turning to advantage the panic of the Vendeans. He hurried away in the direction indicated; and with that handful of brave men the two commanders kept the enemy at bay till the curé of St. Marie-de-Rhé arrived with his two thousand followers. Stofflet, recovering his presence of mind, had also returned to the town in time to take part in the renewed struggle. This unexpected reinforcement decided the day; the Blues soon gave way, and the Vendeans remained masters of the town. The curé, who had stood in the thickest of the fight, with his crucifix reared high in the air, returned to Dol, chanting the *Vexilla Regis*. But on the 21st the battle was renewed, when the Blues were again routed; and the insurgents entered Antrain, after defeating a regiment of the line. By this series of gallant victories they found themselves again masters of their own movements.

Now was the time to retrace their steps, surprise Granville, gain the coast, and wait for the English succours. But the peasants were immovable; they insisted on returning to La Vendée. And when Larochejacquelein enumerated the obstacles which they would have to encounter, they replied, "Angers may be walled with iron, but we will take it." He knew that they overrated their own strength, but he was obliged to yield, and the order was given to march. Before quitting Antrain, they sent to Rennes one hundred and fifty wounded republicans, with a letter recounting the atrocities which the Blues had committed, and ending with these words: "It is by acts of mercy that the army Catholic and Royal takes vengeance on its enemies for the massacres they have perpetrated." This noble act of forbearance was due to the curé of St. Marie-de-Rhé.

Chapter VIII

The army advanced upon Angers by Fougères, (where they sang a *Te Deum*,) Ernée, Laval, and La Flêche. They encountered no opposition; but the road was lined with the mournful traces of their disastrous expedition. The sick, the women, and the wounded, who had fallen behind on their march to Granville, had been murdered by the Blues. All who had shown the slightest sympathy with the poor sufferers had shared their fate, and at every step fresh corpses met the eyes of the wretched peasants. The survivors were in scarcely better plight, and many of them envied the happier lot of the dead. Drenched with a cold November rain, clad in rags, without shoes, and, worst of all, faint with the direst hunger, that retreat was more fatal to the Vendeans than the loss of a battle. Nor even when they caught sight of Angers, did their courage revive; rather, with a presentiment of defeat, they dreaded the coming fight. It seemed to them easier to lie down and die than make one last effort to save their lives.

Chapter IX

Siege of Angers and defeat of the army—Retreat on Baugé—Occupation of Mans—Defeat and massacre of Mans—Larochejacquelein and Stofflet fly before Westermann—Final annihilation of the whole army at Savenay—Atrocities of the republicans—Reflections on the expedition beyond the Loire—Charette's successes in Bas Poitou—Successful stratagem of Joly at Quatre-Chemins—Charette named commander-in-chief—His interview with Larochejacquelein—Recapture of Noirmoutiers—Execution of D'Elbée.

ANGERS WAS PROTECTED by fortifications crumbling indeed into decay, but strong enough to withstand the attacks of an army unprovided with any engines of assault. Its garrison consisted of about three thousand five hundred men, commanded by Generals Danican and Boucret. But its chief strength lay, not in the garrison, some of the officers of which were little worthy of confidence, but in the determined spirit of the bulk of the population and in the presence of Beaupuy. That general, who had been dangerously wounded at Laval, was not yet recovered; yet he personally superintended the arrangements for the defence, and inspired the whole town with ardour. It was decided to remain on the defensive, and wait the attack of the Vendeans. The inhabitants of the faubourgs retired within the walls; the houses thus abandoned were occupied by the besiegers, and served as a cover from which they could commence their operations.

The insurgents began their fire on the 4th of December, about eleven o'clock in the morning; but whether dispirited with the

Chapter IX

difficulty of the enterprise, or deprived of their usual energy by their long sufferings, they exhibited none of that vigour and fury with which other towns had been suddenly carried. The whole of that day they spent in directing against the walls a fire of musketry and artillery, and night came on without any change having taken place in the relative positions of the besiegers and the besieged.

The next morning, at five o'clock, the cannonade commenced again; and before long St. Michael's Gate gave way, and a few of the Vendeans, with their usual ardour, marched up to the assault. But it was impossible to animate the mass of the army; they had no spirit for the battle. Some of the generals promised them the sack of the town; but so far from being excited with the hope of pillage, they were scandalised by the very proposal; they cried out that God would abandon them if they formed any such projects. Still it was necessary to bring the siege to an immediate termination, as the advance of a fresh body of republican troops, under Westermann, Kleber, Marceaux, and Marigny, was reported. The artillery, which had been directed with considerable energy, had at last effected a practicable breach; and the chiefs, with wonderful intrepidity, rushed forward alone, as the last means of rousing their broken-hearted men; but without effect. None followed them; and all except Larochejacquelein, Piron, and Forestier perished in the attempt. These returned, and in vain endeavoured to strike from the peasants a spark of enthusiasm. The flint had become clay—all vigour was gone; and the men who had taken Saumur, and fought at Laval, now looked listlessly on at a few crumbling fortifications, which one hour of their old courage would have made their own.

Soon the opportunity was passed. The time spent in vain exhortations had served to bring up the enemy at their rear. Marigny arrived with a column of light cavalry, and the very sight of him caused the assailants to beat a retreat. He followed in pursuit with an ardour which Westermann himself would have approved. Repulsed by the insurgents, who could fight when it was absolutely

Defeat of the army—Retreat on Baugé

necessary, he returned again to the charge, and was killed with a cannon-ball. Yet the man who exhibited a devotion like this to the cause of his party was then about to be cashiered, his sole crime being that he bore the same name as the brave commander of the Vendean artillery. Nothing is more astonishing throughout this war than the undaunted fidelity of the republican generals to an ungrateful and bloodthirsty Convention. After the repulse at Dol, Marceaux accepted the command-in-chief, on condition that Kleber, who was to have been suspended, should be left with his troops. Kleber accordingly remained, simply observing to Marceaux, "Never mind, we shall be guillotined together." Such was the future in store for the best officers of the Republic; yet it seems to have had no effect on their devotion.

In miserable plight, the insurgents took the first road they saw, and arrived at Baugé, where they encamped. All hope had now died away. It was impossible not to see that the last hours of the army were rapidly approaching. Nothing was heard any longer of a fresh invasion of Maine and Brittany; the peasants had not even the hope of returning to La Vendée. All their prospects had turned on the capture of Angers: they were now retreating from its walls, and farther and farther from the Loire, which still rolled its broad and rapid waters between them and their desolate homes. To famine and cold succeeded sickness; and to add to their disasters, desertion had commenced: hourly, chiefs and peasants dropped off, to try and find their own way into La Vendée, and thread their passage through the Blues unarmed. A few succeeded; but the greater part were seized and massacred.

From Baugé the army advanced to La Flêche, hotly pursued by Westermann. At the bridge of La Flêche they found four thousand men drawn up to oppose them, and the bridge cut down. Thus they were between two enemies. Larochejacquelein charged Piron with the duty of arresting the progress of Westermann, while he, with a picked body of four hundred horsemen, each with a foot-soldier

Chapter IX

on the crupper, went up the river till he found a ford,—dangerous indeed, but still passable. Here he crossed, and then attacked the garrison in flank, which soon yielded to so unexpected an assault. In a few minutes the bridge was replaced, and he crossed the river again to succour Piron. The Blues were soon put to flight, and the army retired in safety into La Flêche. It was a gallant little affair, executed with equal ingenuity and daring; but the army were in such a state, that the victory could only prolong its agony.

At La Flêche they remained two days, enjoying a slight interval of repose; but still suffering from want. They then pushed on to Mans, a town situated on the high road between Angers and Paris. On arriving at Foultourte, they were attacked from the heights; but they still advanced, and in three quarters of an hour routed the enemy. In Mans they found, to their inexpressible delight, abundance of good provisions, and abandoned themselves to the enjoyment of the present, regardless of the rapid pursuit of Westermann, who, although repulsed at La Flêche, had never lost sight of them for a moment. Larochejacquelein endeavoured to rouse them from their apathy; but in vain: deprived so long of repose and food, they cared for nothing now but to eat, drink, and sleep. Very different was the conduct of the Blues, who made preparations for a grand battle. The supreme command was given to Marceaux, who immediately assembled all his available force at the village of Foultourte, determined at last to strike a decisive blow. Here, then, were the sad remnants of La Vendée, first reduced by famine, and then enervated by indulgence, exposed to the attack of a numerous and well-appointed army, under one of the ablest generals of the Republic. Larochejacquelein was fully alive to the danger; yet, with all coolness and diligence, he posted his forces to the best advantage.

The advance-guard of the Blues, consisting of Westermann's and Müller's columns, commenced the attack on the 12th of December. Larochejacquelein had posted three thousand men in ambush in a fir-plantation, and by them Westermann was repulsed, and Müller completely routed. But Marceaux came to the support of the retreating troops, and the battle was restored. Presently the Vendeans in their turn were driven back. Still no advantage had been gained on either side; but disorder began to spread among the ranks of the insurgents, and though Larochejacquelein three times with the utmost bravery precipitated himself on the enemy, his men refused to follow. All clamoured for a retreat within the walls; and thither they retired pell-mell, and immediately gave themselves up to drinking. By this time night had fallen, and the republican generals held a council of war. Kleber had not yet come up, and Marceaux was for awaiting his arrival. Westermann, however, contended for a night attack, and his advice prevailed. When it was quite dark, they crossed the Huisne without opposition, and possessed themselves, almost without striking a blow, of the faubourgs, the bridge, and the first intrenchments. Of the twenty-five thousand fighting men who still remained of the Catholic army, twelve or fifteen lay prostrate with fatigue and drunkenness; many others were enjoying themselves in the houses, and refused to go out: "What did it signify," they said, "whether they were massacred a few hours sooner or later?" Larochejacquelein, frantic with rage and despair, rushed in every direction to rouse them from their lethargy; and at length he and the other chiefs succeeded in assembling several thousand men. But still there was no plan determined upon, no orders were given, or at least none were obeyed: every one went whither he chose; and it may be imagined what success such a defence was likely to have against the systematic attack of disciplined soldiers. And yet a very bloody combat ensued: the Vendeans were forced to retire, but the Blues hesitated to advance until the appearance of Kleber made resistance no longer possible; then the republicans spread themselves over the town, and the handful of gallant men who had held them in check retired with the mass of fugitives by the Laval road. The flight had been proceeding for some time, and many officers, among whom was Stofflet, seeing

Chapter IX

that all was lost, now joined in the retreat. Charged with a bundle of the white flags of which the army was so proud, tattered as they were and half-burned, Stofflet was removing them that they might not fall into the hands of the enemy, when he perceived De Scepaux, with two other Vendeans, serving a gun which they had mounted in a narrow street to protect the retreat of the royalists. He cried out to him: "Now, M. de Scepaux, it is my turn; mount my horse, and let me take your place." "Not so," replied the other, "I stay here while there is a grain of powder and a cannon-ball left. You, general, save our flags; they are in good hands." "The Blues shall have me before they have them," replied Stofflet. "If they send these to the Convention, they will be able to send my head also." Yet in that horrible flight Stofflet could stay to listen to the cry of distress. A poor Vendean mother, wounded and half-dying, lay on the pavement weltering in her gore, amid the heaps of the slain. She recognised the royalist chief as he passed; and holding up to him her infant, she cried, "Save it, save it!" "Give it here," said Stofflet roughly; and he placed it before him on the flags and galloped off. He afterwards restored the child to its mother, who was saved by the charity of others of the insurgents. After his departure, Larochejacquelein, Marigny, Forestier, Duhoux, and others, together with Jean Chouan and Georges Cadoudal, two Bretons destined to render Brittany as famous as La Vendée, maintained an obstinate resistance. They kept up the fire of a battery long after the cannoniers had been slain, and so covered the crowded road. But they were at length compelled to retire, and then Westermann followed the flying masses, and slaughtered them by hundreds.

Meanwhile the aged and infirm, the wounded, the sick, and the women, great numbers of whom had been left behind in the town, fell into the hands of the Blues, and were massacred amid jeers and laughter. They spared neither age nor sex: they killed the babe upon its mother's breast, and the mother fell a corpse upon its mangled body. They killed the old man, who had never drawn a

Larochejacquelein and Stofflet fly before Westermann

sword in that disastrous contest, but had simply followed the army when driven by fire from his own home in the Bocage; they killed young women, after subjecting them to even greater injury; and not content with these outrages, wreaked their fury upon the bloody corpses of their victims. The unhappy people, flocking together for mutual safety, only facilitated their own destruction: it was easier to slaughter them *en masse*, and artillery were deliberately pointed at the terrified crowd, who were at length destroyed by round after round of grape-shot, and repeated volleys of musketry. No fewer than twenty thousand men, women, and children fell in the battle and the subsequent massacre.

At Laval the leaders of the Catholic army ascertained more clearly their forlorn situation. It was here that for the first time the whole extent of the late disaster was revealed to their view. They found themselves not only devoid of ammunition and artillery, but destitute of food and clothing; and, to crown their misery, a fearful pestilence had broken out among their enfeebled followers. Still, to remain at Laval was to invite certain destruction; and Larochejacquelein, as the Blues approached, evacuated the place.

Their destination was Ancenis, and the peasants approached the Loire with some little animation; but their march was a veritable rout. As they went along baggage, women, and wounded were abandoned—in a word, whatever was troublesome to save. The Blues soon despatched the dying; and as their own bulletins remarked, they had no need of scouts to ascertain the track of the enemy, for their road was sufficiently indicated by the number of corpses.

At length they arrived at Ancenis, and occupied it without resistance; and there it was resolved to attempt the passage of the Loire. But their only means of transport were two little boats; and they accordingly set to work to construct large rafts, on which the army might cross. On the other side lay four large vessels laden with hay, upon which every one cast a longing eye; but no one was

Chapter IX

bold enough to attempt their capture. Then Larochejacquelein, with Stofflet and eighteen men, cast themselves into the two skiffs; they landed safely on the other side, followed by the gaze of the whole army, who felt that the future depended on the success of the attempt. But scarcely had Larochejacquelein and his companions set foot on the Vendean soil, when they were attacked by a republican patrol. The peasants fired off their muskets, and then dispersed, selfishly consulting their own safety, and careless what became of their comrades on the other side of the river. Larochejacquelein and Stofflet, to save themselves from the Blues, were compelled to hide themselves in the country. Thus the army was separated from its leader in its greatest need; and to complete the distress, a gun-boat descended the river and sunk the rafts; and at the same time the advanced guard of Westermann made its appearance in the rear.

The sight of their dear country so animated the hearts of the Vendeans, that, weak as they were, they drove back the enemy; but the advance of the main body, under Westermann himself, compelled them hastily to quit Ancenis, and they took the road to Nort. Two or three hundred men succeeded in crossing the Loire at Ancenis, and their good fortune excited the envy of their comrades, numbers of whom forsook the expedition and sought to save themselves separately. Others, relying on the faith of the republicans, who had promised an amnesty to all who would surrender, laid down their arms, and were immediately shot. So that when the army entered Nort, it numbered no more than seven thousand men. And even this small number was soon diminished by the departure of Forestier and some other officers, who forsook the main body, in spite of the reproaches of Marigny, to join an insurrection said to be in course of organisation in the forest of Gâvre. The principal officers remaining were Talmont, Fleuriot, and Donissan; of whom Fleuriot, who has been styled the Nestor of the Vendeans, was chosen commander-in-chief in the absence of Larochejacquelein. Talmont, thinking himself slighted by this election, presently

Final annihilation of the whole army at Savenay

departed to raise the Bretons in the neighbourhood of Laval. Here he fell into the hands of the republicans, before whom he displayed the most noble bravery; and he was subsequently guillotined in front of the principal entrance to his own chateau.

There were still many who, despairing of a passage, would even now have penetrated again into Brittany; but the Abbé Bernier combated that proposition, and the peasants chose the road to Savenay, still keeping the Loire in view. At Savenay Fleuriot took such measures of defence as were possible; but nothing could avert the impending annihilation of the Catholic army.

Pitiable indeed was their condition; dying of hunger and fatigue—in want of arms, ammunition, and clothing—they had traversed a marsh, often up to the middle in water, during a heavy fall of snow in the depth of winter, harassed by an enemy who allowed them not a moment's repose, and of whose brutality they had received terrible proofs; and now, hemmed in between the Loire and the Velaine, and not far from the sea, they were at the mercy of their foes. We may imagine their despair when, on the night of the 22d December, they found themselves invested on all sides. The soldiers were fainting for want of rest; but just as they were about to lie down in the mud, shots were heard: in dogged despair, they only said, "then we must die without resting," and at the call of their chiefs marched forth to battle. All honour to the brave men—all honour to their chiefs, who at such a moment were wanting neither in words to encourage their soldiers nor in energy to lead them on to the fight!

Westermann and Kleber, who had followed their prey in hot pursuit, lost no time in attacking the advanced posts. Lyrot, one of the bravest of the Vendean captains, rushed to encounter them, followed by a large body of horsemen; and so vigorous was their onslaught, that the republicans gave way. But the main body coming up, the advantage was of short duration; although all the generals, Fleuriot, Marigny, Piron, Dessessarts, and Donissan, took up their

Chapter IX

position with promptitude and vigour. However, darkness now began to spread, night came on, and as a nocturnal battle offered the best chance of success to the Vendeans, they began to entertain slight hopes of escape. Westermann, aware of this, with greater patience than he usually exhibited, postponed the main attack till the morning; by which time the peasants were utterly exhausted, having been kept under arms the whole night by repeated alarms, amid torrents of rain.

During the darkness, some of the officers warned the women to make their escape with their children. "All is lost," said Marigny to Madame de Lescure, who had followed the army through all its troubles. "It is impossible to stand tomorrow's attack. In twelve hours the army will be exterminated. For my part, I hope to die in the defence of my flag. But you—fly while you can!" She obeyed. With Madame de Donissan, under the guidance of the Abbé Jagault, she left the town some hours before the battle commenced, and threw herself upon Breton hospitality. She lived to write that thrilling story of her adventures, known as the *Memoirs of Madame de Larochejacquelein*. Nine years afterwards she married Louis, brother of Henri de Larochejacquelein. A great number of women saved themselves in the midst of the darkness, although a few preferred to remain and share the fate of their husbands or brothers. Many priests might have saved themselves; but they stayed to exhort the soldiers, to confess them before battle, and bless them in death. The officers were equally faithful. M. de Donissan, a man who had shared all the dangers, and claimed none of the honours, of the whole campaign, was entreated by his child and his wife to share their flight. "My daughter," he replied, "save your child and your mother. I must remain with the army as long as it exists. Adieu; take care of all that I love." These were the last words Madame de Lescure heard her father utter. As he had said, he remained to the end; and died crying *Vive le Roi!* During that fearful night all prepared themselves for the last desperate struggle. Even

Final annihilation of the whole army at Savenay

the wounded dragged themselves into the ranks; and the sick who were unable to stand caused themselves to be tied on horseback and led into the battle. So that when the morning dawned, the relics of the grand army still presented an imposing appearance. At the first rays of the sun, the republicans sounded the charge. Fleuriot cried, "Forward—forward! *Vive le Roi!*" and the Vendeans, repeating the cry, precipitated themselves on the enemy. The shock was, as usual, so great, that the soldiers of Kleber and Westermann fell back in astonishment at such unlooked-for intrepidity. The royalist chiefs performed prodigies of valour. Marigny, bearing a white flag, which Madame de Lescure had embroidered, specially distinguished himself. Thrice he cast himself, like a lion, on the ranks of the republicans; but to what avail all this heroic devotion, against the overwhelming numbers of the revolutionary army? Westermann soon found himself sufficiently strong to turn Savenay; he executed the manœuvre without difficulty, and the royalists saw that all hope was gone. Fleuriot, then, crying, "After me and the white flag!" rushed upon the enemy's line, holding a sword in one hand, and a flag, pierced with a thousand balls, in the other. The Vendeans followed, broke through the circle, and rushed into the forest of Gâvre. Marigny and Lyrot, who had just seen Piron fall by their side, returned to Savenay, not with any view of holding the town, but of saving the lives of such of the women, old men, and children as had not fled during the night. As at Mans, these brave men succeeded in keeping the enemy at bay for several hours. Two cannons they placed on the Guerande road, now thronged with fugitives. One brave cannonier, who fought by the side of Marigny, had sworn to Madame de Lescure that he would die defending the fleurs-de-lis which she had embroidered. In spite of all their efforts, the carnage of the unhappy women was dreadful. As far as Montoire the road was choked with corpses. A great number of the Vendean women took shelter in the wood of Blanche Couronne. Some days afterwards, their bodies were found frightfully

Chapter IX

mutilated; never had the republicans been guilty of such atrocities as were perpetrated in that wood. At length, when nothing more was to be gained by remaining, Marigny and the brave few who had served the cannon retired, and joined those who had found a shelter in the forest of Gâvre.

After the battle, the Blues dispersed on all sides in pursuit of runaways, and cut down without mercy all whom they found. It is impossible to narrate all the horrible facts which have been recorded; but some are too characteristic to be omitted. In a moment of weakness or despair, twelve hundred Vendeans laid down their arms, crying *Vive la Nation!* They were all shot. Another band of five or six hundred men were surrounded: unable to resist, they all surrendered, and begged for quarter; a discharge of musketry was the only answer they received. After the first volley, the commanding officer cried, "Let all those who are not wounded rise; the great and generous Republic pardons them." First those who had not been wounded, and then those who had been struck but were still alive, stood up, and were all mown down by a second round. So much for the generosity of the Republic! Near a cross which still stands by the road-side, at some distance from Montoire, some poor wounded fugitives dropped down in sheer exhaustion. "Let us stop here," they cried; "we cannot escape. Let us die, then, at the foot of the cross." Among them was an old priest, who had watered the whole road with his blood; for he had been shot in his ministry to the dying. Like his companions, he too was unable to proceed farther; but he said, "Sleep you; I will watch the meanwhile." The women with their children, and the men too, lay down and slept; while the priest, not less exhausted than they, knelt by the cross and watched along the road. For some hours he continued thus praying and watching; but no enemy appeared. At last some runaways passed by, crying, "The Blues are close behind—fly!" He instantly awoke the sleepers; and at his voice mothers arose with their children, and the wounded and sick sought to make their escape. But suddenly a party of republicans appeared in their front, and stopped the way. The old priest then, in imitation of the Good Shepherd, who laid down His own life for His sheep, advanced towards the Blues, and in a loud voice cried out, "These wounded and unarmed men, these feeble women, these little children, are not worthy of your weapons; I it is who deserve your vengeance—on my head fall the weight of your anger. For the sheep have but followed their shepherd. It was I who bade them take up arms in defence of their God and their king. Spare them, therefore, in the name of all that is honourable; and kill me alone."

"You shall die first," said the officer coolly, "and your flock shall quickly follow you;" and in a couple of volleys the priest and his faithful people were all slain beneath the shadow of the cross. A few of the republican officers, feeling that these executions detracted from the honour of their victory, contented themselves with making prisoners of some of the insurgents who fell into their power. But the reprieve was of short duration; they were all conducted to Nantes, and Carrier with his myrmidons sent them to the guillotine!

Nor is this the *ex-parte* statement of the royalists; the republicans avowed their own atrocities. In his official report to the Committee of Public Safety, Westermann thus announces his victory: "In obedience to your orders, I have crushed the children beneath the hoofs of our horses, and massacred the women. They at least shall bring forth no more brigands. Not a single prisoner can be laid to my charge. I have utterly exterminated the enemy. The roads are strewn with bodies, and in some places they lie in actual pyramids. At Savenay the firing was incessant; for every moment brigands were coming in who thought to render themselves prisoners." This was in consequence of the amnesty promised to all who would submit; upon the faith of which many left their hiding-places and gave themselves up. Another republican writer says: "For eight days the Vendean fugitives were hunted

Chapter IX

like wild-beasts." Out of eighty or a hundred thousand souls, who, on the 18th October 1793, crossed the Loire at St. Florent, there were left at the end of the year but a few solitary individuals. The men who had left the field of victory to discharge their Easter duties, little thought of the dreary Christmas they should spend, if it were their rare fortune to survive at all. A few contrived to gain the Bocage; others obtained shelter among the Bretons; but the vast majority had fallen victims either to disease, or famine, or the sword of the Republic.

The fugitives who had escaped to the forest of Gâvre must have died of famine and cold, but for the generous hospitality of the Breton population. At the risk of certain death in the event of discovery, the peasants gave them shelter, and frequently fell victims to their own charity. In return for this kindness, many of the insurgents of Anjou, unbroken in courage, and faithful to the Catholic cause, remained in the woods, and attached themselves to the various bands of Chouans which had already been formed under the Maine and Breton generals. Others sought shelter in Nantes, and Nort, and other towns, in which there existed many Christians ready to conceal them at the risk of their lives. But no independent attempt was made to renew the expedition beyond the Loire. As an army, the Vendeans no longer existed; the rout at Savenay was not a defeat merely,—it was an annihilation.

This disastrous campaign lasted sixty-five days. The movement cannot be defended; yet success would probably have attended it, if the Vendeans had received any of the support they were justified in expecting. In the passage of the Loire, the chiefs had in view not merely an escape from an enemy in the rear; their object was to approach the coast, and so establish relations with England, and obtain from her reinforcements and ammunition. They also reckoned, and with justice, on a general rising of the Breton population, and the immediate arrival of some member of the royal family. In all these calculations they were disappointed. The English fleet appeared off the coast of Granville a fortnight after the luckless attack on that place, and when the insurgents were in the last extremity beneath the walls of Angers. The Bretons joined them in very insignificant numbers; and not a sign of the royal princes appeared. The army, already virtually defeated, was thus thrown entirely on its own resources, at a distance of forty leagues from home, encumbered with a crowd of women and children, and surrounded with truculent enemies. And yet before its destruction it took twelve cities, gained seven battles, killed twenty thousand of the republicans, and took from them one hundred pieces of cannon,—"trophies greater," as Dr. Alison has remarked, "than were gained by the vast allied armies in Flanders during the whole campaign."

They were, indeed, defeated. Still the glory cannot be denied them of dying for their faith. It is possible that the presence of an English force or of a royal prince might have saved the army; yet the one would have detracted from the patriotic, the other from the religious character of the insurrection. A foreign or a political element would have been introduced, and sullied the memory of an event which now glows with the merit of martyrdom. No assistance from Great Britain, nor even the personal countenance of the house of Bourbon, could then have set the king upon his throne. But that for which the Vendeans struggled they obtained. The expedition beyond the Loire failed, but the insurrection was not suppressed; nor did it cease till the nation had restored to the west the liberty of the Catholic Church.

La Vendée was not subdued. Charette, in the Bas Poitou, was still waging a successful war. It will be remembered that that general had quarrelled with Bonchamps, and had left D'Elbée and the other chiefs to stand the brunt of the invasion with which the Bocage was threatened; while he himself planned and executed an expedition against the Isle of Noirmoutiers. That attempt was completely successful: after a slight skirmish, he obtained, on the

Chapter IX

11th October, possession of Barbastre, a small town on the shore of the island, under the command of Wieland, the governor; and as the situation was extremely favourable for communication with England, and afforded abundant resources for the army, he proceeded to fortify himself in it.

He had scarcely achieved this success, when his satisfaction was damped by the news of the defeat at Chollet, and the passage of the Loire. At first he refused to credit the intelligence: but he was soon compelled to acknowledge his error in absenting himself from the main army; for on entering the Bocage to ascertain the truth, he met D'Elbée, escorted by fifteen hundred Angevins, lying on his litter. The wounded commander-in-chief accepted the place of refuge afforded him by the Isle of Noirmoutiers; and hither he retired to die in peace. But another lot was reserved for him.

The passage of the Loire, and consequent evacuation of the Bocage by the enemy, left Bas Poitou also a little repose, which Charette employed in organising his forces. He was soon, however, disturbed by General Haxo, who left Nantes at the head of a column of six or seven thousand men. Success at first attended the operations of the republican commander, and Charette found himself hemmed in on the Isle of Bouin; but the insurgents, by a convulsive effort, forced their way through the enemy, and escaped. They then made an incursion into the Bocage, to raise the peasants who had not crossed the Loire.

At Quatre-Chemins they found themselves in the presence of a republican division of fifteen or eighteen hundred men. Charette divided his troops into two columns, one under his own command, the other under Joly. He himself took the St. Cécile road, Joly that from Essarts. The latter, ready to engage, and impatient at not seeing Charette appear, had recourse to a stratagem exhibiting a degree of audacity rare even for him. Mounting a tricolor cockade, and commanding a few horsemen to do the same and follow him, he marched straight into the enemy's camp. To the *Qui vive* of the sentinels, he answered *Républicain*, and was allowed to pass. Being asked by some soldiers what news: "The battle is going to begin," said he; "the brigands are not far off." "Have you any reinforcements?" "I have a column in ambush in the wood. I will return. Remain where you are." He gained the other side of the camp, carried off the last sentinels, reached Charette, and urged him to attack instantly. He then returned a second time through the ranks of the enemy, and reappeared with his own division. A simultaneous fire from both sides first taught the Blues their mistake; the camp was soon taken, and the republicans lost artillery, arms, ammunition, and nearly a thousand men.

It was Charette's misfortune always to have his authority contested. From the day that he was chosen to supersede Souchu to the present moment, he had always had to endure the presence of a rival. It became indispensable therefore to elect a commander-in-chief; and, in spite of the manœuvres of Joly, Charette was chosen. Joly was at first much chagrined; but, as he was sincerely devoted to the cause, he restrained himself, and, as far as was possible, obeyed. The old soldiers of the Catholic army were not, however, so submissive. They had not yet learned Charette's military genius; and ascribing to his secession the defeat at Chollet, they could not reconcile themselves to his command; so that the new general was often compelled to use violence to obtain recruits. But he was indefatigable, and contrived to collect in Haut Poitou a small body of three thousand infantry and three hundred horsemen, which, to his infinite credit, he converted into efficient troops, and succeeded in keeping under arms in face of great hardships and a superior enemy. From Poitou he passed into Anjou, in which province he counted on collecting the *élite* of his army. Pierre Cathelineau, the brother of the saint of Anjou, was already at the head of a detachment; and he did not doubt but that the peasants would acknowledge his authority. But the arrival of Larochejacquelein and Stofflet defeated his calculations.

Chapter IX

The general-in-chief of the grand army, on finding himself and his men on opposite sides of the Loire, and unable to rejoin them, penetrated into the Bocage; and after running great risks from the republican patrols, having once fallen asleep in the same inn with a party of Blues, at length found his way to a body of insurgents in the neighbourhood of Chollet, under the command of Charette. That chief took no pains to conceal his displeasure at Larochejacquelein's unexpected arrival; for he well knew that the influence of the brave young hero was paramount in Anjou. But he acquainted him with his plan of attack upon Chollet, and asked him to follow in his train. "Monsieur," replied Larochejacquelein haughtily, "I am accustomed to lead, not to follow;" and he withdrew. Eight hundred men immediately quitted Charette's army to join their old general, and the two Vendean columns turned their backs on each other without having formed any plan of campaign against the common enemy. As the fortune of the insurrection declined, its leaders appear to have exhibited less generosity of soul.

After this interview, which took place on the 29th December 1793, Charette returned to his own country; but not in time to save his stronghold in Noirmoutiers from the Blues. His march was unmolested; but an incident occurred in connection with it worthy of record. The enemy had despatched three hundred national guards from the south of La Vendée for the purpose of watching his movements. Instead of Charette and his insurgents, they fell in with a detachment of the army of the north, and joined it, singing aloud the Marseillaise. In spite of that hymn and their tricolor cockades, they were taken for Vendeans. Nor could they undeceive their comrades by the most solemn protestations. The soldiers insisted that they would not be tricked, that they knew how to distinguish patriots from insurgents, and actually shot them all upon the spot. Charette, their real enemy, was far away on his road to Noirmoutiers. During his absence in Anjou, General Haxo had traversed the Marais in all directions without effect; and Turreau, a man for ever

Recapture of Noirmoutiers—Execution of D'Elbée

execrated as the organiser of the infernal columns, had been sent to supersede him. Upon this Haxo determined to attack the isle of Noirmoutiers, an enterprise he had hitherto deferred from want of sufficient strength; and on the 3d January 1794, the defenders of Barbastre capitulated, upon the faith of General Haxo's word, that those who laid down their arms should save their lives,—and he was known to be a man of honour. Unhappily Haxo had no longer the command in chief, and Turreau ordered all the prisoners to be put to death. More than fifteen hundred men were thus murdered.

The value of their victory was doubled by the discovery that D'Elbée was among the vanquished. "Look," said one of the commissioners of the Convention, "here is D'Elbée!" "Yes," was the answer, "here is your greatest foe; and had I been able to fight, you had not been here." "What will you do, if we give you your life?" "Commence the war again." Turreau attempted to worm out of him some information about the insurgents, but in vain; he was much struck with his firmness, but could not understand his religious principles. It seemed to him incomprehensible that a man of intelligence should attach the slightest importance to this or that form of worship. When he saw that nothing was to be learned from him, he ordered him to be shot; and after five days' torture, he was led out to the tree of liberty along with two of his comrades. As the word was about to be given to the executioners to fire, one of the commissioners observed that there were "only three victims; the number four, as being square and symmetrical, was more agreeable to the eye." "Well," said another, "there is Wieland, take him." Wieland was accordingly taken, although he was a sincere republican, tied to the stake, and shot. The next morning the wife of D'Elbée shared her husband's death, and showed herself worthy of her lord.

Charette, unable to succour Noirmoutiers, kept up a guerilla warfare in the Bocage, harassing the Blues without suffering loss. "It is not an easy thing to find Charette," said Turreau, "still less to make him fight. Today he is at the head of ten thousand men;

Chapter IX

tomorrow he has only a score of horsemen. You think he is in front, and you find him in your rear. Yesterday he threatened such or such a post, and today he is ten leagues off. Thus he constantly deranges your combinations, and is ever seeking to surprise you by snatching off your patrols and killing your stragglers." Larochejacquelein too was at the head of a numerous body of insurgents, and obtained several victories over the republicans. Such was the state of La Vendée when Turreau proceeded to put in execution the designs which had been laid down by the Committee of Public Safety. But the account of his exploits must be ushered in by the history of Carrier and his *noyades* at Nantes.

Chapter X

The reign of terror under Carrier at Nantes—The infernal columns.

FROM THE FIRST outbreak of the civil war, Nantes had claimed, on account of its position, the special attention of the republicans. Commanding the passage of the Loire, and affording easy communication with England by sea, it became of the utmost importance both to save it from falling into the hands of the insurgents, and to imbue it with republican principles. At an early period of the revolution, the inhabitants had been able to augur the probable fate of their town from the conduct of their judges, who, after acquitting a prisoner, immediately condemned him to death out of fear of a club of jacobins, and to save appearances pronounced a new judgment. Soon after this infamous abuse of judicial power Nantes beheld her chief offices filled by miscreants of the lowest of the people, under whose government not merely royalism, but even moderatism, came to be considered a crime worthy of death, and a great number of sincere republicans, but rich and advocates of a conciliatory policy, were led to the scaffold. It was soon a favourite maxim at Nantes, that it mattered not whether a man was guilty or not, so long as the Republic required his head. The mass of the population were rather favourable to the clubbists than otherwise. Inspired with a terror of the Vendeans, who had twice attempted to take their town, they readily acquiesced in the destruction of those who were represented to be their accomplices. Such was the feeling of the population, when the Committee

Chapter X

of Public Safety wrote to Carrier in these terms: "Go to Nantes, and purge the city." The Nantesmen thought they had been long living under a reign of terror; but in fact it was only now beginning.

The committee knew in whom they had placed confidence. Carrier surrounded himself immediately with a number of abandoned demagogues, whom he made his principal agents, and invested with formal functions. With the assistance of these men, he commenced by setting up an office for the denunciation of the victims, called the National Vengeance Office. The first class against whom he declared was one which the revolution had always considered as "suspected," that of the rich. Carrier declared them criminal, and ordered their wholesale incarceration. "People! people!" he cried, "up with your clubs, and smash all those fat merchants, all those men who have grown rich on your sweat; away, break into their chests, and exterminate the wretches. People, you may depend on my assistance in taking vengeance on all public vampires! the guillotine shall do justice on them all. I will set their heads rolling on the national scaffold!" The next day he said, "Good *sans-culottes*! all that the fat merchants have is yours. Show them up, and away will go their heads! No proofs are necessary; the denunciation of a good *sans-culotte* will be quite sufficient." The effect of such proclamations may easily be conceived. All who had any thing to lose were instantly denounced; and so eager for prey were the bloodhounds of Carrier, that false crimes were unnecessarily invented, and the most frivolous pretexts were given when a bare denunciation would have sufficed. Men were seized and put to death for being the friends of the rich, or for having accepted office without a certificate of citizenship; for being monopolists of turnips; for having been domestics in some old family;—on such charges the best blood of Nantes was brought to the scaffold.

Encouraged by the praises which he received from the Committee of Public Safety, Carrier redoubled his cruelty. He organised, under the twofold name of the Marat army and the revolutionary army of Brutus, three corps worthy of their leader. Each had a distinct province and a particular title. The first was the Marat company; the second, the American hussars; the third, the spies of the Mountain.

The Marat company was specially appointed to arrest suspected persons, and make domiciliary visits. On the day of their formation they swore death to royalists, fanatics, dandies, monks, and moderates. Their pay was ten francs a day; but they knew how to increase it by robbery.

The American hussars were negroes and mulattoes brought over to France as slaves from St. Domingo, but of whom the revolution had made citizens. They seemed to have no intelligence except for crime, and were employed chiefly in the wholesale executions.

The spies of the Mountain were charged with inspecting the environs of Nantes, and of effecting such arrests as they judged necessary. These were mostly German deserters; and many of them wore a soldier's uniform, which they disgraced by the perpetration of the most horrible crimes—burning alive men, women, and old people; dishonouring and massacring women, and flinging from bayonet to bayonet, like so many balls, the bodies of little children before the very eyes of their mothers, from whose arms they had torn them. One day a party of unhappy victims who had escaped from these spies of the Mountain went to beg for justice of Carrier. "Why did not you kill those ——," he cried (giving them an infamous name), "instead of letting them come here to bother me?"

In consequence of the efforts of these different bands, the most honourable citizens were soon cast into prison. They employed a means as simple as it was expeditious to discover the enemies of the people, or, as they expressed it, to *nab* the rich,—*pincer les riches*. Report was spread of a conspiracy; the *générale* was beaten, and the *sans-culottes*, the true children of the nation, repaired to their posts. But the rich, the selfish, remained as usual at home. The inference was obvious. All who would not turn out to suppress a conspiracy,

Chapter X

either must be actual accomplices, or in their hearts must wish it success; and of course incurred the doom of conspirators. Nothing could be more simple; and every available building in Nantes was soon choked with the crowds that were apprehended in so summary a manner.

To these innumerable victims, taken from the rich inhabitants, were added the Vendeans brought in every day from the country, who had accepted the amnesty proclaimed to all who would lay down their arms and acknowledge the Republic. The Nantes authorities ventured to plead the cause of these unhappy men. But Carrier, with an oath, replied, "You do not know your duty. I will have you all guillotined if one of them escapes."

The question naturally occurs, in what way were these crowds of prisoners disposed of? It soon became evident, that the "*national razor*," as the guillotine was flippantly called, was quite insufficient to keep down the numbers, although a great many had been sent to Paris. Carrier consulted his inventive genius; and first tried volleys of musketry in the quarries of Gigant. In order to carry out this horrible plan, he had, what was called, to *regenerate his authorities*, some of whom refused to obey his orders. Their places were soon supplied by less scrupulous agents. Under their management, a large number of men, women, and children were marched out to the quarries of Gigant, and there shot promiscuously. They varied the fusillade day by day. Sometimes the massacres were indiscriminate, sometimes special; sometimes the victims were all men, sometimes all women. The bodies were for days left exposed without any covering, tainting the air and outraging decency. Some of the fusillades numbered several hundreds of victims. Seven hundred Vendeans, and a large number of republican soldiers made prisoners by the Catholic army before the rout at Savenay, presented themselves to the Nantes authorities. The Vendeans claimed the amnesty; the Blues begged either to be permitted to return to their homes, or to take up arms for the Republic. Carrier had them shot

NANTES.

Chapter X

indiscriminately. At another time five hundred were massacred in the same way. The details he gives in his own report to the Convention: "There have arrived at Nantes," he says, "five hundred brigands, whom the inhabitants of the country seized in the act of laying down their arms, and asking for mercy; but the only mercy which can be shown the rebels is to give them a speedy death."

The national guards and the troops of the line were commissioned to inter the dead; but the duty was discharged so ill, that a burying corps was specially appointed for that service. These auxiliaries to the revolutionary army of Brutus had so much occupation, that they could scarcely cast more than a few shovelfuls of earth over the corpses: and soon bands of dogs scented out the horrible charnel-house, and regaled themselves upon human flesh. This revolting fact was left unnoticed by the authorities till it was observed that morsels of flesh, and even whole limbs, were dragged into the town, where they infected the air; and then, but not till then, an order was issued commanding all dogs to be tied up.

Notwithstanding this wholesale butchery, the guillotine was still in incessant demand; and so lavish was the expenditure of blood, that the basin constructed to receive the stream of life was insufficient for the purpose; and it was necessary to form a conduit between the scaffold and the Loire. Twice the executioners demanded an increase in pay, and twice it was admitted that, on account of the increase of labour, the demand was just. Sometimes Carrier gave a night exhibition; and a batch of heads was chopped off by torchlight.

And yet a third, and, if possible, still more efficacious method, was required for the execution of the vast number of prisoners still remaining alive. Carrier thereupon invented the *noyades*,—an inhuman device with which his name will be for ever associated, and which casts into the shade the most atrocious of his other acts, or indeed the worst cruelties of the other revolutionary tyrants. Before, however, they were formally avowed, they had been once or twice secretly practised. On announcing to the Convention the "regeneration" of the Nantes authorities, Carrier concluded his despatch in these words: "Ninety of those whom we call refractory priests were shut up in a boat on the Loire. I have just learned, and the news is certain, that they have all perished in the river." It was pretended that this was an accident; but in a few days a new noyade was reported in more express terms: "Fifty-eight individuals, known as refractory priests, were shut up in a boat on the Loire; last night they were all swallowed up. It is a true revolutionary stream, that Loire!"

Horrible to relate, it appears that this wholesale murder was due to an apostate prelate, the constitutional bishop Minée. In a special meeting of the club to which he belonged, he declared that reason and philosophy commanded him to break the ties which attached him to a caste to which the Republic owed all its misfortunes; and that he did break them accordingly, and abjured his priesthood. Many of the constitutional priests followed his example; and, according to the report of a republican, "it was soon difficult to believe that there had ever been in Nantes priests and saints, and an absurd religion called the Catholic. The priests who durst resist the general vote, were put on board a boat along with the refractory priests who were already there. By a little republican ingenuity, a plank was easily detached. The boat filled with water on all sides at once, and sank with its priestly cargo."

Eight days afterwards was celebrated the *fête* in honour of the Goddess of Reason. The new worship was inaugurated at Nantes by the drowning of a hundred priests. Minée celebrated the occasion by a grand speech, in which he pronounced a panegyric on Marat, his venerable patron. Carrier gave a grand banquet in a Dutch galliot, from which the victims were precipitated, bound two and two together, into the water.

Enraptured with the success of his noyades, Carrier determined to employ them more frequently. People of every class, sex,

Chapter X

and age were now to suffer a mode of death first devised only for priests. The Marats used to repair to the prisons, and bring enough for a freight to the Isle of Chavirée, as they used jokingly to say. If the unhappy inmates asked what they were wanted for, the answer was, "You will be employed in the construction of an under-water fort." Whenever there were not victims sufficient in any particular prison, others were brought from elsewhere to make up the number required.

The patriots exerted themselves to bring the system of noyades to perfection. At first they used to content themselves with throwing their victims into the water tied two and two together. As there was a risk of the cord breaking and the victim being saved, they afterwards sank the boat itself with the hatches down. There was, however, a dispute among the *noyeurs* as to which of these two methods was to be preferred—if the one was the more safe, the other was the more diverting. Carrier used to say, that one of the greatest pleasures was to stand by and see the grimaces which a priest or an aristocrat made in dying; and his myrmidons were much of the same taste. With a refinement of cruelty, the republicans were very fond of making a jest of the sufferings of their victims. Often instead of at once arresting a man, they would let him run, and hunt him down. With the same object they invented the civic marriages, as they were called,—a more horrible device perhaps than any that they had yet conceived. Tying two persons of opposite sexes together in a state of nudity, they left them exposed to the jeers and laughter of the crowd, and then threw them into the water. Modesty has no language to express the outrages which were perpetrated on the banks of the Loire.

"The Nantese," said Carrier, "have the ancient Breton spirit; iron, fire, and water must nationalise their town." The guillotine, the fusillades, and the noyades,—these were the iron, fire, and water that were to do the work of regeneration. But they were not his only agents; pestilence was added to the dreadful three. The air was corrupted by the heaps of unburied bodies, and by the pools of blood that flowed from the guillotine. The water was tainted by the corpses that lay and rotted at the bottom, and were washed up by the waves, or dragged to the surface, as they were for long after, by the anchors of ships. In vain the authorities enforced the burial of the dead, and forbade the use of the water of the Loire. The pestilence had begun; and was bred, moreover, afresh in the filth and abominations of the prisons. From the prisons it spread into the town; and by a just retribution the murderers died of the disease which their own cruelty had engendered.

Many of the old convents had been turned into prisons, and yet room was wanting for the immense multitudes who were arrested; so that a thousand were crammed into a space that was scarcely large enough for three hundred. It is not to be supposed that the pitiless ruffians cared to feed the wretches whom they thus cooped up. The prisoners died alike for want of food and of air. Nay, to give them nourishment or comfort of any kind was inevitably to incur the same fate. Nor was any attempt made to remove the dead, or to cleanse the floors. Imagination may depict, but decency forbids to describe, the horrors which even a very short time must have produced in a hot and crowded prison. There women brought forth their children and saw them die, and there was no one to pity; and died themselves, and there was no one to bury mother or infant. A horrible stench bred an incurable fever, that often spared the starving wretches in the prison, and struck down rich and poor outside. Persons coming in from the street were often seized with asphyxia; and when the authorities, from personal fear, desired to cleanse one of these dens, they were unable to find workmen courageous enough to enter: none but thirty or forty prisoners condemned to death would undertake the labour. These men, under a promise of liberty, performed it; it cost some of them their lives, but the survivors were guillotined notwithstanding the promise. "That was only fair!" said the Marats.

Chapter X

The exact number of victims during Carrier's reign of terror can never be ascertained. According to the indictment against him, it was from ten to twelve thousand. But this is far below the real truth. Some time before his departure, this execrable delegate of the Convention said, pointing to the Loire, "There are already two thousand eight hundred brigands in the national bath;" and the expeditions to the Isle of Chavirée continued long after that. Hundreds were suffocated and starved in prison, of whose death no one took any account. Hundreds expired of famine—hundreds were daily beheaded by the guillotine—hundreds, nay thousands, were slaughtered pell-mell in the Quarries of Gigant, stabbed in the streets, or drowned in the Loire. Never will the exact number be ascertained till the awful day when the grave and the sea give up their dead.

So utterly prostrate was the town, that none dreamed of resistance. To withstand Carrier, or to be thought desirous of withstanding him, was to incur instant death. When every one feared for his own life, no one was bold enough to attempt the defence of others; and when the Marats appeared with their summons, those who were called followed at once without delay or remonstrance. They found it easier to die than to defend their lives, and courage vanished, to appear again only on the scaffold.

At last the very dregs of the populace sickened of blood;—the clubs themselves, from which Carrier had selected his Marats, began to weary of the guillotine. This result was chiefly brought about by the execution of the Biliais family. The head of the house, an old member of the Breton parliament, lived on his estate in the neighbourhood of Nantes, occupied solely in works of charity. He was denounced and condemned, on the ground that he had harboured a priest. On hearing his sentence, he exclaimed, "May our Lord give me grace to die a good death!" Some days afterwards the same sentence was pronounced on his wife and two daughters, for having endeavoured to keep the people in the Catholic faith. Already acquainted with the fate of M. de la Biliais, they heard their own with indifference; and the people, observing their calmness, supposed them to be acquitted, and felt an involuntary pleasure. The next morning they were marched out to suffer; and they went reciting aloud the prayers of the dying. On arriving at the scaffold, the mother desired only one favour—that she might die last, and feel sure that her daughters lost no more than their lives. Her prayer was heard.

Another execution also tended to change the tide of popular feeling,—that of four sisters, the Demoiselles Mello de la Metairie. Deprived of both their parents, these young ladies had continued to live in their native city, devoting their lives to the care of the sick and the consolation of the poor and afflicted. No other crime was ever laid to their charge; but it was enough to draw down upon their heads the fury of the "patriots." They were denounced as exercising a baneful influence over their countrymen, dragged before the revolutionary tribunal, and condemned to be guillotined on the morrow. The eldest was only twenty-four years of age.

They were immediately taken to the dungeon of the Clock Tower, which was then used as the condemned cell; there all were imprisoned who had only a few hours to live. The place was selected with a refinement of cruelty. Lying under the huge pendulum, the victims could count, not only the hours, but the moments which remained to them. They felt their life ebbing drop by drop, and saw themselves pushed, second by second, by the hand of time, into eternity. When the innocent girls heard the door close upon them in their living tomb, they knew that they were shut up from all hope on earth—they were beyond all human aid; yet no groan of despair burst from them. They fell upon their knees, and prayed to Him for whose consolation no dungeon could be too deep: and they prayed also to their mother, who had gone before them into heaven, to obtain for them grace to make a happy death. They, so young, so beautiful, for whom so many days seemed to be in store!

Chapter X

In prayers and tears and mutual embraces the hours passed on, the night fled, and day dawned; at length the moment of execution arrived. Steps were heard on the staircase leading to the dungeon; the door creaked on its hinges; and they flung themselves again upon the ground and invoked the God of martyrs. Then rising, they embraced each other, and in a firm voice said to the jailer, "We are ready."

A crowd had been assembled in the *place* for several hours; and when the four young girls appeared, a murmur of pity was heard on all sides; but this feeling was soon repressed, and cries were heard of "Down with the aristocrats! the aristocrats to the guillotine!" These cries, at first raised by a few, were taken up by the whole multitude, for each feared to be suspected of sympathy with the unhappy victims. The executioner could with difficulty force a way through the crowd, but at length they arrived at the guillotine. The eldest of the four mounted first, pointing towards heaven as she embraced her young sisters for the last time. In a few moments she was there. The second and the third followed her with the same assurance.

Only the youngest remained. Her last moment had arrived. She rose from the earth, and then mounted in her turn the bloody way. The executioner, in order to bind her eyes, took her hands, as she held them over her face that she might not see the mutilated bodies of her sisters. Then the maiden appeared in all the beauty of her youth. She was but fifteen years old; and as she cast her eyes towards heaven, with a divine enthusiasm in her countenance, she looked like an angel ready to fly away from the abode of crime. Even the executioner felt a sensation of pity; and turning towards the people he exclaimed, "She is too young, she is not yet fifteen!"

"Mercy! mercy!" they cried from every quarter. "The Republic pardons her—she is not yet old enough to die!"

From the scaffold the young girl said to the crowd, "I am more than fifteen. You have killed my sisters, and I am as guilty as they were!"

The reign of terror under Carrier at Nantes

"No, no," replied the multitude; "come down. You are pardoned!"

"I do not want pardon, I want to die," cried the innocent child. "I see my sisters, they are ascending up to heaven. They are calling me, they are waiting for me. O, have pity, executioner, and let me die. I am guilty—just as guilty as they were. I hate the Republic—I detest it! *Vive le Roi! Vive le Roi!*"

"Ah, well, let her die, then," said a few voices. "Let her die, then," said the crowd.

The executioner, with a sigh, seized his victim; and soon the angel had rejoined the angels. The man of blood, whose very calling was murder, and who with the utmost indifference had put so many innocents to death, could never efface from his mind the death of that young girl. The next morning he was absent from his post, and in a few days he died.

The people too, who had seen floods of innocent blood flow like water, shuddered at the murder of the four sisters; and the tide of popular feeling turned at last. Carrier was the only man unaffected. He joked as usual upon the weakness of the executioner: and in spite of the demand for mercy, the guillotine continued its measured stroke; still the fusillades rattled in the quarries of Gigant; still the living cargo was swamped in the Loire. All longed for a cessation of bloodshed, yet no one dared to beard the tyrant; and the reign of terror was only stopped at last by Robespierre himself, who had heard that Carrier was too indiscriminate in his zeal, and who accordingly recalled his delegate. Yet, strange to say, the noyades continued after his departure; although his successors opened the prisons to a multitude of captives, who had little dreamed that they should ever again see the sun till they were led forth to die.

Public opinion, now in its revulsion, demanded satisfaction for the crimes of the reign of terror at Nantes; and the agents of Carrier were arraigned before the Paris tribunal. They demanded that their master, who still sat free on the benches of the Convention, should

Chapter X

be placed by their side. Their prayer was granted; an indictment was drawn up against Carrier himself amid the acclamations of the multitude, and he was condemned to death. He died protesting his innocence; and, revolting as his words may be, they were in a legal sense true. He was put to death by his own accomplices; he acted under the orders of the Convention, who condemned themselves in condemning him.

The narrations of affecting suffering, of Christian fortitude, of providential escapes that have been recorded are innumerable. Some of them we will here set down. In the midst of all the cruelty of the terrorists, they awarded to the pregnant woman and nursing mother a respite from death. But this show of mercy only concealed the greater barbarity. A lady named Madame de la Roche Saint André was arrested and condemned as a royalist. She pleaded her pregnancy, and was led back from the scaffold to prison. There she was safely delivered, and for some time continued to nurse her child. Thus the helpless babe preserved the life of her who had given it life; and in the depth of her dungeon the companions of Madame de la Roche Saint André bestowed incessant care upon the infant, on the frail thread of whose existence hung the safety of its mother. But in spite of their care, one night it died, stifled with the foul air in which it first drew its breath. The next morning, the man employed to select the victims accosted the bereaved lady thus: "Your child is dead; we only allowed you to live that you might nourish it; today you shall die." In vain her sister, Mademoiselle de Janon, begged, as a great favour, to be permitted to die in her stead. The ruffians who sat on the bloody bench, replied, "No, you would be too happy to make the sacrifice;" and Madame de la Roche Saint André was punished for the death of her infant, and died on the scaffold with all the resignation of a Christian.

Although a great number of children were sacrificed, the republicans seem to have made some attempts to save them. The *entrepôt* was a huge building, used before the revolution as a storehouse for merchandise. During the reign of terror it was turned into a prison, as its proximity to the river adapted it for the noyades. There, on one occasion, a vast number of Vendean women were confined, many of them with babes at the breast; and it was announced that any women of Nantes who wished to save the children of the Vendeans might be admitted to the *entrepôt*, and that each might rescue one of the little creatures. A great number of charitable women rushed to the prison; and the Christian mother can alone picture to herself the scene which ensued. On seeing them enter, the broken-hearted Vendeans fell upon their knees, and holding up their infants in their arms, appealed to the strangers to take them away and save them from a cruel death. But scarcely were their prayers heard, when they besought the strangers to restore them again; they begged to be allowed one last embrace, and then one more; and the little children, struggling to escape from the strangers, threw themselves into the arms of their mothers, and clung to their bosoms, and refused to be taken away; and then was the same scene of heart-breaking misery to be enacted over again.

The widow of an insurgent was among the prisoners who were to die the next day. She saw among the women who had come to the prison to save the children a person whose appearance denoted easy circumstances. The widow thought she could not do better than confide her child to her care. "Madame," she said, "have pity on me, and adopt my child." "Yes," said the unknown, "I will, and will educate him." "God bless you!" said the widow comforted; "teach him to love God, and imitate his father, who died for the king."

"Do not distress yourself," said the stranger, embracing the child; "I am rich. He shall want for nothing. I will teach him to love and serve the Republic."

"Give him back to me! give me back my child!" cried the royalist widow; "you will destroy his soul. I had rather he should die with me than live to be perverted and forget God and the king." And

Chapter X

with a mother's strength she snatched her child away, and together they were engulfed in the Loire the next day.

Madame de Jourdain perished in the noyades with her three daughters. A republican rushed to save the youngest, who was of remarkable beauty. He seized her as she was about to be precipitated from the boat, but she burst from his grasp into the river. Falling, however, on a heap of corpses, she cried to the executioners, "Push me in! push me in! There is not enough water!" Her prayer was heard. This heroism was universal. A maid-servant of the Viscountess de Lespinay heard an officer say to her mistress, "Wait here till I return. I will fling my cloak over you, and save you." He came back with his cloak; but by mistake threw it over the servant. The poor girl might have been saved; but with wonderful generosity pointed out to the republican the mistake he had made, and herself followed the executioners.

Notwithstanding the danger with which the least kindness shown to any royalist or Catholic was attended, there were not a few of the inhabitants of Nantes who braved the fury of the terrorists, and concealed in their houses both priests and insurgents. A touching story is told of the devotion of two young ladies to an abbé who had been denounced by an old schoolfellow, one of the most active of the Jacobin party. The republican had professed a great friendship for the priest till the revolution broke out, when the latter refused to take the constitutional oath, and was compelled to fly. He took refuge in Nantes, at the house of two ladies, who hid him in a secret chamber, the very existence of which was unknown to any but themselves. The republican had, however, some suspicion that they were acquainted with his place of concealment; and by professing a great anxiety to save his friend, he practised on their inexperience, and obtained from them an acknowledgment of the truth. Unable to believe in such treachery, the poor women revealed the secret of the unknown chamber; they opened the door, and showed the monster his prey. With a yell of triumph he pounced upon the priest, and dragged him forth to the tribunal; and the ladies, broken-hearted at having betrayed their guest, suffered with him the next day on the same scaffold.

The blood recoils at this treacherous conduct towards a friend; but in those days the dearest ties, not of friendship only, but of blood, were forgotten. There lived at Nantes two brothers, of whom the revolution found one a fencing-master, and the other a student in a seminary, destined for the ecclesiastical state. The former became a Jacobin, and the latter joined the flag of the insurrection in La Vendée. In one of the successful engagements of the Vendeans, the Jacobin fell into the hands of a party of peasants who had sworn to be revenged for the ruthless massacre of their families the night before. He was brought before the officer for trial before execution. The wretched man hung down his head, in anticipation of his approaching doom. "Hand him over to the chaplain," said the judge; "perhaps in a few days he will convert him." At the sound of the officer's voice, the criminal looked up and caught his eye. The two brothers recognised each other. In a moment the royalist forgot the difference of party, and embraced his brother; but the Blue repulsed him, saying, in a low voice, "Do not pretend to love me; you hate me, and I detest you." "I swear by our mother that I love you," said the other. "Then prove it by sending me back to Nantes." "So I will," said the royalist. "Let him die, let him die," said the peasants; "get out of the way, commandant, and let us shoot him." "Not before you have shot me," returned the officer: "it shall never be said there was a Cain in our ranks." At that moment came up Bernier the chaplain: "Why are you resting on your arms?" said he to the peasants. "We want to finish with that man. He is one of those who massacred our wives and children. We will avenge them." "You cannot do it, my children, without crime." "We have sworn it," they cried. "Is it by this that you have sworn?" replied the priest, drawing a crucifix from his bosom; "have you sworn by the cross not to have mercy?" The Vendeans were mute, and laid down their

Chapter X

arms. "God bless you!" said the officer; "you have saved my brother." "I did not know he was your brother," said Bernier; "I only saw in him a wretched man condemned to death. What have I to do in the camp but to preach forbearance? There are enough here who cry vengeance; I always cry mercy." The peasants took up the word, and the men who a moment before had been foremost in demanding the death of the prisoner, now exclaimed, "Mercy! mercy!" The republican was astonished; but his pride revolted at the indignity of being saved by a priest, and no word of thanks passed his lips. And on being released he departed without embracing his brother, or acknowledging his debt to the Abbé Bernier.

Time passed on, and the fortune of war brought about the annihilation of the grand army at Savenay. The royalist officer was one of those who had shared the dangers of the expedition up to that point; and at the close of the day he and three others were all that remained of the company of Lyrot. The latter were bent on regaining their village in the Bocage: he resolved to seek an asylum at Nantes. He walked all night, taking advantage of the darkness to approach the town. In the day-time he hid among the thick bushes on the road-side, and when evening came set forth again. "If my mother were alive," said he, "with what tenderness she would receive me! But I have no friends. I have a brother; to him I will go. I once saved his life; he will now save mine." This hope sustained his courage in the midst of the darkness and cold and rain of a December night; yet with a beating heart he knocked at his brother's door. The republican opened it himself. "O my brother," said the fugitive, "I am come to ask an asylum." "An asylum?" said he with a sneer; "O, then, you fierce Vendeans, who were going to upset the Republic, have had to fly? Well, come in!" The royalist entered. "Wait here till I have got my hat and cloak." "Whither will you take me?" said the unhappy Vendean. "Don't you want an asylum? Follow me, I will take you to one." "But why not here, my brother? I am weak and faint." "Never mind; follow me, and ask no questions." The poor wretch obeyed. His brother seized his arm, and dragged him along at a rapid pace. At length they stopped at a vast hotel. At a word from the republican, the porter let them pass, and they entered; they ascended by a superb staircase, leading to a bed-chamber luxuriously furnished. Two women were preparing a bath near the bed. On their entrance the women retired, and a man came in. It was Carrier. In an imperious tone, he asked what they wanted at that hour. "This," said the fugitive's brother, "is a brigand, a friend of priests, and a captain in the Catholic army." "Who gave him up to you?" "Himself." "And how do you know him?" "He is my brother." "Your brother?" "Yes, I have brought him; he came from Savenay just now to ask an asylum." "And what do you want me to do with him?" "Put him to death." At these words Carrier, wretch as he was, started back, and cried: "What, your own brother?" "Yes, my brother. I denounce him. I have done my duty; now do yours." Carrier knew what these words meant: that if he hesitated, he should be himself denounced. His natural thirst for blood aided his resolution; and he called the guards, and gave orders that the Vendean should be taken off to the Bouffay; "and," added he to the unnatural informer, "be at the place of execution tomorrow morning, and you shall see if I let the foes of the Republic live." The unhappy royalist had no need of these last words to know the fate that was in store for him; but he only said to his brother, "Is it so you repay me? you, who owe your life to me, give me up to death? Adieu! tomorrow you shall see my blood flow." He spent the night in the dungeon, praying God to have mercy on the murderer, and to give him grace to pardon him from the heart. When he was conducted to the scaffold, the very crowd were filled with horror at his brother's crime. Before laying his head down, he said, "For our mother's sake, and for the sake of God, I pardon you." "And I," replied the fratricide, "curse you. Go into nothingness; and let me hear no more of your God." The next moment the Vendean died, praying with his last breath for the unnatural brother who was the cause of his death.

Chapter X

Of the multitudes who were plunged beneath the waters of the Loire, few ever escaped. When they rose to the surface, there were always in readiness some inhuman wretches to cut off the last hope from the gasping victims. But instances of miraculous preservation were not unknown; and more than one heroic Christian constantly devoted himself to watch for any bodies floating down the stream from which life was not yet extinct. The story of the Abbé Landeau, curé of St. Lyphar, is not the least affecting of these cases.

This good priest had lain long in the prisons of Nantes, and had seen a vast number of his brethren led out, never to return. At length his own turn came. In the middle of the night he heard his name called by the fatal voice which awoke the victims. He rose instantly. By his side lay an old priest, who was also summoned. The Abbé Landeau stretched out his hand to him. The old religious, with a smile, said, "My brother, I accept your support. We have long suffered together; give me your arm for our last journey."

Embracing the priests, and they were many, who were not yet summoned, the two friends left the prison, and were dragged through the silent streets by the national executioners. Not a word was breathed, not a sound was made, lest the pity of the inhabitants should be roused;—for the noyades were as yet in their infancy.

At length they came to the Loire, where they found a boat in readiness. A few of the priests were still ignorant of their destination. "Where are you going to carry us," they asked; "to Spain, or to Cayenne?" To this question no answer was returned but a ferocious laugh or a grim pleasantry. Impatient to accomplish their work, the executioners hurried them on board with blows and insults; after which they shoved off into the stream. The victims were most of them shut up below; but a few, among whom were the abbé and his friend, were left standing on the deck.

It was a calm and beautiful night, the stars were shining brightly, and the boat fell merrily down the stream, as for a fête.

Suddenly, in the stillness, was heard a voice, crying, "Citizens, rid the Republic of its foes!"

At this order, the executioners, who had appeared to be asleep, cast themselves on the wretched priests, tied them two and two together, and, opening the infernal plugs, pushed them overboard into the river.

The abbé was precipitated from the deck tied to his old prison companion. Together they cried, as they were falling, "Merciful God, have pity on us, and receive us together!" Their prayer rose to heaven along with the groans and cries and ejaculations of scores of victims. The noise was terrible. The unhappy wretches, before sinking, beat about in the water. Some tried to climb up again into the boat, but the executioners, with their boat-hooks, pushed them back into the Loire. In the midst of the tumult and confusion, the cord which bound the two priests became loose. They did not, however, separate. The abbé was strong, and knew how to swim: he still continued to support the old man, and for some time both entertained the hope of being saved. But at last the old religious said, "My strength is exhausted; let me go. Why should we both drown?" and he attempted to untie the cord. The abbé perceived it, and said, "I will not leave you, O my brother; I will save you, or we will perish together. Mount on my back. Perhaps we shall fall in with some fishing-boat. Let us hope in God, who saved Jonas."

The old man obeyed; but unfortunately the spot selected for the execution was one of the widest parts of the Loire. The banks were a long way off, and the strength of the abbé was well-nigh exhausted. The religious saw it, and with one word, Adieu! let go, and was carried away by the current.

The abbé had hitherto been sustained with the hope of saving his aged brother, and now was ready to give way in despair at his fate. At the dead of night, in the midst of the waves, what could be the use of prolonging the struggle? And even if he were saved, he would live but to encounter new perils. Better the death of martyrs

Chapter X

than the life of the dungeons. Such were his thoughts, when he heard the sound of a boat not far off. He strained his eyes, and distinguished a sail through the gloom, and the figure of a sailor praying. The priest swam so that the boat should pass by him; and when it was close, raised his cold hand out of the water and placed it on the sailor's arm. The man started. "Have pity on me," said the abbé; "I am ready to sink." "Hold on by the boat," said the other; "I have two strange passengers on board. I will go and see if they are sleeping." Presently he returned, and pulled up the abbé into the boat, and hid him under a heap of sails. "Don't stir," said he, "till the passengers have gone ashore."

After some hours they touched at St. Nazaire; and the fisherman roused the abbé, and said, "Now we are alone, monsieur; get up, and take some brandy, and put on this cloak; my wife will be glad to know the use it has been put to. Often at night she says, 'Good man, let us get into the boat, and see if we can find any poor wretches to save;' and we frequently see the bodies of the people who have been drowned floating down the stream. With our boathooks we pull them into the boat. Sometimes they are women and children—sometimes priests, tied two and two. And there are at Nantes good people who let us know when there is going to be a noyade. Then we push off, and wait for what may pass. And the good God has blessed our labour: we have saved one woman; her clothes had kept her up. Another time my son saved an old man."

The sequel to this history is too interesting to be omitted, although not bearing on the particular subject of this chapter. But it illustrates the fervour of the Catholics during those times of persecution. The fisherman was afraid to land the abbé at his own destination, on account of the vigilance of the Blues; so he set him ashore higher up, and showed him the way to a cottage inhabited by trustworthy people, giving him a piece of paper, which he was to show the man who opened the door. He then asked his blessing, and left him. The abbé reached the house in safety. An old man opened to him, but started back in a fright at his strange appearance. But when he saw the paper, he made him welcome. "We have agreed among ourselves," said he, "when we have saved a priest, to give him a leaf out of one of our prayer-books, as a token to all true Christians." He then gave him food and a bed.

The next morning the fisherman's family came to see the priest. They were compelled to have recourse to a thousand stratagems to disarm the suspicions of the republicans. It wanted two days of Christmas; and the good people, who had not heard Mass for so long, entreated the priest to offer the holy sacrifice for them on Christmas night. He gladly consented. There was no church in which to celebrate the mysteries, and they were compelled to choose an old barn. The women of the village decorated it during the night before: hangings were spread all round; a rustic table, covered with the whitest linen, served for the altar; branches of holly, with their red berries, were placed upon it; and an ebony crucifix, and two rosin candles in iron candlesticks, completed the equipment of that lowly sanctuary. Without doubt it was not despised by Him whose birth in a stable it was designed to commemorate.

The hour which recalled the greatest of mysteries arrived; each family of the hamlet awaited the approach of midnight, assembled round the hearth relating old stories and singing Christmas carols. Then singly and quietly the faithful repaired to the barn, which had been prepared for the festival. With what piety they knelt before that humble altar! and with what courage! for to assemble thus for prayer was a crime worthy of death. The shepherds who heard the angels announce the birth of Christ had not more lively faith.

When the priest appeared before the altar, sobs and tears burst forth. Scarcely three days had elapsed since he had been snatched from the very jaws of death; and this secret assembly might involve them all in the horrible fate from which he had just been rescued. According to usage, the abbé said the three Masses of Christmas; the congregation received into their hearts their incarnate God;

Chapter X

and when all was over, returned to their own homes, confident that no unfriendly eye had watched their proceedings. But a republican peasant was aware of the presence of a priest in the village, and gave notice to the authorities. A rigorous search was instituted, and for some days the priest was hidden in an oven. At night the good fisherman and his wife brought him out, and lavished upon him all their care; in the morning he was restored to his hiding-place.

In this hamlet the abbé lived till the days of persecution were over. At length the time came when France permitted her children to worship God. Then his former parishioners of St. Lyphar, who knew that their curé had been saved by the fisherman of the Loire, repaired in great numbers to the village, and entreated him to return to his old church. He obeyed the call of duty, and the day of his return was fixed.

From the first dawn young men came flocking in from St. Lyphar, dressed in their gayest attire; later arrived the ancients of the parish, leading a horse, saddled but without a rider, destined for the curé.

Before leaving the fisherman's hut, the abbé raised a cross hard by, and prostrating himself in prayer, he and all the multitude invoked God's blessing on the family which, at so great danger, had succoured him. Then they set out, conversing on the virtues of their pastor and the wonderful dealings of God towards him. When they drew near to St. Lyphar, and the curé saw the tower of the old church in the hollow, he exclaimed, "O my God, remove me no more from this village! Let me die here in peace!" "May you live long," said the peasants, "to bring up those who have been born in your absence!" Presently they saw the women, who had come out to meet the procession, bearing their infants in their arms. The old curé blessed them with tears in his eyes, and the procession swelled as it approached the town. At the entrance were drawn up all the sick and infirm, who had not been able to meet their pastor sooner. There also were stationed two other priests, bearing the golden cross and banner belonging to the parish, and which they had succeeded in hiding from the revolutionists. Then the choir burst out into the psalm, "Blessed is he who cometh in the name of the Lord;" which the crowd took up in their turn. And soon the cassock, surplice, and cope were placed on the shoulders of the priest, and the procession turned towards the church. So great was his emotion, that he was compelled to lean on the arms of the priests on either side.

Presently the cross and banner are lowered to enter the church; the doors open, and the old priest advances to kiss the altar of his youth. The tapers are lit, and the incense rises, and a great silence reigns throughout the congregation: the thanksgiving commences; and while the words *Te Deum laudamus* are on his lips, the priest sinks to the ground. The canticle which he had commenced on earth, he had gone to finish in heaven; for God had called him to Himself.

The reign of terror at Nantes stands out from the page of history with a fearful prominence; but throughout the department of the west the guillotine and the fusillades were long in constant use. Some days after the siege of Angers, Westermann proclaimed an amnesty; and twelve hundred Vendeans put faith in his word, and surrendered themselves, with their children and wives, to the republicans. They were seized and confined in the cathedral, for the prisons were all full; and there they were left for several days,—a crowd of every sex and age, without food or covering. At last the twelve hundred men were taken out and led to the plain of St. Gemmes; when there, they were marshalled by the side of an immense dyke ready excavated to receive their bodies, and there shot. The children were all sent to the "coral fishing," at Nantes, as the Angevin committee facetiously termed the noyades in their letter to Carrier. The women were put into a separate prison, which most of them left only to be executed. According to the most trustworthy accounts, about three thousand four hundred

Chapter X

persons were massacred at Angers, besides an unknown number at the Ponts-de-Cé, and at the Port de l'Ancre, and at Erigné. Similar atrocities took place at Doué, at Saumur, at Mans, at Laval, at Brest, and at Rennes. At Rennes they compelled the children of the royalist prisoners to perform the office of executioners; putting the muskets into their little hands, they made them take aim with weeping eyes. But the unhappy boys turned away their heads and fired. Their fathers only suffered the greater tortures from their want of skill; and the revolutionists derived a double pleasure from the novelty of the execution and the prolonged sufferings of their victims. At Vannes, at Redon, at Antrain, the guillotine was in incessant operation. Besides the exceptional tribunals established in all the chief towns, there were movable committees, which adjourned their sittings from place to place as they might be wanted. Every where prayer was considered a crime. To regenerate the human species by draining their blood,—this was the maxim of the day; and for several months the departments of the west saw it literally executed.

Turreau, the new general-in-chief of the republicans, was an officer of no mean ability; and it did not escape him, that the Vendean leaders, notwithstanding the multiplicity of their attacks, possessed very restricted resources, and were nowhere assembled in any force. He determined to prevent the concentration of their strength by simultaneous action on every part. With a view of showing himself every where at once, and extinguishing the sparks of insurrection as they arose, he divided his army into several columns. He also gave orders that the republican communes, whose courage was not undisputed, should be disarmed, lest they should be attacked and beaten by the enemy; that all neutral inhabitants should be banished; and that the supplies of the country (grain, forage, and cattle) should be seized. Entrenched camps were to be formed in the chief positions, and gun-boats were set to pass up and down the Loire; and thus La Vendée was to be cut off from Brittany, and its several provinces isolated from each other. Turreau's plan was to starve out the insurrection, by shutting up all possible channels by which the country could be supported.

To the various generals who were to be intrusted with its execution, he issued an order, of which the following is an example:—

"LIBERTY, FRATERNITY, EQUALITY, OR DEATH.

"General Huché will depart at once for Luçon; he will take the command of all the armed forces there and in the neighbourhood. He will then seize, by all military means, all supplies and forage, on his right, from St. Hermine to Chantonay; in front, as far as St. Hilaire de Vouhys, La Chaise, and Chateau-Fromage; on his left, from La Roche-sur-Yon to La Claie; the whole inclusively. All supplies which he may find, he will lay up at Luçon, as also all horned cattle. *As soon as the seizures have been effected, all the towns, villages, hamlets, bakeries, and mills, without any exception, shall be burned*; the inhabitants who shall be known to have taken part, directly or indirectly, in the revolt of their country, shall be exterminated on the spot.

(Signed) "TURREAU, *General-in-chief*."

Orders precisely similar were given to each of the twelve generals in command of the expeditionary columns; so that the whole province was parcelled out for destruction. Thirteen towns were at first excepted from the fire-warrant, although all were to be subjected to pillage; but eventually several of these shared the general fate. It was the peculiarity of Turreau's invasion, to pass over the claims of any person or thing to exemption. There were several communes which had never taken part in the insurrection, and many republicans who had all along opposed it; but no distinction was made between Blues and Royalists. The general directions given by each general to his soldiers were, "Burn every living thing, and

Chapter X

exterminate at the point of the bayonet all the inhabitants you meet." By the reckless brutality with which these orders were obeyed, Turreau's troops justly acquired the designation of *the infernal columns*.

Any recapitulation of the outrages which were perpetrated by the infernal columns, would be but a catalogue of butcheries and pillage. Neither age nor sex were spared; and the most horrible injuries were inflicted on helpless women. Dishonour was invariably followed by a cruel death; and decency forsook the very highway. Robbery was carried to its height. Many of the common soldiers acquired sums of fifty thousand francs and more; and were to be seen covered with jewels, and living in riotous luxury. Chapelain, a republican of rank, thus speaks of Grignon, one of the twelve generals: "Grignon told me, that on entering La Vendée he had sworn to kill every one he met; that a patriot could not be supposed possible in that region; and that, at any rate, a patriot's death was of little consequence, if the public safety demanded it. One day he said, 'How clumsy they are! They begin with killing. They ought to extort the money first by a promise of mercy; and when they have obtained what they can get, then kill all the same.'"

Of the same general another republican officer writes: "Grignon sacrificed to his rage whatever he met, and the massacre was horrible. At one place, under the ridiculous pretence that an altar-cloth found in the belfry was a flag of the brigands, he slaughtered the whole municipality, though they had presented themselves before the army decorated with the republican scarf, and also all the good citizens of the commune who had joined the national guard. He satisfied his rage by the indiscriminate massacre of every individual he could find, and the burning of numberless houses. The same horrors attended his whole march."

General Dufour was accused of the same wholesale pillage of republicans and royalists alike. General Huché's conduct was thus denounced: "The barbarous orders of General Huché are expressly aimed at the Republic. . . . Universal alarm has seized on all hearts.

The infernal columns

The rights of the man and the citizen are outraged by a monster, whose conduct, we are bound to say, surpasses the cruelty of Nero." In consequence of these excesses the authorities of Luçon placed him under arrest. Forthwith the commissioners declared the town suspected, and placed it in a state of siege. Thus did the Convention sanction the worst acts of its officers. A municipal officer, speaking of General Grammont, says, that his column slaughtered old men, women, and children; not even known patriots and constitutional priests being spared: and when any republicans came to complain, he used to answer: "You may think yourselves very lucky you have not been shot with the rest!" In a formal complaint against General Commaire, we read: "Every day Commaire is seen to take the first children he meets,—offspring of republicans or royalists he cares not,—seize them by one leg, and cleave them down the middle, as a butcher cleaves a sheep. His men do the same." Of General Amey it was said, "He caused the ovens to be heated; and when they were hot he cast in women and children. We expostulated; and he gave for answer, 'That is the way the Republic likes its bread baked.'"

Cordillier wrote: "Independently of the universal conflagration which is still raging, I have *passed up the hedge* (*i.e.* shot) about six hundred individuals of both sexes."

Duquesnoy sums up his own campaign with the following confession: "I consider I have destroyed three thousand men, of whom two thousand were under arms. At Les Hertiers I had more than a hundred men slain, without counting the women."

Grignon, against whom we have enumerated the testimonies of others, thus speaks of himself: "On our way my rear-guard burned a number of mills and farms, slaying men and women. I burned St. Lambert, and slew a quantity of men and women." Yet, strange to say, even Grignon had his moments of weakness; for which he incurred the reproof of more consistent republicans. One day he failed to shoot the whole of his prey; and Francastel, a commissioner, exclaimed, "What! prisoners in La Vendée?"

Chapter X

The infernal columns were not wanting in the same ingenuity which invented the noyades of the Loire.

In revenge for the terrible defeat of the army of Mayence at Torfou, the neighbourhood of Clisson was made the scene of a massacre equal in atrocity to any thing which Carrier ever devised. A crowd of men, women, and children, to the number of two hundred—some say four and even five hundred—driven by the flames, which had destroyed their cottages, took refuge in the vaults of an old chateau. For several weeks these unhappy people remained in the damp dark cellars, without once daring to venture out. At night the children had to go out to obtain food. At the least noise they had orders to return; and they were always closely questioned as to what they had seen and heard. "We have seen nothing but the fires all round the country," they generally replied; "and heard nothing but the noise of the river, and the wind among the trees."

But one evening a little girl was surprised by a party of men concealed in the ruins. The moment she saw them she threw down her bundle and ran away. They watched her, and saw her enter a dark passage. The poor child narrated to the terrified people what she had seen; and the soldiers outside heard the dull murmurs of alarm which followed her recital. With savage joy they sent off for assistance; and the men of Mayence, overjoyed at the prospect of revenge, rushed to the chateau. In an instant all the old men, little children, and women were dragged out of the vaults. Then arose a difficulty. What should they do with these royalists? There was a pause—the republicans looked round—one of them pointed to a large well in the court-yard; his comrades perceived the gesture, and understood it; and in another instant the whole crowd, fathers and mothers, women and children, were pushed over the side, and thrown down alive into the depth. In vain they shrieked for mercy, in vain they struggled, in vain they clung to the clothes of their executioners, to the grass of the court, to the rough stones of the parapet—down they went, one after another, pell-mell, drowning with their cries the oaths of their murderers, till all was over. Those who came last fell without injury the short distance between the heaving heap of mangled half-suffocated bodies and the top of the well. Then earth and heavy stones were flung down. Every now and then, with a convulsive struggle, an arm or a leg would be seen to move above the layer of mould; but soon all was still, the shrieks died away, and the victims were for ever at rest. At their leisure the murderers filled up the pit, and the bodies have never been disturbed.

Other acts of brutality have been recorded. It is said that the violators of female honour scratched with the points of their swords upon the flesh of their victims inscriptions setting forth the outrage they had committed. Can the records of history parallel,—they cannot surpass,—iniquities like these?

For nearly four months the infernal columns had the range of the country. On the 20th January 1794, the first invasion was made, and Turreau was superseded by Vimeux on the 13th May. For nearly four months La Vendée was abandoned to pillage, fire, massacre, violation, and every crime which could outrage humanity, or cry aloud for the Divine vengeance. The unhappy population fled into the fastnesses of the forests; but, alas, the sick, and the aged, and the pregnant woman, and the innocent babe—these could not escape from the destroyer; and their blood was spilt like water in every parish. The men did, indeed, make oftentimes the most heroic resistance; but what could avail the efforts of a handful of starving peasants against the armed fury of regular soldiers? Yet the deeds of heroism which have been recorded surpass the most glorious achievements of ancient story. The parish of Chanzeau is prominent for the number of brave men that it produced. It will be remembered that it was from Chanzeau that Forêt, in the first days of the insurrection, gathered his troops. Marie Jeanne also was from Chanzeau. When the infernal columns ravaged the country, the village had been more than once a prey to the flames; and it

Chapter X

was announced to the terrified inhabitants that the few remaining houses were to be levelled to the ground. A handful of men armed in haste: but it was necessary to save the women and children; and by a sublime act of resignation, they resolved to sacrifice themselves to gain time for their escape into the woods.

The old sacristan of Chanzeau, Maurice Ragueneau, whose name will be remembered as long as the insurrection in La Vendée, put himself at the head of seventeen men. Ten women, who preferred death with their husbands to life without them, followed them; and the Abbé Blanvillain, their curé, joined the glorious band. He had taken the oath to the civil constitution of the clergy; but repenting of his error, he recanted, and remained among the good Christians of Chanzeau to encourage them to die well. Ragueneau caused ammunition and victuals to be taken into the belfry, where they all shut themselves in; and the remainder of the inhabitants escaped out of the village before the Blues came.

Caffin, the republican general, entered the town, and finding no one, invested the church, and summoned its defenders to surrender. He promised them their life. They knew better than to trust the promises of a republican; and replied with the cry, *Vive la réligion! Vive le Roi!* Upon this the battle commenced. Ragueneau placed the best marksmen at the apertures of the tower, and the women stood by to load, which they did with inconceivable rapidity. Many of the Blues had been slain before they could force their way into the church; and then Ragueneau poured his fire through the spaces between the bells and framework. For five hours this strange battle lasted, during which the assailants were decimated by the shot from the tower, without being able to reach the defenders. At last they conceived the idea of setting fire to the ruins, which had been twice burned before. They brought the straw and wood to pile against the wall; but were forced to retreat before a general broadside from the insurgents within. However, by means of corpses, they raised an immense pile, and the belfry caught fire. The flames soon began to roar with fearful fury, and mounted up to the vaulting. In perfect calmness the peasants inside looked at the horrible death before them; but they made no effort to escape. The Abbé Blanvillain, who was wounded, spoke of demanding quarter. "Ah, Monsieur le Curé!" cried Ragueneau, "what an opportunity for you to wipe off your sacrilegious oath by martyrdom! and will you not make the most of it?" The abbé was silent, and devoted himself to death. The fire had by this time reached the planks to which they had retreated. The abbé had a ball through his thigh; but seeing a parishioner dying, he was anxious to give him the last sacraments; and gave the ciborium, in which the Hosts were, to a woman to hold, while he tried to leap the space between. He missed his leap, and fell upon the burning vault below.

By this time their ammunition was all expended. Ragueneau alone remained fighting in the midst of the flames. At last he was wounded mortally. Marie Jeanne, his sister,—she who had given her name to the bronze cannon,—cast herself on his body; and when the survivors tried to draw her away, she cried, "Let me die. It is no offence in the sight of God to escape by death from those monsters. My God! have pity on me!"—and with these words she precipitated herself anew into the flames.

Five women and thirteen men still lived, waiting their fate in prayer and silence. The Blues themselves trembled at the sight, and a cry of pity burst from their lips. "Surrender," they cried; "we won't do you any harm." They hesitated even now; and one of Stofflet's chasseurs absolutely refused to capitulate. He was shot through the head; and he fell, saying, "I die for the God who died for me." The soldiers now placed ladders, to save such as would surrender. Two did so, and they were instantly taken into a garden and shot. But at the sight of the bloodstained countenances of those men and those young women, who had braved so great dangers, and had escaped as by a miracle, their hearts softened. Caffin had mercy upon them;

Chapter X

and they were taken to Chemillé, and kept there till the 2d May, when Stofflet signed the pacification with the representatives of the people.

Turreau, the instigator and the immediate author of these crimes, himself seldom left his head-quarters. He lived in a perpetual state of drunkenness; writing letters to his generals to stimulate their zeal, and addressing reports to the minister-of-war, that he might gain the reputation of an indefatigable officer. The Convention afterwards attempted to disown his system: but those reports reached them during a period of four months, and the whole of that time they took no steps to arrest his infernal columns; and when, on his recall, he was arraigned before the bar of the Convention, he was acquitted of the charge of excessive violence.

Strange to say, this man lived to be named chevalier of St. Louis, under Louis XVIII. He, who of all others had most wasted that king's most loyal province, was promoted to honour; while Stofflet and Cathelineau, names for ever memorable for their devotion to the crown, were refused admission into the royal gallery of Vendean generals, because they had come of peasant blood! Such conduct is of a piece with the cowardly indifference which looked on for seven years while La Vendée and Brittany were suffering loss of life and property in the royal cause, and made no attempt to uphold the insurrection!

Chapter XI

Death of Henri de Larochejacquelein—Stofflet elected to the chief command of the grand army—Successes of Charette—His guerilla warfare—Death of Haxo—Turreau receives one month to finish the insurrection—Confederation of Charette, Stofflet, and Marigny—Death of Marigny and Joly—Partial cessation of hostilities—Tinténiac appears again in La Vendée—Pacific change in the attitude of the Republic—Renewed successes of Charette—Bernier civil commissary-general—Pacification of La Jaunais—The secret articles—Triumphal entry of Charette into Nantes—Stofflet ratifies the pacification.

While Turreau was thus devastating La Vendée, where were Larochejacquelein, Stofflet, and Charette? Had they forgotten their country and its cause—were they deaf to her cries of distress? Charette still fought in the depths of the Marais; Stofflet in the recesses of the Bocage; but Larochejacquelein, the young, the brave, the chivalrous, the peasants' idol and the terror of their foes, lay stiff and cold in a soldier's grave. He was treacherously slain by two republicans, whose lives he had spared. On the 28th of January he met and defeated the enemy near Chollet. After the battle, he found two grenadiers hiding behind a hedge. He advanced towards them, crying, "Surrender, and you shall have quarter!" They cast themselves upon their knees, and when he was at barrel's length from them, one of them shot him through the head. So died Henri de Larochejacquelein, aged only twenty-two. Other chieftains may have displayed more judgment, and others more piety; but none were so brave, none so noble-hearted as he. He was the type of all that was heroic and

Chapter XI

high-minded and generous; and well might the unhappy survivors exclaim, as they laid him in his grave, "At last it may be said with truth that La Vendée is no more."

He was buried secretly, lest the knowledge of his death should discourage his own soldiers and animate the enemy. The supreme command of the grand army devolved upon Stofflet; and the new general-in-chief accepted the responsibility in tears, but without allowing himself to be disheartened. He showed himself equal to the emergency, and his activity and devotion seemed to increase with the danger. Seconded by other Vendean chiefs, he allowed the Blues no rest, but perpetually engaged them in harassing skirmishes; and was victorious over them in a pitched battle at Chollet. After these affairs he retired to the forest of Vezins, where the enemy were afraid to follow him. In this retreat he formed a regular camp, under protection of which there sprung up a sylvan town. Thither repaired all the fighting-men of the country; and stores, ammunition, and artillery were there accumulated. Every forest in the same way became a *refuge* for the aged and infirm, and the children, who were happy enough to escape the bayonet of the enemy. In the forest of Grala there were to be seen a church, a hospital, a magazine, a shop, and a manufactory for repairing weapons; and wooden huts, or wigwams, were built in regular streets. Stofflet had under his command about seven thousand men.

Charette had taken refuge in the extremity of his territory, the whole of which was traversed in every direction by the infernal columns. Here he endured the bitterest hardships, and displayed the greatest energy. He was in want of every necessary, not only of war, but of life; he had no victuals, no clothes, no arms, no ammunition. His soldiers, worn with fatigue, and hunted like wild-beasts by packs of soldiers, and in despair at the sight of their ruined houses, their burning farms, their starving or starved children, deserted from their leader. A few officers and a handful of peasants, who were determined to die with him, formed his whole army. It was then that he displayed that consummate resource which Napoleon declared amounted often to genius.

On the 9th of January he seizes St. Fulgent; he leaves it to surprise and rout a column of the enemy; he returns to St. Fulgent, and is himself defeated, and escapes with ten followers. A few days afterwards he assembles a troop and attacks Dufour. He is shot in the shoulder, and, of course, his men run away. Somehow he contrives to rally them, and the next day he finds time to bind up his wound. To his great joy recruits come in; for fight he must, surrounded as he is by the infernal columns. He learns that Sapinaud and another chief are anxious to join him, and he marches on the 2d February to meet them half-way. He arrives at Chauché just in time to see them beaten by Grignon. Without thinking what may be the disparity of force, he instantly charges the victorious columns, and utterly defeats them, slaying four hundred men. Grignon retires; but his place is supplied by another "infernal" general, and Charette beats him, as he had beaten his colleague. The blood on his sword is not yet dry, when a third column comes up, and shares the fate of the other two. We might imagine we were reading a page of romance, not of history.

Turreau, uneasy at these defeats, despatches Duquesnoy with a body of picked men to pursue him without intermission. In vain. Duquesnoy could never come up to him. Charette knew where and when to fight. At last he risks a battle at St. Columbia with three or four thousand men. His troops are at once disordered by a charge of cavalry, and Charette gives a signal of retreat. In a moment the Vendeans are nowhere. "I cannot say," wrote Duquesnoy, "which way the brigands fled: they vanished." Three or four days afterwards they appear again and defeat Duquesnoy.

So it was when Turreau sent fresh troops. Charette continually retreated, and appeared in unexpected places, outwitting the enemy in their most deep-laid combinations, and never once allowing

Chapter XI

himself to be surprised. However, his position was becoming extremely perilous. The infernal columns were drawing a circle round his army; and the lion must infallibly have been captured in his lair, if the Convention had not interposed at the very moment of success, and called off Turreau to Nantes with five thousand men and his own column. This reprieve inspired the Vendeans with new courage. Charette and Joly immediately determined to attack Légé. They took it by a *coup-de-main*, with a loss of eight hundred men to the republicans, and restored the fortunes of the insurrection in Bas Poitou. That day was marked by one of those terrible incidents which are the inevitable offspring of civil war. Joly had three sons; two fought under his own orders, the third commanded a troop of republicans. Of the two who were with him, one was killed, the other wounded: the third was made prisoner by the Vendeans, and his father commanded him to be shot. This act of barbarity excited the indignation of the whole army. Joly simply said, "I have done my duty." But the old surgeon was never the same man after the bloody deed.

The Blues were scarcely less active, and Haxo is now sent to command in Bas Poitou. This general made no attempt to overreach Charette by crafty manœuvres. He marched straight forward without stopping, always engaging in battle with fresh troops, and giving each company a rest in turn. "Charette," said he, "shall perish by my hand, or I will fall by his." The Vendeans were now reduced to the direst extremity. They durst not cook, or even bake their bread, lest the smoke should betray them; and often they were compelled to rise at night in haste and abandon the little provisions which they had. At length Charette said, "My friends, rather die than be continually flying. Let us show the Blues that La Vendée still exists!" So they halted to wait for Haxo. Haxo came up, and the battle began in a field of broom with incredible fury on both sides. After a fearful struggle the Blues gave way. Haxo was wounded in the breast, and his horse was slain under him. He got up, and leaned his back against an oak, and cried, "I no longer fight as a general, but as a soldier." The Vendeans surrounded him, and called upon him to surrender. Strokes with his sabre were the only answer he deigned to give. He was soon shot; and he fell exclaiming, "Is it possible? I perish by the hand of a coward!"

The death of Haxo and the defeat of his troops gave the Vendeans a few days' repose, and crowned the campaign of Charette with glory. For three months he had been constantly pursued, or rather, surrounded by forces five or six times exceeding his own. He had been often defeated, and as often victorious; and he finished by conquering the general who had been sent, in official phraseology, to *annihilate* him. This glorious result was owing, indeed, partly to the very violence which threatened him with destruction. Turreau had promised the Convention that fifteen days of his system, properly carried out, would suffice to extinguish the remaining embers of the insurrection. But he soon wrote to say that he knew not when the *incomprehensible* La Vendée would expire. His indiscriminate pillage, and slaughter of friends and foes, decided many to join the insurgents who had hitherto held aloof. The character of the war lost all its first generosity and chivalry: it soon became a war to the knife; and the war was more terrible to the Blues than to the peasants. "A soldier," wrote Turreau, "who would be a hero on the Rhine is good for nothing here. The very name of a brigand strikes terror to his heart." Thus the failure of the infernal columns became more intelligible; and Charette's successes are accounted for, primarily, by the indefatigable energy, resource, and courage of the Vendean commander; secondarily, by the indignation roused against the invaders by the republican portion of the population. The Convention at last perceived this, and passed some faint censure on the system of the general-in-chief, commanding him to distinguish for the future between the innocent and the guilty, and to finish the war within one month. Turreau replied that the time was too short; but he formed a new plan of campaign, the principle of which was to change the

Chapter XI

blood of the country. The patriots were all to remove to a distance of twenty leagues from the seat of war, or be considered rebels; all of whom, without regard to sex or age, were to be exterminated, and their places supplied by pure *sans-culottes*. At the same time the insurgents were invited to lay down their arms and give up their chiefs. Fifteen thousand of the most devoted republicans withdrew, and were abandoned to the utmost destitution; the rest joined the insurrection. Meanwhile the soldiers of Charette and Stofflet paid no attention to the offer of amnesty; that offer had been too often made and violated, and it was now treated by the peasants with contempt. Turreau's new plan had no better success than the old one.

Three generals commanded the Vendeans; Stofflet upon the banks of the Loire, Charette in the Marais and the Bocage, and Marigny near Bressuire. Marigny had endeavoured, after the failure of the expedition beyond the Loire, to raise the Bretons in the neighbourhood of Nantes and Savenay. Upon the failure of this attempt, he had returned to the Bocage, and was now surrounded by followers. In the extremity to which the insurgent army was reduced, it was obviously of the utmost consequence that its leaders should act with the most entire unity and concord, and that their measures should be concerted with a sole view to the general good. Unhappily, each acted as if he had no interest in common with the others, and fought and manœuvred, and manœuvred and fought, without reference to the common cause. Jealousy existed, to the full as bitter, among the enemy; but the military operations of the republicans were directed by a commander-in-chief; and rivalry, therefore, was the less fatal to success. Because there was no supreme authority in the insurgent army, there could be no concentration of force. Nevertheless, the necessity of united action forced itself upon the convictions of the three leaders, and frequent conferences were held with a view to that object. At one of these, Charette proposed the nomination of a generalissimo, and claimed the office for himself. Stofflet, it is said, under the

Confederation—Death of Marigny

influence of the Abbé Bernier, objected; and Charette gave way. But a treaty was formed between the three chieftains, by which each continued independent, but bound himself, under pain of death, to follow concerted plans. Stofflet first derived benefit from this arrangement, it being agreed that it was of primary importance to dispossess the Blues of the posts on the Loire. With that view a general rendezvous was proclaimed at Chemillé, and thence they advanced on Jallais.

The incidents which follow have been variously related. But it seems certain that Charette and Stofflet, jealous of Marigny's influence over the insurgents of the Haut Poitou, wished him to content himself with the command of artillery as formerly. But that arm was now of very inferior importance, consisting only of a few miserable pieces; and Marigny would not consent to take so subordinate a part. It appears also, that while yet indignant at the slight put upon him by his colleagues, in their proposition about the artillery, his soldiers complained of an unjust distribution of the victuals by Charette, and tumultuously withdrew from the army. Marigny unhappily followed them, and Charette and Stofflet immediately met and pronounced him a deserter. The former insisted that an example should be made; and he was condemned to death.

Marigny received the news of his sentence with indifference. The more so as the two judges took no steps to put it into execution. Two months passed away, and nothing further was done; but at length Stofflet heard that Marigny was in hiding in a chateau near Cerisay. He accordingly despatched a party of the German deserters to shoot him. No Vendean would undertake the office. Some of the officers remonstrated against a crime that, independently of its guilt, must be fatal to their cause. He hesitated a moment, but at length repeated the order.

Sick, and taken by surprise, Marigny offered no resistance, but simply demanded a priest and time for confession. With inconceivable cruelty, the request was refused. Yes, in the Catholic army,

Chapter XI

among a people in arms for the cause of religion, an officer is basely condemned by his fellows, and denied the consolations of his faith! The very republicans were less cruel at Noirmoutiers, when D'Elbée was shot. But Marigny, confiding in the Divine mercy, met his fate with courage. "My death," he said, "will not diminish the divisions; it but proves the speedy ruin of our party." Then to the soldiers he cried, "Aim at my heart—aim straight. Fire!" and he fell pierced with many balls.

Scarcely had he fallen, when each of the judges sought to lay the blame on the other. Stofflet pretended that he was innocent of his blood; Charette declared that he had offered Marigny an asylum; and both accused Bernier. But the priest was doubtless innocent. It is impossible to acquit the two leaders of the murder; for the one deliberately ordered, and the other took no pains to prevent, the execution of a sentence which both had passed two months before. It is the one great blot in the history of the insurrection.

Marigny was right; his death but increased the divisions of the army and hastened its decline. His soldiers refused to serve under the murderers of their beloved chieftain; and Charette and Stofflet incurred the indignation of their own troops. They professed a hearty contrition for the deed. Stofflet was one day in the woods, accompanied by only two soldiers, when they met a party of Marigny's men. "There goes the assassin of Marigny!" cried the insurgents of Haut Poitou. Stofflet halted; and in a voice full of sorrow and bitterness replied,—"You accuse me of a crime which I deplore, which I never wished to commit. But if you think me guilty, shoot me." They passed on in silence.

Yet this most sad event did not prevent the commission of another act of violence. Between Charette and Joly there existed an old rivalry; and Joly alone, of all the officers of the army of the Marais, held himself independent of its general. He had made enemies, too, among the soldiers, by his readiness to punish the least resistance by the pistol; and at length reports began to be spread

Partial cessation of hostilities—Tinténiac appears again

against his probity. The army were clamourous for an investigation; and Charette was not the man to discountenance a movement against his old competitor. Joly, in indignant silence, withdrew from the command, and took refuge in the forest of Aizenay. Thence he moved towards Anjou, intending, doubtless, to quit La Vendée. There he was taken for a spy, and a party of peasants went to apprehend him. Joly, always above giving explanations, blew out the brains of the first of the assailants; but he was soon massacred. When it was too late, his body was recognised. The news of his death was received by his former enemies with the same sorrow as that of the murder of Marigny; they forgot all but the courage of the old surgeon. Yet it is impossible to recall his assassination with the sorrow with which we read the tragic history of Marigny's death. He was identified with the bravery of the Catholic army, but not with its religious spirit. His first exploits had been performed when the rest of the insurgents had left the field of victory for their Easter duties; and in his end it is not unnatural to read the just anger of God against a father who could deliberately put his own son to death.

After the death of Marigny, Stofflet and Charette separated. The war was carried on languidly on both sides. The troops employed by the Republic in the west were wanted at the frontier; Turreau was recalled, and Vimeux appointed to the armies of the west in his stead. The new general abstained from any active operations, and commenced by adding ten to the five entrenched camps formed by his predecessor. At the same time, the two Vendean generals attempted to organise their forces. Charette formed eleven divisions, and Stofflet eight; and a breathing-time ensued. The Convention appeared at last to see that another system must be tried.

Towards the end of May, Tinténiac appeared again in La Vendée, bearing despatches from the English government and from the Count of Artois, second brother of Louis XVI., and afterwards Charles X. Fifteen months had the country been in arms for the

Chapter XI

royal cause, and till this moment no member of the royal family had displayed the slightest sympathy with the movement. The Prince now announced his intention to appear in the Bocage, and the English government made the same offer as before, viz. of men and ammunition, on condition that the Vendeans should possess themselves of a sea-port at which they could be landed. Aiguillon Roads were indicated as a very favourable spot for the purpose. The prince, however, said nothing of the time of his arrival; and the Vendean chiefs charged Tinténiac to inform him that the performance of his promise was indispensable to success.

Will it be believed, that at this favourable moment Charette and Stofflet allowed their petty rivalry to prejudice the public cause? It was determined to attack Challans preparatory to further steps. Now Challans lies in the heart of Charette's country, and its capture would have given him a great preponderance of influence in the army. In the heat of the battle, Stofflet, not to permit his rival to acquire so great an advantage, withdrew his men in good order; and the day was lost.

However, defeat was of the less moment in consequence of the change in the mind of the Convention. Peace was not yet possible; but many circumstances indicated its approach. In his orders of the day, Vimeux enjoined respect to private property, and protection to individuals; acts of pillage were to be visited with punishment, and military operations to be suspended to *facilitate the harvest*. It is true, that while the general-in-chief showed a conciliatory spirit, his subordinates continued their old system of indiscriminate slaughter of men, women, and children. Still the tide had evidently turned, and crime became the exception where it had been the rule.

The natural consequence of this change in the enemy's tactics, and of the incessant divisions of the two great chiefs, was the decay of enthusiasm in the insurgent territory. If men were required to fight,—and occasional conflicts still occurred,—a few thousand soldiers were with difficulty collected. Not that the peasants believed in the expressions of good-will with which the republican proclamations abounded; even the fall of Robespierre was received with indifference. In that remote district, they were more closely acquainted with the system than the men who worked it; and when Charette assembled his army and said, "Give up your chiefs, and you shall receive the pardon of the Blues," they answered with one voice, "No, we would rather die with you."

But, weary of fighting, they were glad to rest when they could. Charette, nevertheless, took advantage of the momentary enthusiasm which his meeting with his men called forth to attack the enemy. On the 8th September, he seized La Rouillière, one of the republican entrenched camps; and six days afterwards he obtained a still more decisive success, when the camp of Fréligné, defended by a numerous division, fell into his power, with abundance of arms and ammunition. The Blues lost more than a thousand men. It was the greatest victory that had been achieved since the campaign beyond the Loire; and was useful in hastening the desire of the Convention for the termination of hostilities by revealing the still energetic spirit of their peasant adversaries.

The example of Charette had little effect on Stofflet. The Abbé Bernier kept him quiet; and Charette, unable alone to undertake any enterprise of importance, retired to his head-quarters at Belleville.

Meanwhile fresh causes of hostility arose between the two chiefs. The Abbé Bernier, whose influence over the mind of Stofflet was supreme, endeavoured to erect in Vendée a regular government; and in order that its decrees should not depend for their force on the authority of this or that military chief, he caused himself to be elected civil commissary-general. Each parish was invited to send a representative to the Château Mazière, and the generals of division received the like summons. Charette, and those who acted with him, took no notice of the Abbé's attempt; the meeting was, however, very numerous. Nearly eight hundred members attended

Chapter XI

it, and with a single exception gave a unanimous vote in his favour. Bernier placed his opponent under arrest, and found himself invested with supreme authority. Charette warmly protested against his self-constituted power; but the ecclesiastic proceeded with energy to act as if it were unquestioned. He ordered assistance to be promptly given to the widows and children of insurgents who had fallen in the war; he issued regulations for the administration of the property of refugees, police, commerce and agriculture,— greatly, it must be acknowledged, to the benefit of the country, although not without some disadvantages also. He even pretended to exercise authority in military matters, and to claim superiority over Stofflet himself.

The administration of Bernier, by giving an impulse to trade and agriculture, disclosed the great difficulties under which the arts of peace lay from the absence of a circulating medium. Most of the coin in the country had been concealed by its possessors, and for the sake of safety withdrawn from circulation. Thereupon Bernier proposed to create, and did create, a paper money to an immense amount, payable at the peace—that is, the restoration. It was an ill-advised measure; for a paper currency can only be valuable at a time of great commercial confidence; at this moment confidence was impossible. Bernier fell into the error which so many statesmen have committed, of seeking to bolster up a government by fictitious resources. It was not, however, on this ground that Charette opposed the issuing of promissory notes. The measure excited his indignation, not so much from its intrinsic impolicy, as because it was adopted without reference to his opinion; and he and his generals proceeded to judge the "conduct of the ambitious man who dared to act on his sole authority." Some of the subordinate officers would have condemned the offending chief to death, unmindful of the unhappy consequences which followed the assassination of Marigny. Stofflet and Bernier replied to the condemnation which was passed upon them by an able and energetic call to union; to which, however, their adversaries paid but slight attention. An external coalition was, indeed, brought about. Hostilities ceased by their publicity to invite the aggression of the Convention; but they were not the less active. Still there ensued an appearance of reconciliation; and the Republic, instead of pursuing the war with fresh vigour, at last judged the time to have arrived for terminating this long and grievous struggle by a treaty of peace.

The first official overtures came from the Committee of Public Safety. On the 2d December 1794, Carnot, in the capacity of member of that committee, introduced a proclamation, the purport of which was, as usual, "to bring back the rebels to their duty;" but couched in a more conciliatory form. It commenced with declaring "that the Convention considered the Vendeans more misguided than guilty, and was anxious to pardon its erring children." This preamble was little likely to weigh with the insurgents, who knew what reliance was to be placed on the promises of the Convention. But the proclamation terminated with a significant phrase. Hitherto the amnesty had been promised to the peasants alone, the officers were to be delivered up to the vengeance of the nation; now "all the persons known as rebels of La Vendée and as Chouans, who would lay down their arms during the month following the day of publication of that proclamation, should be left undisturbed and secure from all penalties in consequence of their revolt."

However, even with this concession, the proclamation was fruitless. The Vendeans refused to receive a pardon; they would only treat on terms of equality.

The attitude of independence which the insurgents maintained,—an attitude even dignified by its calm determination,—made a great impression on the republican party, and rendered them the more eager for peace. The general feeling was shared by none more warmly than by the representatives of the Convention in La Vendée, Ruelle and Canclaux. But the Vendeans were afraid to trust the most solemn protestations of their foes, and for

Chapter XI

a long time Ruelle in vain sought to obtain an interview with his redoubtable antagonist in the Marais. This was at last effected by the intervention of a woman. There lived in Nantes a creole lady who, by the insurrection of the negroes in St. Domingo, had been forced to seek an asylum in that city. Here, by some strange good fortune, she had acquired the confidence alike of Royalists and Blues; and notwithstanding the known fact of her having harboured some of the stragglers of the expedition beyond the Loire, had passed unmolested through the reign of terror. Convinced of the upright intentions of Ruelle, Madame Garnier Chambou obtained for him an interview with the sister of Charette, who was then lying concealed in Nantes; and she promised to be responsible for the safe conduct of any messenger from the Republic to her brother. While Ruelle was considering to whom to intrust that delicate commission, there arrived a man named Bureau de la Batardière, who had been proscribed by the Convention as an agent of the Vendeans, though he belonged to neither party. He was a *Moderate*, anxious for peace, and glad of an opportunity of doing a service to the Republic which would remove the ban under which his person and property lay. Active, insinuating, cool, and determined, no fitter mediator could have been selected. The first interview between Charette and Bureau took place on the 28th December. Appearing to yield more to the entreaties of his sister than the arguments of Bureau, Charette agreed to an amnesty; but he declared that if negotiations were to proceed, he must have an interview with Canclaux and Ruelle; and he added, that his first conditions were the free exercise of the Catholic religion and the return of the Bourbons.

Charette was anxious for peace on account of the jaded condition of his soldiers. He was perfectly aware that it could not give all that the insurrection demanded; yet he trusted that the disposition evinced by the revolutionary authorities for more pacific measures was an indication of the return of better times, of a reaction from the republicanism of the age to the old royalist principles of France; and, however temporary or insufficient for the full restoration of the church and throne, he expected to employ the interval in the better organisation of his troops, and the recovery of the province from the ravages of war. With this view, he summoned all the principal proprietors and gentlemen of La Vendée to discuss the question, while Ruelle repaired to Paris to obtain powers to conclude a treaty of peace with the insurgents; for as yet he was only commissioned to proclaim an amnesty. At the meeting, which was numerously attended, only three were in favour of a continuation of hostilities; and Ruelle returned with full authority to concede to the Vendeans the liberty of conscience which they made their ultimatum. Under these circumstances the pacification proceeded rapidly; and on the 17th of February 1795, at La Jaunais, eleven Conventionists on one side, and twenty Vendean officers on the other, signed a treaty of peace, the object of which was, according to the terms of that document, "to reunite to the great family of the French those who ought never to have been separated from it." By this treaty the Convention not only conceded religious liberty to the insurgents, but engaged to defray the expenses of the war to the extent of two millions; to leave under the orders of Charette a corps of two thousand *territorial guards*, consisting of inhabitants of the district and paid by the public treasury; to give the Vendeans indemnity for their losses, and assist them in the rebuilding of their houses; and to dispense with the usual military service of the young men, in order that they might re-establish agriculture in the country. On the other hand, the insurgents declared that they submitted themselves to the Republic one and indivisible, and entered into an engagement not again to bear arms against it.

The reader may think that by this treaty Charette and those who were with him abandoned the cause of the crown. But the submission to the Republic was confessedly nominal and fictitious. It was impossible for the Convention to treat upon any other than

Chapter XI

republican terms: they could not stultify themselves by acknowledging the claims of the Bourbons; liberty of conscience was the utmost that they could concede, or that could be reasonably expected of them. But there were besides several articles agreed upon between the negotiating parties which reduced the submission of the Vendeans to a temporary toleration of the Republic. These were, first, that the monarchy should be restored; secondly, that the Catholic religion should be set up again in all its splendour; thirdly, that the royalists in the interval should be masters of their country; besides others of less importance. These unpublished articles acquit Charette and his party of the crime of abandoning their principles, as Stofflet indignantly insisted at the time; but they raise a question upon which there has been a good deal of discussion. Ruelle is accused of double-dealing, in agreeing to articles which the Convention had never any intention of carrying out. It is absurd to suppose that what all the arms of Europe failed to effect, a handful of peasants in the last extremity, and at a distance from Paris, should have wrung from the government. On the other hand, Charette is charged either with folly and credulity in believing the promises so made, or with treason to his king if, as is most probable, he placed no faith in them at all. But to us there appears little difficulty in the transaction. There was neither duplicity on the one side, nor credulity or treason on the other. Both parties were anxious for peace. The insurgents stipulated first of all for liberty of conscience. "That," replies the delegate of the Convention, "you can have; the Republic is not compromised by that concession." Farther, we must have the throne and monarchy restored. "That," replies the delegate, "is absurd; the Republic will not consent to its own dissolution." Is, then, peace impossible? No; why maintain a useless struggle? Not all the blood of La Vendée will set Louis XVIII. on his throne. Give us your nominal submission to the Republic; we, on the other hand, will give a secret promise to restore the old constitution of the country. The former will justify the Convention in the eyes of

The secret articles—Triumphal entry of Charette

the world; the latter will justify yourselves in the eyes of your own party and to your own consciences. Be it remembered, that from first to last the Vendean was a religious war—a war in which the political element was secondary, and, as it were, accidental. To have held out now that the main object of the insurrection had been attained, would have been inconsistent with the whole tenor of the struggle. Our opening remarks went to show that the population of La Vendée were indifferent to the political changes which were taking place, and only took up arms when the civil constitution of the clergy was forced upon them. Now that, by their blood and sufferings, they had won for their country the repeal of that constitution, could they be expected to wage a hopeless war for a cause which had failed to excite them at the first?

As is usually the case when a compromise is made, some of both parties were offended. The more violent revolutionists exclaimed with cries of rage that this pacification was the first step towards the restoration of the monarchy; the extreme royalists declared that it had adjourned that event *sine die*. But it was received with the greatest enthusiasm by the vast majority both of the republicans and insurgents. When Bureau de la Batardière appeared at the bar of the Convention, and did homage to the Republic in the name of Charette,—when he unfurled the white flag, and laid it at the foot of the tribune,—the whole assembly rose at the sight of the royalist standard, and for some minutes continued to shout *Vive la Nation!* Under the excitement of that enthusiasm, all the articles of the pacification which Ruelle had concluded were ratified by the Convention without one dissentient voice. Not less joy did the Vendeans manifest, on their part, when Charette made his triumphal entry into Nantes, to ratify in public what had been previously arranged in secrecy at La Jaunais.

On the 26th February 1795, salvos of artillery announced to the men of Nantes that Charette and his staff were at the gates of their town. An immense crowd thronged the streets; for it was

Chapter XI

no common ceremony that they were about to celebrate, but the inauguration, as they trusted, of a happy peace. The royalist general rides between Canclaux and Beaupuy. The generals of the Convention are in the military costume of the day, with plume, cockade, and scarf of the republican colours. Charette, mounted on his own charger, appears dressed with all the magnificence in which he delighted. Clad in blue, and girt with a white scarf fringed with gold and embroidered with fleurs-de-lis, and on his head the well-known white plume around which the brave men of Bas Poitou had so often rallied, he now advances through the midst of a population who seem drunk with joy. Behind him follow four of his officers, with four of the officers of Canclaux; and after them the staffs of the two armies, side by side, wearing the white and the tricolor cockades. The national guard line the road. The cavalry and *guides* of Charette advance in order of battle, bearing aloft the Vendean flag; and behind them are drawn two chariots surmounted with the bonnet of liberty. Inside are the representatives who had signed the treaty; the chariots are preceded by military music. The whole procession is closed by the republican cavalry.

At the sight of Charette, to whom Canclaux with all the courtesy of the old school did the honours of the day, the crowd about the bridges was at first too much astonished for noisy applause; but the cries soon rose loud and high of *Vive Charette!* Presently a few voices cried *Vive le Roi!* With infinite tact, Bureau de la Batardière, who had the disposal of the arrangements, cast himself into the midst of the throng, and in tones of thunder shouted *Vive la paix! Vive la paix!* repeated the representatives within the chariots, waving through the windows the tricolor banner; *vive la paix!* took up the officers and soldiers of the two armies.

Excited with joy, the people hailed Charette with acclamations; no prince on entering his capital could have been received with more enthusiastic welcome. And at these demonstrations his habitually severe expression of countenance softened; he bowed

Triumphal entry—Stofflet ratifies the pacification

his thanks in kingly style towards either side, as with the cavalcade of royalists and republicans he traversed the chief streets and squares of his native town. Every where he was received with the same enthusiasm. As he passed through the *place* of Bouffay, the stones of which had been so often flooded with Vendean blood, his brow contracted, his eye shot forth its old fire, he raised his hat and bowed to the memory of the martyred dead. Canclaux and Beaupuy, touched with the same thought, joined in that simple mark of respect; and it was repeated throughout the whole procession.

The pageant ended; "brigands" and "patriots" met as if there were no bloody memories to disturb their friendship. The Loire flowed on like an ordinary stream; all swore never to renew the horrors of that civil war—all doubtless in good faith. Yet a very few weeks saw it raging again with unabated fury. Charette alone, though flattered by the reception, distrusted that goodly show of peace. He was led to the theatre in the evening, and the whole audience rose to repeat the plaudits of the morning. But he received them with a sort of remorse, forseeing a speedy termination to all their rejoicings.

Stofflet, on hearing of the treaty of La Jaunais, vociferated, *Au diable la République! Au diable Charette!* in a perfect frenzy of rage. But many of his officers were secretly on the side of peace, and before long abandoned him. Some of them, and those, shame to say, men who had distinguished themselves in the insurrection, allowed themselves to be bought over by the Convention, in revenge, it is said, for the tyranny of Stofflet and Bernier. However that may be, his adherents fell away. He found it impossible to carry on the war without the support of his rival, or to engage the sympathies of the peasantry in a strife which was now purely for the royal family, no members of which had exhibited the least gratitude for the lavish expenditure of blood in their favour; and after a long and hopeless struggle, he concluded at Varades, on the 2d May, a treaty of peace with the republicans upon the identical terms which

Chapter XI

Charette had obtained. He agreed to support the Republic till the establishment of the monarchy, in return for certain concessions, the most important of which was the restoration of the Catholic faith. Thus the objects of the insurrection were accomplished; not in vain had Cathelineau, and Lescure, and Bonchamps, and a host of other glorious men, fought and died. They fought for their God, His altars, and His priests; and now, after two years of bloodshed and horrors, the cross of Christ prevailed against the tricolor flag of His enemies.

Chapter XII

The Chouannerie—History of Jean Chouan—He joins the Vendean army at Laval at the head of the Little Vendée—Tactics of the Chouans—Measures of the Convention—Puisaye's system—His departure for England—Pacification during his absence—Family of Jean Chouan—Jambe d'Argent—M. Jacques—False Chouans—Anecdote of Madame Huneau.

HERE WE MUST for a while retrace our steps, and pause to consider what had been doing the meanwhile in Brittany. The reader will bear in mind, that in the spring of 1793 Brittany had shown the same symptoms of insurrection which, about the same time, appeared in La Vendée; and that the Convention, by the advice of Canclaux, resolved to conciliate the one, in order that it might with greater effect coerce the other. It has been said that the result of this manœuvre was at once to appease the discontent of the Bretons; in that the clergy, perceiving themselves at liberty to celebrate the Catholic rites as formerly, exhorted their flocks to return to their labours. But this tranquillity was not universal, nor was it permanent. There were many Bretons who were not to be deceived by a policy in direct contradiction to the whole tenor of the revolution; and these held themselves in readiness to act as occasion might require. Nor had they to wait long. France soon outstepped the bounds it had assigned to itself; and by an easy transition, passed from a national, which had supplanted a Catholic Church, to the rejection of a Church of any kind. Then arose a fresh persecution in Brittany; and with persecution came resistance. The spirit which had been lulled woke again; not as in La Vendée by the simultaneous insurrection

Chapter XII

of the whole population, but by separate risings in various parts of the country. These were at first of small importance; but after the passage of the Loire, the war became more active; and we must now return from the pacification of Charette and Stofflet to trace the progress of the Chouannerie.

This name the insurrection in Brittany derived from its originator Jean Chouan, a peasant of St. Ouen-des-toits, near Laval. The history of this remarkable man is full of the deepest interest; and the influence which he exercised over his countrymen renders it necessary to record here the prominent events in his life.

In Maine there existed a heavy impost on salt, called the *gabelle*, which was not levied in Brittany. Salt, therefore, the sugar of the poor, as the poet Beranger called it, cost only a sous per pound in the latter province, while in the former the price was thirteen sous. The gentry, by the odious privileges of the time, were exempt from this tax; but the poor were compelled not only to pay the higher price, but to consume a certain quantity. The minimum of consumption was fixed by the excise.

Hence arose a very active contraband trade between the two provinces. The smugglers of *faux sel*, as the salt which had never paid duty was called, were very numerous. Almost all the peasants on the boundary were devoted to this dangerous traffic; and among others, a family of the name of Cottereau. This family had been *sabotiers** for generations, and lived in the recesses of the woods in huts constructed of leafy branches, where they plied their trade. Here the women brought forth their children without nurse or other assistance; and the boys grew up like wolves, and lived like their fathers before them as *faux-sauniers*, smugglers of salt. So savage did the whole family become by this wild existence, that the country people called them *chouins*, that is, in the patois of the district, *chats-huants*, screech-owls. From this the word *chouan* is a corruption.

* Makers of wooden shoes

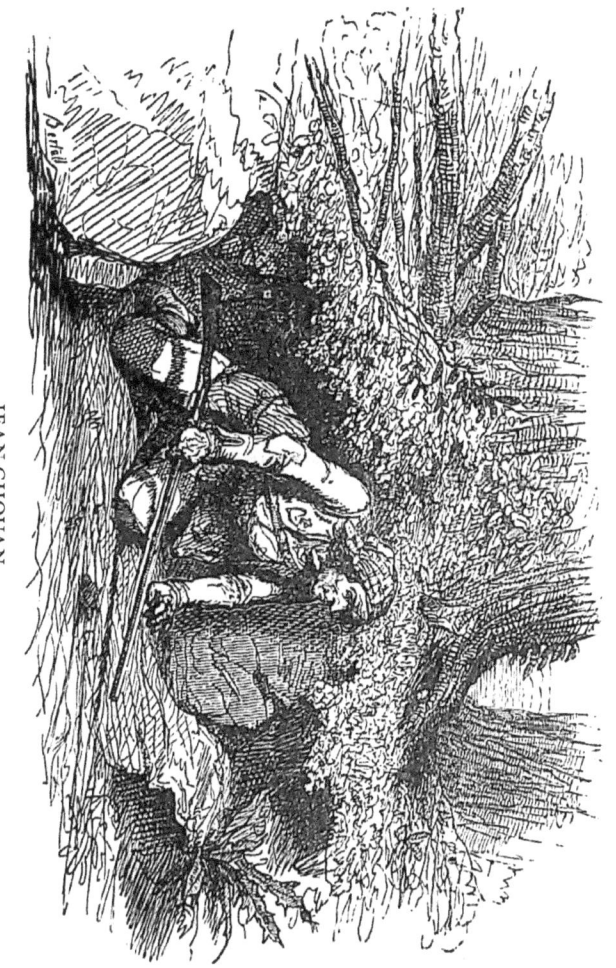

JEAN CHOUAN.

Chapter XII

Some time before the revolution, the then head of the family was of a more civilised nature than his race. He was to a certain extent educated; and on Sundays he used to visit the hamlets, and after Mass read the lives of the saints to the men, and teach the young girls hymns. In this way he became acquainted with a farmer's daughter named Jeanne Moyné, and the two fell in love with each other. But the father could not, without dishonour, give his child to a man who had never tilled the ground, much less to an outcast like Cottereau; and Jeanne was told to turn her heart another way. She said nothing; but some days afterwards her place was vacant, and her distaff was found broken at the door of the stable. Cottereau met her, and brought her to his cabin in the forest of Concise; where, however, she refused to stay till they had been married by the priest. On Sunday, therefore, they set off for St. Ouen-des-toits. The young girl entered the church alone to speak to the rector; but he was just ascending the pulpit to read the *monitoire*, in which the names of his parishioners who had neglected their duties, or laboured on days of obligation, were read out.* The priest then announced, that a girl in the neighbourhood had given great scandal by leaving her home to follow a man; and called upon her to confess her fault before the parishioners. Jeanne, who was on her knees among the other women, and had till that moment kept her head down to avoid recognition, rose up immediately with a calm countenance, and began the *Confiteor* aloud. The excitement among the congregation may be conceived. The priest scarcely knew whether to praise or blame. He questioned her; and her replies drew tears from the women, and even the fathers of families who were present could not withhold their sympathy. As for the priest, he recommended her to the prayers of the congregation; and the next evening he brought her back to Cottereau, and they were

---

* This custom of public admonition of offenders, under pain of excommunication after three warnings, existed in all the parishes of the west before the revolution.

married. From this marriage issued two daughters and four sons, among whom was the famous Jean Chouan. Before many years Jeanne was left a widow.

Long before he declared war against the Blues, her son Jean was the most noted salt-smuggler in all Maine. He went by the sobriquet of the *gas-menton*, the lying lad, which he had acquired from his tricks on the excise officers, and his habit of saying "there is no danger," by which he frequently led the smugglers into great scrapes. He himself not always escaped scatheless, notwithstanding his address and courage; and his family were frequently fined for his exploits. One day the bailiffs arrived, to seize his furniture in lieu of the fine; but Jean and his brothers, aware of their intention, had removed all their goods and chattels to a neighbour's house. Not a whit disconcerted, the bailiffs ordered their men to pull off the roof, to sell the slates. With the greatest good-will in the world, Jean himself lent a helping-hand; and when only the four walls were standing, invited the officers to examine whether the work had been done to their liking. They came in triumph, suspecting nothing; but scarcely were they within, when Jean fastened the door upon them, saying, that as they had unroofed other people's houses, it was but fair they should themselves have experience of the comforts of a night in the open air; and as it was beginning to rain, he bade them good evening, and left them to their meditations.

After this, Jean and his brothers were tracked like foxes; all their property was seized, and the family reduced to ruin. At length, the *gas-menton* made up a party of young men like himself desperate and reckless, to meet the officers, and have their revenge. The encounter resulted in the death of the most unpopular of the excisemen. Jean was advised to run away, and keep himself close in the woods of Brittany. But he replied, "there is no danger;" and the next night he was taken; and as the excise authorities had to judge him, he had little mercy to expect. His mother, the widow, on hearing of his apprehension, instantly perceived the danger. "He will be

Chapter XII

hanged," she exclaimed in despair. Her first impulse was to hasten to the Prince de Talmont, who had always been a friend to her. But unfortunately he was then at court. Suddenly she took the resolution of going up to plead her son's cause before the king himself. Seventy leagues she performed barefoot in five days, without stopping except for a morsel of bread which she begged as she walked, and a little sleep on the straw of the barns by the way-side. When she reached Versailles, she learned to her dismay that the prince, through whom alone she could gain access to majesty, was absent, and would not return for some time. One whole night she spent on her knees before the crucifix without ceasing to weep. She knew no one at Paris but the prince's coachman; and this man, touched by her distress, asked her if she would have courage to speak to the king herself. *"Have I not been speaking to the Blessed Trinity?"* she replied. "Very well," said the man, "then I will risk my place to serve a countrywoman. You shall get into my master the prince's carriage; it will be thought that he is inside going to court; and they will let us pass the barrier. Then, when the king comes out of the grand vestibule to enter his coach, you must go and throw yourself at his feet, and pray God to give you grace to speak well, for the fate of both of us depends on how all turns out." The thing was done the same day. Jeanne entered the prince's carriage, waited for the king, and as soon as he appeared, ran to him crying, "Mercy, monseigneur; the excisemen have ruined us, and now they are going to take my son, because he is a salt-smuggler. Save Jean, monseigneur; we are seven to pray to God for you."

The king stared to hear himself called monseigneur by a woman in an outlandish dress; and the people about him cried out that she was a mad woman, and that they should seize her. But when she had finished her story, all were lost in admiration of her conduct; and the king returned to the palace to sign with his own hand a reprieve till the pardon should be made out. In a few days afterwards her son was liberated.

History of Jean Chouan

Though he had felt the hangman's rope round his neck, Jean Cottereau continued his contraband trade as a salt-smuggler. In an encounter with the excisemen one of them was again slain; and as Jean's antecedents pointed him out as the murderer, he was compelled to throw himself upon the protection of the Talmonts, who could only save him by placing him in the army. He accordingly enlisted in Turenne's regiment, then quartered at Lille. He remained in this new post a year, when he grew home-sick and deserted. This new offence was not to be pardoned. But to save his life, his protectors obtained a *lettre de cachet** in his favour, and Jean spent two years in captivity. During this period he became a man; and on his return to his own country, he gave evidence of a solid conversion. He had lost his vagabond habits, and his piety showed itself to have been fortified by confinement. Just then the revolution broke out, and Jean immediately espoused the royal cause more warmly than all his neighbours. The king was more to him than to other Bretons; his mother had been received in the palace, she was acquainted with the king's face and the sound of his voice. She had seen him sign her son's pardon, and used to say with pride, that from that hour there was a link between the Bourbons and the Cottereaus.

It was the 15th August 1792. An order from the directory of the district had summoned to St. Ouen-des-toits all the young men of the neighbouring parishes, to enrol themselves in the national guard by voluntary enlistment. Most of them obeyed the summons; but the very sight of the officers with their registers inspired them with indignation, and when the names were called over, they replied only with hootings. The gendarmes threatened to arrest the ringleaders, and were about to put their menace in execution, when Jean Chouan shouted, "No national guard! no volunteers!" The cry was repeated on all sides. "If it is the king who commands us, we will all of us march for the king." "All of us, all of us," cried

---

* *Lettres de cachet* were warrants for the secret arrest of persons at the will of the court. They were one cause of the revolution.

Chapter XII

the peasants. "But not a man will march for the nation," added Jean. "Not a man! not a man!" echoed the crowd. Upon this they fell upon the commissaries, tore up their registers, upset the tables, wrenched off the legs, and therewith beat the gendarmes. This exploit was crowned by a general tumult, in the streets of Laval, between the insurgents and Graffin the mayor, at the head of the soldiers, for the possession of the tricolor flag; which ended in the discomfiture of the republicans.

Jean Cottereau took advantage of the enthusiasm created by their first success to organise an avowed insurrection. He announced to all the young men of the country, that the time had arrived for their formation into regular companies, and promised them on behalf of the royal family a daily pay. This argument was all-powerful with the Bretons; and therein consisted one great difference between the Chouannerie and the insurrection in La Vendée. Cathelineau and his men were animated by no hope of temporal reward; they fought for the cause of religion, and looked forward to a recompense hereafter.

The national guards of Laval, who had lost their flag, revenged themselves by excursions against such of the neighbouring parishes as they suspected of royalism. Jean Chouan thereupon determined to try the valour of his men. He attacked the patriots at Launey-Villiers, and repulsed them, with the loss of twenty men. The Chouans were now denounced by Graffin, and condemned to death. They accordingly took refuge in Misdon Wood,—a little band of forty men, the most determined salt-smugglers of the country. Among them was a man of the name of Mielette, who contested with Jean himself the sovereignty of the contraband trade. With this small force, Jean kept up a continued war with the authorities; and in some instances with considerable loss to the Blues. The insurrection, however, failed to spread on account of the pacific policy of the Blues; and Chouan was still in the woods, when the Vendean army, after achieving its vast successes, and

He joins the Vendean army at Laval

sustaining that great reverse which prostrated the energies of the insurgents, crossed the Loire, and attempted to carry on the struggle in Brittany.

Besides Chouan's party in Misdon Wood, there were similar bands of insurgents in most of the forests of Brittany, who had all of them more or less distinguished themselves in encounters with the republicans. These separate and independent bands were in themselves but little formidable; yet they offered, as Canclaux perceived, all the materials for a numerous army. Their union was prevented by the judicious measures of the Convention. But one, whose name is scarcely less celebrated than that of Jean Cottereau himself, Count Joseph de Puisaye, attempted, and with wonderful success, the concentration of their force.

Count Joseph de Puisaye was born at Mortagne, and neither spoke the Breton tongue nor shared the Breton character. It would not have been surprising, therefore, if he had failed in obtaining influence over a people proverbial for their fierce jealousy of foreigners. He was, moreover, although courageous enough, not remarkable for daring; and though a Catholic, still devoid of that firm devotion to the Church which characterised the men whom he aspired to lead. But he had taken refuge in Brittany from the fury of the Jacobins; and although the inhabitants had been forbidden to harbour him under pain of death, he had received from them the most generous hospitality. They had forgotten the foreigner in the refugee, and thus he had gained an ascendency over them which enabled him to carry out his project with success. The peasants gave him their entire confidence; the nobles seemed at once to recognise his authority; and the priests came forward as his devoted advocates. And so vigorous were his measures, that at Laval he was in a position to offer to the council-general of the expeditionary army fifty thousand men on its appearance at Rennes. The offer, and the manner of its being declined, have already been related. Not satisfied with the rejection of his proposal, he sought

Chapter XII

an interview with the chiefs at Laval; but on arriving at that city, found that they had advanced to Fougères. Thither he followed, but was still unable to meet them; and at length he took refuge in the forest of Pertre, where he was soon joined by Jean Chouan and a number of the Breton peasants, who, under the name of the Little Vendée, had fought with the grand army and escaped its disasters.

Jean Chouan had been aware of the expected passage of the Loire, although not of the precise point at which it would be effected; and one day he had given a rendezvous to Puisaye, in the forest of Pertre, with a view to concert measures for a coalition of the Breton with the Vendean insurgents, when one of his men exclaimed that he heard thunder. "It is La Vendée," said Jean, putting his ear to the ground; "it is the sound of cannon. Let us on to Laval, the Prince de Talmont expects us there." The troop set off in the middle of the night, recruiting as they went; and Jean entered Laval at the head of four hundred men, besides four thousand five hundred other combatants who came in from other parts of Maine. Their arrival excited the greatest transport in the Vendean army; for Jean's reputation was well known on their side of the Loire. This Breton contingent was known as the Little Vendée; they performed good service at the great battle which took place the next morning, when the republican army sustained their memorable defeat.

The Little Vendée, with Jean at their head, followed the grand army through all its fortunes, and shared with it the reverse at Granville and the glorious victory at Dol. When all seemed lost, and the entire army had taken to flight, amid the reproaches of the women and the recriminations of the men,—when Stofflet himself was at the head of the runaways, and the very cavalry suffered themselves to be carried away by the general panic,—then Jean Chouan stood firm with his Little Vendée between the army and certain destruction. He it was who, with Talmont, kept the enemy at bay, till the return of Larochejacquelein, and the heroic exhortations of the curé of St Marie-de-Rhé, had restored some degree of courage to the enfeebled Vendeans, and the disaster was changed into a triumph. At La Flêche he was again instrumental in beating off Westermann. At Mans he kept up the struggle from house to house long after every vestige of hope had fled the Vendean party; and after the rout of Savenay, when there was no longer an army to fight, he returned with a small remnant of his followers to his old quarters in Misdon Wood.

Two or three thousand Bretons perished in the ranks of the Vendean army. This, however, did not check the progress of the insurrection: the feeling of abhorrence to the Republic increased day by day; but Puisaye was compelled to abandon his original plan of uniting in one the various bodies of insurgents which appeared all over the country. The Bretons could be induced even less than the Vendeans to leave their own immediate district. Their general, therefore, endeavoured to perfect the mode of warfare naturally adopted by the natives; and the Chouannerie, which was originally an accident, became a system. The insurgents were formed into stationary divisions, varying from three to seven or eight hundred strong. As soon as a republican column ventured into the country, it found itself surrounded by invisible enemies, against whom no tactics were successful. The Chouans rarely showed themselves to the enemy, or engaged in battle. Concealed behind trees, and dispersed every where, they harassed the invading party without suffering in return. Never appearing in masses, they could not be routed. If silenced in the morning, by mid-day they collected in greater numbers than ever, as the noise of the musketry summoned fresh combatants to the spot. Scarcely was one conflict over, when another commenced, and the soldiers knew no rest. Brittany and Maine, like La Vendée, are countries of bocage. Each field is surrounded by ditches and thick hedges; with large trees at intervals, stretching out their branches on all sides. The ground is crossed by a multitude of water-courses; and the forests and woods offered to the insurgents an inviolable asylum. These natural advantages

Chapter XII

Puisaye and the Chouans were not slow to discern and turn to the discomfiture of the enemy; and the republicans were bewildered by a foe whom they could least grasp when he was most destructive.

In the heart of the forests the Chouans constructed cabins, to which they could always resort after each battle. In woods of small extent, like the wood of Misdon, Jean Chouan's retreat, these were mostly subterranean, for greater security; but in the larger forests, as the forest of Pertre, they were thus formed: stakes were driven into the ground, and woven with branches with the leaves on; the roof was framed of long poles, crossed and tied together at the top, and fastened at the bottom by ropes to the stakes, which were thus rendered more secure; turfs were laid upon the poles, and the cabin so made rain-proof; a hole in the middle, plastered with several layers of earth, served for a chimney. In a cabin so constructed seven men could obtain shelter; and in such a one Puisaye lived continually, sharing all the hardships of the Chouans.

The Convention, occupied with the war in La Vendée, and trusting to its policy of conciliation, paid little attention to the Chouans. They appeared to them rather in the light of a horde of brigands, than as political enemies. But by accident they became acquainted with the correspondence which Puisaye had from the first carried on with England. It was Puisaye's error to believe that the whole success of the insurrection depended on the support of Great Britain; and when the British emissaries appeared at Laval, and proposed to the leaders of the grand army to possess themselves of Granville, for the debarcation of troops and ammunition, he had commenced a negotiation for assistance with Lord Dundas. Surprised in his cabin one morning by a party of republicans, he barely escaped with his life; and all his papers fell into the hands of the enemy.

The Convention then for the first time perceived the danger they were in from these despised Chouans, and took measures to repress them with their usual promptitude. Fresh troops were sent into Brittany; a part of the forest of Pertre was searched by General Beaufort, and several hundreds of peasants captured. General Rossignol, Beaufort's superior officer, thereupon reported the war terminated. Carrier, not so easily satisfied, ordered terrorism to be established throughout the country, the property of rebels to be confiscated, absentees to be judged rebels, suspected persons to be imprisoned, and fire and sword to be employed for the subjugation of the insurgents. He was obeyed, but still the insurrection spread.

Then Kleber was charged with its suppression. That general proceeded with great vigour and ability. Establishing himself in various villages, he converted the churches into fortresses and thence he issued in eight divisions to traverse the whole country, enveloping the forest of Pertre, disarming all suspected peasants, and skilfully dealing with such as appeared peaceable and harmless. This system, without being crowned with entire success, was slowly putting a stop to the Chouannerie, when Kleber was recalled, and superseded by Vachot, who pursued opposite tactics, and the Chouans appeared again more numerous and daring than ever; so that after a long struggle the Convention had the mortification to receive from their representative on the spot the assurance of his conviction that "the Chouannerie was the radical disease of the country. Wherever there was a man, he was either a Chouan in fact or in intention; patriots were in an insignificant minority."

It would be impossible to give a detailed account of the Chouannerie, from its broken character and its absence of plan. Distributed all over the country, not a day passed that was not marked by numerous irregular encounters with the Blues. The whole province, from Laval to Brest, and from Vannes to St. Malo, was in arms. Here the insurgents showed themselves to the number of five or six hundred men, there not perhaps above fifty or sixty; but the smallest companies would make their attacks, and a single man would fire on a regiment and be gone. A few chiefs whose districts joined might now and then unite their strength for some

Chapter XII

common undertaking; but such concerted movements were very rare. The spirit of absolute independence was universal, and formed the greatest obstacle which Puisaye had to encounter. Nevertheless, in this war of skirmishes and ambuscades he perceived a means of training his soldiers, and of wearing out the patience and spirit of the Blues. But he desired more than that. He hoped to form an army which should be ready when the moment arrived, to appear in force and strike a decisive blow; and in order to accomplish this, he made it a practice, when he went to inspect a distant company of insurgents, to take with him a party of Chouans from some other neighbourhood. Thus, by little and little, both soldiers and officers became habituated to leaving home, and familiar with the idea of undertaking some general enterprise. The presence of certain of the Vendean generals who remained in Brittany after the rout at Savenay, conduced to the success of his design; especially as the Chouannerie presently extended into Anjou.

And yet, notwithstanding the activity of Puisaye in the organisation of his men, he fell into the error of restraining their ardour by useless delays, and negotiating with England, when he should have been fighting with the Republic. Many a Vendean chief who had placed himself under his orders withdrew in vexation at seeing neglected so many favourable opportunities for a general insurrection; and Marigny, who had lingered in Brittany after the final catastrophe at Savenay in order to spread the insurrection in Brittany, speedily returned to join his old comrades on the left bank of the Loire.

When, in the beginning of June 1794, Tinténiac made his second mission to the Vendeans, he took the opportunity of examining for himself the exact condition of the Chouannerie. Puisaye received him warmly, confided to him his most secret plans, and obtained from him the promise of assistance from the English government and the Breton refugees. But Tinténiac especially urged on the Chouan chief the advantage of a personal visit to London.

Puisaye's system—Departure for England—Pacification

"You will do more yourself," he said, "in one fortnight than all those who are there can do in years; and one hour's conversation with you will be more effective than volumes of correspondence." Puisaye was flattered by the notion of appearing in London as the representative of the west, and determined to accept the proposition; but before starting he took care to fortify the work he had so well begun, by appointing a major-general in his place, of the name of Cormatin, a council, a committee of parishes, and whatever else was necessary for the well-being of the insurgents, who had now become so numerous and so well organised, as to merit the title they had assumed of the Catholic and Royal Army of Brittany. When he had thus secured his work, he sailed for London towards the end of September 1794.

But while Puisaye was engaged in negotiations with Pitt, Windham, and Dundas, an event occurred which he had not foreseen. The Convention attempted to conclude a treaty of peace with the insurgents. The amnesty of the 2d December was published in Brittany as in La Vendée (the reader will perhaps recollect that both provinces were included in its offer of pardon); and General Hoche, who had been recently nominated to the chief command of the armies of Brest and Cherbourg, exhibited a desire to conciliate the Chouans. As in La Vendée, the preliminaries were difficult. The good faith of the republicans was suspected; and many, like Stofflet, were opposed to any pacification at all. However, on the 3d January 1795, a suspension of hostilities was agreed upon between the royalist committee and the representative of the republicans. Military operations were nevertheless carried on after that date. Many of the insurgents refused to recognise the authority of the committee; and it was not till the 17th February that Cormatin signed the treaty of La Jaunais at Nantes, along with Charette; the example of the renowned chief of Bas Poitou having great weight with the advocates for war. But the peace was not established even yet; acts of aggression continued on both sides. Still, the longer it was delayed,

Chapter XII

the more anxious the republicans became for the cessation of hostilities, as the extent of the danger became daily more apparent. On the 20th March, Hoche wrote thus to the Committee of Public Safety: "What I can discover of the projects of the Chouans is sufficient to make me tremble as a good republican. To starve towns into insurrection, to intercept all communication, to assassinate patriots and public officers, to obtain gold from England by forged assignats, to bribe our soldiers and sailors and buy our secrets, to seize on our arsenals, organise a large army, extend the Chouannerie over the whole surface of the Republic, and spread terrorism every where;—these, in few words, are their atrocious designs." And as the only means of averting the danger, he recommends the immediate liberation of the refractory priests. To his own generals he speaks in the same strain, and exhorts them "not to let a little religion stop them; but to go to Mass, if necessary—to speak of God with reverence—and to give out that God will punish acts of violence and blood." The mind recoils at the thought of blasphemous hypocrisy like this; but it is impossible to deny the wisdom of the advice. And at La Mabillais, near Rennes, on the 10th April, the peace was finally concluded, upon the terms which had been granted to La Vendée. The great advocate for peace on the part of the Bretons was Cormatin, who forged Puisaye's name to a document giving him plenary powers to negotiate with the Convention. But of the hundred and twenty-five officers who took part in the discussion, only twenty were on his side; and Georges Cadoudal especially, one of the principal chiefs of Morbihan, protested against the pacification. He and many others had sworn never to make peace with the Republic; knowing this, the Blues distrusted the pacification; and while Cormatin made a triumphant entry into Rennes, each party continued to prepare for war.

When hostilities commenced, the family of Jean Chouan consisted of seven persons: his mother, his four brothers, Pierre, Jean, François, and René; and his two sisters, Perrine and Renée. By the 1st

Pacification—Family of Jean Chouan

August 1794, the youngest of the four brothers was the only one of the seven left alive; the rest had all perished. The heroic mother had been killed in the rout at Mans; François had died of his wounds; Pierre had been taken and guillotined; the two daughters had also perished on the scaffold, as sisters of the great brigand. The story of their death is of a piece with the history of the whole family. On being brought before the judges, Perrine displayed extraordinary courage. "You treat us as brigands," she said; "but the good God will judge us, and you also, and will award to each what is just. I throw myself on His mercy. From you I expect neither justice nor pity. I glory in being the sister of Jean Chouan." Renée, on the other hand, wept at the thought of the terrible death which they were going to suffer. Still she would condescend to ask no favour at the hands of her executioners on the bench. On her way to the scaffold, her limbs failed her at every step; but her more courageous sister sustained her, exhorted her to resignation, spoke of the glorious reward in store for them, and saw her die; and then, when her own turn came, calmly made the sign of the cross, and said, *"Vive le Roi! Vive Jean Chouan! God protect them, and have mercy on me!"* Mielette, Jean Chouan's friend, was in the crowd; and after their death rushed up to the scaffold, and dipped a handkerchief in their blood, and brought it to their brother. He received the news of their death in silence; took the handkerchief, and placed it in his bosom, and went away. It was found there shortly afterwards, when he was killed in the defence of his sister-in-law, René's wife. He died surrounded by his men, whom, with his last breath, he encouraged to be true to their God and their king. He was buried carefully and secretly, to protect the body from the vengeance of the Blues, by whom he was regarded with the greatest terror; and who did not cease, after his decease, to blacken his memory with the charge of the most atrocious crimes.

Such was the end of this extraordinary man, who gave his name to a civil war, "compared to which," said General Hoche, "all others are but child's play." However, he was only the precursor of

Chapter XII

that strife, of which Jambe d'Argent and M. Jacques were to be the heroes. Jean Chouan had no idea of organising or extending the insurrection. In the particular combat in which he happened to be engaged, he was resistless; but he had neither the ambition nor the genius to become a great captain; and therefore his death had little influence on the insurrection. His work was accomplished; and he disappeared when others were only commencing theirs.

After the destruction of the Catholic army, a fresh force was formed out of the few remaining Vendeans and the inhabitants of Maine. These had no regular chiefs, the boldest, or he who struck out the best plan for the occasion, marching at the head of his comrades; if his plan failed, or a better was suggested by another, he resigned the command and became a private soldier,—to resume it again perhaps later in the day. But as the most able or the most courageous man naturally found himself at the head most frequently, he came to possess a certain authority in the eyes of the others. There was a lame beggar named Louis Treton, who soon acquired a supremacy of this kind. This man was born to govern others. When a lad, he had kept a farmer's flocks; and even the brute beasts had acknowledged his power. The most restive horse, the fiercest bull, quailed beneath his eye. However, in an unequal combat with a famished wolf, he received a wound which crippled him for life; and he was a beggar from village to village when the civil war burst forth. Louis Treton joined the insurrection not for pay, nor to defend the crown, but for the Church. He was a man worthy in every respect to be ranked with Cathelineau himself. When, after the disasters of Mans and Savenay, all Maine was prostrate with terror, he went from farm to farm, and called the young men by their names to take up arms. He spoke to them only of their ruined churches and their proscribed faith; and when he spoke none could choose but hearken. His voice, strong enough to be heard above the din of battle, was at other times winning and sweet; but alike irresistible when agitated with passion, or calm with the very earnestness of his purpose.

Jambe d'Argent—M. Jacques

He was soon marked out to be the proper leader of his countrymen; by two victories that were due to him, and one defeat that they suffered from disregarding his advice. Jambe d'Argent, so he was called in allusion to the tin plate which covered his wound, immediately gave proofs of his great sagacity in the manner with which he treated the few rivals who contested his sovereignty. He then set to work to rekindle the insurrection. He had long studied all the chances of that war of flies against the republican lion; and he knew that the secret of success in an unequal strife lay in the art of enveloping weakness in mystery, and keeping the stronger party in the constant fear of an unseen antagonist. The difficulty was to get this plan accepted. The peasants had long ceased to think of his lame leg; but the nobles of Maine, unlike their brethren in La Vendée, would not have a crippled beggar to lead them. He might die for their sakes, but they would not follow his counsels. Jambe d'Argent, with a nobility of soul worthy of his cause, sought out for some step-father to his plans, by whom they might be executed; though he should lose thereby the honour of their conception.

His choice fell on a gentleman strange to Maine, and known by the name of M. Jacques. This officer had appeared on the right bank of the Mayenne soon after the destruction of the royal army; but he was in command of no troops; he was only seen in moments of great peril: then he suddenly showed himself in the first rank, where he gave some order or executed some movement which at once changed the rout into a victory. He, like Jambe d'Argent, had the power of fascinating all hearts: in the chateaux the ladies praised his manners; in the hiding-places which he found for the clergy, the priests extolled his learning; and the peasants averred that no man ever handled a musket or rode a horse with greater skill than he. He could tire out the strongest walkers; he seemed insensible to hunger or thirst, and proof against wind and sun and rain. He spoke little; but every word sank into the memory. He possessed also the rare power of Cæsar: at the same instant he would

Chapter XII

give an order, hear a report, and write a despatch, without distraction or confusion. No one knew his haunts, or his resources, or his means of communication. He appeared and disappeared like the knights in ancient story, who would suddenly arrive, carry off every prize in the tournament, and then vanish in a cloud of dust. That M. Jacques was an assumed name no one doubted; and the general belief was that he was the Duke d'Enghien, and the precursor of the Count d'Artois, whose coming had been so often promised.

Whether true or false, this report invested M. Jacques with that rank for lack of which Jambe d'Argent was unable to influence the nobles. The latter accordingly resolved to intrust to him the execution of his plan for the new Chouannerie, and for that end demanded an interview. M. Jacques at once embraced the lame beggar's principle of action, and the details were arranged between them. Each band was to remain in its own parish, under the command of its own leader; but a supreme chief was to give unity to the war, and when need were, assemble the various corps. A regular service for the transport of despatches was to be established; magazines of victuals were to be set up in the several forests; the herdsmen were to serve as sentinels, the beggars as spies, the women as messengers. Head-quarters were appointed, and new names given to them for the embarrassment of the Blues. Jambe d'Argent chose for his own retreat the farm-house of Grand Bordage, which he called the camp of the High Meadows. There he repaired to organise the insurrection. His first care was to contrive in it a retreat for fugitive priests, proscribed women, and the wounded; and so ingenious was his arrangement, that the Blues searched the farm-house twenty times and found nothing. When all these preliminaries were happily accomplished, the agitation commenced every where at once.

While M. Jacques, who was only a private gentleman from Anjou, who chose to preserve his incognito to protect his mother and sisters from the vengeance of the Blues, acted as the ostensible

M. Jacques

leader, it was Jambe d'Argent who really commanded the peasantry of Maine. With various success, this self-taught general conducted the most difficult enterprises against the republicans; his knowledge and tact increasing with his opportunities of exercising them. The influence which he possessed over his men was, however, hardly realised in the province till he received a wound which threatened to be mortal, and the question of his successor stared his unhappy soldiers in the face; for M. Jacques had absented himself, and was supposed to have been slain, and there was no one left to take the lead. Jambe d'Argent recovered, and lived to take part, very much against his will, in the pacification of Cormatin: not, however, till after the death of M. Jacques, who suddenly appeared again as one bereft of reason; and instead of the cool bravery he had always shown, now seemed less to seek victory than death. Yet death fled from him. Bullets glanced from his plume of feathers, sabres were turned by his silk and velvet; he rode deliberately through volleys of musketry, and came out unwounded. "He tempts God," muttered the awe-stricken Chouans, "and God will abandon him." And it was so. He fell as he was advancing, torch in hand, to fire a church, in which the Blues had as usual taken refuge, not wounded by the enemies' balls, but stricken by God; and he died three days afterwards, carrying with him to the tomb the fortunes of the Chouannerie in Maine, and the secret of his own despair. It was afterwards said that a noble lady, betrothed to a Vendean officer, had followed him across the Loire, and seen him perish at Mans: that she had conceived, in consequence, the most violent hatred against the Republic, and had retired to a ruined chateau of her family, which by chance Jacques had made his retreat; that she had accepted his hand that she might employ it to avenge the death of her dead lover, on whom all her affections were still centered; and that M. Jacques, convinced of the truth on the very day of his marriage, had sought death in a frenzy of despair.

The first epoch in the Chouannerie closed with the death of Jean Cottereau; the second was terminated by that of M. Jacques.

Chapter XII

Every where but in Maine the insurrection had changed its character. Intrigue had taken the place of open warfare. Charette and Stofflet had had recourse to diplomacy in La Vendée; and in Brittany Puisaye was engaged in negotiations of various kinds. After the death of M. Jacques, Jambe d'Argent signed the treaty of Mabillais, or at least agreed to a suspension of arms. But, as we have seen, neither party had confidence in the security of the peace, or the good faith of the other; and perpetual engagements took place, in one of which Jambe d'Argent was killed. He was buried secretly, as all other leaders of the day; but his grave is shown. He was a good and upright man; actuated by no personal ambition or secondary motives, he fought like Cathelineau for the faith of his fathers, and he died like him a martyr to his cause.

This single-minded devotion to the Church alone was rare among the leaders of the Chouannerie. Even Jean Chouan was actuated as much by gratitude to the throne, and love to the house of Talmont, as by the higher motive with which Jambe d'Argent was inspired. But the insurgents generally were devoted Christians. Yet the Chouannerie has been popularly described by the revolutionary writers, who had an interest in concealing the truth, as nothing but a series of thefts and assassinations. That the Chouans did indulge in fearful reprisals for the outrages they had suffered from the Blues, is undeniable; but very little is true of all that is laid to their charge; and the reports of General Hoche, with regard to the designs of the insurgents, had no foundation in fact. There were, however, a set of men who associated themselves with the Chouans for the sole object of robbery; and the acts of this small section have been ascribed to the whole army. By a diabolical device of the Convention, the Chouannerie lies open to the accusation on another account also. The Chouans committed no excesses against the general population of the country, but only against the notorious supporters of the Republic; in consequence, they were universally protected and fed by the peaceable inhabitants. The Convention perceived that

JAMBE D'ARGENT.

Chapter XII

this popularity rendered them invincible; and they formed out of the dregs of their own army a body of men armed and dressed like Chouans, whom they sent into the insurgent camps as fresh recruits from the country. These soldiers were ordered to put to fire and sword all indiscriminately, and so destroy the prestige for order and good conduct which the true Chouans had acquired. The greater atrocities they committed, the better they fulfilled their mission; and the revolutionary bulletins were soon full of details of the frightful crimes of the Chouans. The country, however, was not to be deceived. All the world knew that these were the acts of false Chouans; and the real insurgents were not the less welcome wherever they went. Such deeds of violence were inconsistent with the known practices of the soldiers of Puisaye and Jambe d'Argent,—of men who, to chase away bad thoughts while they lay concealed in their huts, used to recite the rosary aloud for a portion of the day. "Comrades," said Jambe d'Argent, "let us think of God, if we would have Him think of us." The same chief let a column of the enemy escape, rather than attack them in the church where he had been baptised. Another chief declared, that whoever blasphemed the name of God should be put to death; and he executed his threat on a soldier who transgressed. Such sentiments as these, could not have belonged to men given over, as the republicans reported, to every excess. They were not inconsistent, as this penalty for blasphemy shows, with terrible severity; but it is impossible to associate them with cold-blooded murder, robbery, and outrage. The Bretons are naturally a fierce and rugged race. The countrymen of Cathelineau, the men of Anjou, are gentle, quiet, easy in their manners, slow to take offence, fond of pleasure, and as cheerful as their own smiling fields and sunny hills. The Bretons are like the dark forests in which they live; and though fighting side by side, had nothing in common with their neighbours but their love of the Church and of their king.

The Chouannerie, stigmatised by its enemies as a "series of thefts and assassinations," abounds with instances of the most exalted heroism and the most generous devotion. The following is one of the episodes of that eventful war.

When the Chouans first took up arms, there lived as portress in the chateau of Thuré a poor widow woman named Madame Huneau. She was known to all the country round for her works of mercy. Having acquired some practical knowledge of medicine, she was a constant attendant upon the sick-beds of the poor; and when her skill was insufficient to effect a cure, she soothed and comforted the dying with the consolations of religion, for she was of an exemplary devotion. She had an only son, too young to take any part in the insurrection; but he contrived to be useful to the Chouans by carrying their correspondence and watching the movements of the Blues. The partisans of the Republic in the neighbourhood, suspecting the cause of his frequent absence from home, laid wait for him; and as he was returning one evening from one of his expeditions, he was shot in the avenue of the chateau, and within a few paces of his mother. At the same time a man rushed through the bushes, and made his escape. Her skill, poor woman, was useless, for he was mortally wounded; but, in resignation to the will of God, she gave herself up with greater diligence to her works of charity.

Not long after the murder of her son, she heard of the dangerous illness of a notorious terrorist in the neighbourhood. His cries and blasphemies were so frightful, that none of his own people would venture near his bed-side. The poor woman trembled at hearing the name of the sick man; but, with a generosity which grace only could inspire, she approached his house. He was then lying prostrate after a paroxysm of delirium; but at the sound of her voice he started up in a sort of frenzy, crying—"What has brought this woman here? Does she know what I have done? Has she come to enjoy my torments? Away, out of my sight! There is no pity or mercy for me. I am certain to be damned; God Himself could not save me." The poor widow shuddered at his ravings; but she stayed,

Chapter XII

and collecting all her strength, said,—"O miserable man! why blaspheme? Repent, and God will have mercy upon you. Has He not sent me here to you? and now I know that you are the man who killed my son. Ah, since God has sent me here to pardon you, without doubt He will pardon you also. Merit, then, His forgiveness by repentance."

The heart of the reprobate was touched. He was contrite; but to render his conversion more profitable and complete, there was needed still the minister of God, to receive the solemn confession of his sins, and pronounce, in the name of God, his entire absolution. In the canton was a priest, with whose retreat Madame Huneau was acquainted. With great danger both to herself and to him she brought him to the dying penitent, and had the satisfaction of seeing him reconciled to heaven, and able to meet death with confidence. He lived eight days, during which the holy woman never quitted the bedside of her son's murderer; and, as he expired with a blessing on his lips, received his last sigh. One such incident as this seems enough to make reparation for a hundred acts of revenge; and such as was Madame Huneau was, in his way, many a rough Chouan, who fought for his God and his king, and when the fight was over forgave his enemies and spared their lives. It is always the evil which floats to the surface. On a review of the past, the historian sees and relates crimes of bloodshed and violence because they force themselves upon his attention. It is only by accident that he becomes acquainted with acts of generosity and charity.

Chapter XIII

Puisaye in England—The royal agency at Paris—Renewal of hostilities in Brittany and in La Vendée—Aide-de-camp of the Count d'Artois in Bas Poitou—Quiberon.

While Cormatin busied himself in pacifications with the Republic, Puisaye was in London negotiating with the English government for the fulfilment of some of their many promises to the insurgents of the west. In this he was successful. He conducted himself with his usual discretion; not putting himself forward as the leader of a party, but keeping aloof, and shunning rather than inviting attention. By this conduct he secured the confidence of the ministers, who were at first inclined to treat him as an adventurer. His plans were examined with care, and his requests in great measure granted. He asked for ten thousand English troops, and they promised him several regiments of refugees, and the commissions were immediately drawn up. At the same time, the Count d'Artois, in the name of the king, confirmed him in the command-in-chief of the Catholic and royal army of Brittany. This last appointment was of the utmost advantage to Puisaye, as there existed in Paris a "royal agency" which disputed his authority. This agency consisted of men who made it their business to keep up a correspondence with the king, and doing nothing themselves in his service, to misrepresent the efforts of others. The ringleader of these obstructives was the Abbé Bronier, a

Chapter XIII

man of whom the Cardinal Maury once said, "If you want to throw every thing into inextricable confusion, call in the Abbé Bronier; he would set the heavenly hosts themselves by the ears." According to them, Charette was a coward; Stofflet, a *certain monsieur* of whom something might be expected; and Puisaye a Jacobin, badly converted, who wanted to revolutionise Brittany and proclaim the Duke of York King of France. This official recognition of his authority by the Count d'Artois was therefore especially satisfactory to Puisaye.

Although Cormatin had acted without authority in concluding a peace with the Republic, Puisaye was by no means displeased at the event. He had always been averse to premature hostilities, and preferred a policy which would induce the Convention to remove their troops to the frontier; and he wrote from London—*Do not fire a shot*. At the same time he disavowed the act of Cormatin, that he might be free to commence the offensive when the time arrived. He refused to interpret the treaty of Mabillais, except as a truce—a temporary cessation of hostilities.

And, in point of fact, the war never completely ceased. The Chouans, it is true, undertook no considerable enterprise, but they continued to treat the Blues as foes. For example, the farmers refused to sell their grain to the contractors for the republican army. And when, by dint of labour and expense,—for no coin would pass in the province not bearing the stamp of the royal effigy,—they had collected a supply, the means were lacking for its transportation—the peasants had hidden the axletrees of their waggons. No one could with impunity show any sympathy for the Republic; the proprietors of public offices were taxed for the support of the royal army, recruiting went on in every village, and the republican soldiers were tempted to desert. So successful was this system of seduction, that Hoche wrote word to the Convention that "desertions could not be more frequent;" and Commissioner Brue added, "Ours is a most alarming position." The Blues were not behindhand in reprisals; a system of pillage was organised, and the persons and property of the peasants outraged. The chiefs on either side exchanged mutual recriminations, and then hostilities ceased for a time; but both parties were holding themselves in preparation for some decisive struggle. The Chouans were waiting to see Puisaye and the sails of the English fleet—the Blues intended to lull their foes into a false security, that they might arrest all their chiefs at one blow; and though the peace was not formally broken, the whole country was in a state of agitation. It was impossible that this state of things could last many weeks, and at length it was terminated by the interception of a letter from one of the insurgent chiefs, containing evidence of preparations for a new war. Cormatin, and many other generals, were arrested; Cadoudal, Boisguy, Jambe d'Argent, Sol de Grisolles, took arms. Several republican columns advanced into the country, engagements took place, in which the Chouans were at first vanquished, but afterwards completely successful. The Chouannerie had again broken out in all its virulence.

About the same time the peace was broken in La Vendée.

Charette had scarcely signed the treaty of La Jaunais, when he received a letter from the Count de Provence, eldest brother of Louis XVI. and lately proclaimed king by the title of Louis XVIII., declaring that his exploits had rendered him the second founder of the monarchy. The loyal and chivalrous soul of Charette needed nothing more to animate him to the prosecution of the struggle with greater eagerness than ever. Yet several months passed away and no open rupture with the Republic took place. He was, however, preparing for war. He had ardently hoped that the long-expected succour from England would land on the coast of Bas Poitou. But the aide-de-camp of the Count d'Artois, the Marquis de Rivière, intimated to him that Brittany was judged to be the more favourable spot, and that nothing was wanted but a diversion on the part of the Vendean chiefs, to secure the success

Chapter XIII

of the expedition. Charette, notwithstanding his chagrin at this preference of Puisaye over himself, pledged his word to support the movement; and Stofflet did the same. The Marquis de Rivière thereupon, to secure the co-operation of the two chiefs, contrived a reconciliation between them. The renewal of hostilities was fixed to take place about the beginning of July.

As in Brittany, however, the peace, although formally kept, had been all along very imperfectly observed, and an open rupture was precipitated by the impatience of the republican generals themselves. While the Vendeans made fresh recruitings, the Blues applied to the Convention for reinforcements, in order to carry out their plan of arresting every chief on the same day. This attempt was made, and failed, and Charette protested against the violation of the treaty; yet he would not compromise the success of the royalist designs by a premature appeal to force. He was, however, compelled to anticipate the appointed time by an attempt upon his own person. He learned that the republicans had formed the project of surprising him at his head-quarters in Belle Ville. He promptly decided on his course. Instead of seeking to escape, he calmly waited the arrival of the enemy. They entered the town, and occupied the market-place. Their captain then advanced to Charette, and summoned him in the name of the Republic to discard the white cockade and surrender. "It is you," he replied, "who must put down the tricolor cockade, and give up your arms." At these words, the Vendean guards who accompanied him advanced and captured the Blues. The captain was liberated; but the peasant who had been guide to the republicans was shot, and many of the prisoners went over to the Vendean flag. Thus the peace was broken: this took place about the middle of June. The succeeding days of that month were passed by the insurgents in numerous encounters with the Blues, in which they were every where successful. Charette was observed, nevertheless, not to push the war with great vigour, and the Republic believed that he and Stofflet were both anxious for peace. The insurgent leaders were really waiting for the signal from England. Meanwhile the Convention were becoming more and more alarmed at the aspect of the war in Brittany; and at the urgent request of Hoche, the general-in-chief of the army of Brest, Canclaux sent reinforcements from La Vendée to increase his strength in the field, and augment the garrison of Nantes.

Puisaye had at length triumphed over every obstacle. Before his perseverance and energy, the calumnies of the royal agency, the objections of the *émigrés*, the hostility of the princes, had alike given way; and on the 10th June 1795, he sailed from Portsmouth with three ships of the line, and sixteen other vessels, under the command of Commodore Warren, in which three thousand six hundred men were embarked; and another expedition was to follow in two or three weeks. The English government had also provided muskets and ammunition for twenty-seven thousand men, uniforms for both cavalry and infantry, cannon, pistols, sabres, shoes, and victuals for three months. The regiments which formed this first division were the royal emigrant, the royal Louis, the royal marine, the royal artillery, and another. The Count d'Hervilly, colonel of the royal Louis, was named commander-in-chief, under the orders of Puisaye. He was a soldier of the old school, brave, cool, and convinced that it was impossible to make war except upon the most received principles. His unfortunate attachment to routine was one great cause of the subsequent disasters of the army. He insisted on applying to an army of peasant insurgents the rules which had been framed for regular troops.

The Bishop of Dol, Mgr. de Hercé, with his vicars-general, and many other ecclesiastics, added the sanction of their presence to this great effort for the restoration of the Church. That prelate had already published a brief, in which he exhorted the Bretons to shrink from no sacrifice in the defence of their faith. With the clergy came also a number of *émigrés* as volunteers, and also a number of French prisoners, who had fought for the Republic, but

Chapter XIII

preferred changing their flag to wearing out their lives in confinement in England.

Puisaye had received from Dundas a packet which he was not to open till they were in deep water. It contained instructions providing that, in case the debarcation were effected, the troops should be under the command of Lieutenant-General Count de Puisaye. Upon this Hervilly said coolly, "I also have instructions;" and he produced an order from the same Dundas by which the troops were confided to him. "Yes," said Puisaye, "but under my orders." Not to compromise the whole expedition, the two rival chiefs promised mutual concessions; but the insubordination of Hervilly was as injurious to the interests of the army as his rigid adherence to conventional rules.

Fifteen days after leaving Portsmouth, the fleet came to an anchor in Quiberon Bay. Puisaye was informed that all was ready for the debarcation, and would have commenced immediately. Military routine, however, requiring that a reconnaissance should first be made, Hervilly opposed such a very undignified proceeding, and twenty-four hours were thrown away according to rule. The landing took place without opposition; for the Chouans flocked in in crowds from all the country round, and two or three republican detachments had already been driven from the coast by Tinténiac, Georges Cadoudal, and the *élite* of the Breton army. The descent was a sort of triumph. On all sides were heard cries of *Vive notre réligion! vive notre roi!* It was a grand day for Puisaye, and he was elated with the most sanguine hopes. That enthusiasm was, however, not universal. D'Hervilly declared that shouting was contrary to all precedent; and many of the *émigrés* looked on at the poor Chouans with the most supreme contempt.

The appearance of the long-promised succours in Quiberon Bay attracted multitudes of Chouans from all parts of the province; and in three days nearly twenty thousand muskets were served out. These volunteers were formed into three bands, which marched forward, and drove back the Blues in every direction. Puisaye would have followed up these first movements with despatch, and proposed to penetrate at once into the interior. But D'Hervilly protested against a step not in conformity with the tactics of the service, and proposed to form an entrenched camp at Quiberon as the basis of future operations.

Quiberon is a peninsula stretching about ten miles into the sea, the neck of which was defended by Fort Penthièvre. It was this peninsula that D'Hervilly proposed to fortify. The advice was ruinous to the cause; but it was in part adopted, and the first successes were lost. Enthusiasm began to cool; and the Chouans in advance fell back, not finding themselves supported.

Six days passed away, and still Quiberon was not in the power of the insurgents. But the 3d July was appointed for a combined attack by sea and land on Fort Penthièvre. Resistance being almost impossible, the garrison, seven hundred strong, capitulated, and the greater number volunteered into the royal army; the rest were sent on board the English vessels. The fort was then occupied by the besiegers; and by the most inconceivable want of caution, the new garrison was composed, not of tried and faithful royalists, but partly of the very soldiers who had just surrendered, and partly of the old republicans, who, to escape an English prison, had joined the insurrection.

On the first landing of the English expedition, the situation of the republican army had been perilous in the extreme. With a population hostile to them, they were exposed to danger on all sides from the numerous bands starting into existence. But by the time Quiberon had fallen into the hands of the royalists, the relative positions of the two sides had somewhat changed. The republicans were in straits, but they were under the command of a single general,—a general, moreover, of ability and resource; and while D'Hervilly had been childishly fussing about the want of discipline, and the unmartial air of the peasant soldiers, and Puisaye striving to make his authority recognised, Hoche had been busily at work.

Chapter XIII

He had concentrated his troops, obtained succours from Canclaux and elsewhere, and visited the posts most threatened. He had about sixteen thousand men under arms, and this number was daily increasing. With these he determined on a grand attack on the royalist camp, and commenced active preparations at once. At the same time, not anticipating any assault on his own position, his lines were badly guarded. His soldiers abandoned themselves to every sort of disorder, and lived in constant riot and excess, committing all the horrors which La Vendée and Brittany were accustomed to suffer at the hands of republican troops. Puisaye, perceiving this, despatched D'Hervilly to make an attack on the enemy's camp; and the old officer's conduct on that occasion serves well to illustrate the effect which such a leader would probably produce upon men like the Chouans. The attack was made, and succeeded; the advance posts were penetrated, and the foe thrown into disorder. In the very moment of victory, D'Hervilly ordered a retreat. Why? the reader may inquire;—because some of the peasants had winced under the first shots of the Blues! In vain the poor fellows, unaccustomed to fire, eagerly demanded to be led on to atone for their fault. "No," replied the great general, "I am not sufficiently pleased with you today to give you that pleasure." For the sake of punishing a few Chouans, he threw away a great advantage.

Hoche daily received reinforcements, and was evidently making preparations for a decisive attack on the peninsula. The royalist engineers affirmed confidently that Fort Penthièvre and the other works of the defence would hold out for six weeks at least. However, the Chouans felt uneasy, and demanded that some effort should be made to extricate them from their perilous position. The two generals determined accordingly that a simultaneous attack should be made upon the Blues in front and rear. To execute the latter part of this plan, two divisions, respectively three thousand five hundred and three thousand strong, were embarked, under the command of Tinténiac and Jean Jan, one of the chiefs from Morbihan. These were to land, the former at Sarzeau, the latter at Lorient; to advance into the interior for recruits, and then join at Baud, so as to be able to attack the Blues in the rear by the break of day on the 16th. Another diversion was to be made by Count Vauban.

On that day, the troops which remained in the peninsula got under arms about two hours before dawn, so as to attack at the same moment as Tinténiac, Jean Jan, and Vauban. In a short time, they observed the appointed signal, viz. a rocket shot up into the air. "Forward! charge! it is Tinténiac," cried several officers at once. Hoche was perfectly acquainted with the enemy's plan, and had taken all his measures accordingly. He had a full understanding with the republican-royalists in Fort Penthièvre. The *émigrés* charge, and as usual the advance posts stagger under the first onset. "They are Frenchmen, that is plain enough," said the Blues; but the advantage was only temporary. The republican line opened, and two formidable batteries were unmasked, by which the assailants were enveloped in a semicircle of grape. They still continued to advance, however; and D'Hervilly pushed forward a few field-pieces to play on the enemy's guns. Hoche could not conceal his astonishment at such a resistance, and ordered the cavalry to charge. The men who had stood firm against round shot were not to be beaten by such means. But Puisaye, despairing of the arrival of Tinténiac and the others, ordered a retreat, which was made in good order under cover of the fire from the English sloops. In the action D'Hervilly was killed.

It remains to be explained how Tinténiac and Jean Jan had failed to make their diversion. Vauban, with two thousand men, was to have taken one of the enemy's advanced posts during the night, in time to join in the concerted attack. In the event of failure, he was to send up two rockets; of success only one. Arriving too late to surprise the Blues, he abstained from the meditated attack, and shot up two rockets. Only one was seen; and the Chouans in the peninsula, confident of success, rushed to the conflict. However,

Chapter XIII

little importance was attached to that diversion; the success of the enterprise depended on Tinténiac, whom they expected to see come up with at least twenty thousand men. Unhappily, they had not reckoned on the interference of the royal agency at Paris.

The Abbé Bronier and his colleagues had obtained a complete ascendency over the princes, and especially over the heir to the throne. But this influence was exerted but little for the royal interests. The most selfish motives actuated the men in whom the new king placed unlimited confidence. From being simply an organ of communication, the royal agency became a cabinet exercising irresponsible and supreme power; and with a restless jealousy of all rivals, they cared nothing for the cause they professed to serve, so long as others, independent of themselves, were charged with the administration of affairs. Before Puisaye obtained the assistance of the English government, the agency had declared against Charette and the Vendean movement, in favour of the Chouannerie. As soon as success appeared likely to attend the operations in Brittany, they made it their business to defeat them. They turned round, proclaimed their confidence in Charette, sent him a flattering eulogy on his devotion to the royal cause, and sought to obtain a debarcation of the English expedition on the coasts of Bas Poitou. Soon after Commodore Warren had dropped anchor in Quiberon Bay, they sent orders through all Maine, Anjou, Vendée, and Upper Brittany, for the people to remain quiet; and their partisans represented the arrival of the English expedition at Quiberon as a mere stratagem, its real destination being La Vendée. While Puisaye sent emissaries all through the country to effect a general rising, they fabricated counter-orders, and had the incredible assurance to attach his signature to them. Many a chief who was thus actually on the march returned to his quarters. Such was the state of affairs when Tinténiac landed at Sarzeau; and if he had been permitted to fulfil his mission, the design of Puisaye might yet have succeeded. But one of the representatives of the agency (and such were some of Puisaye's intimate friends) ordered him, in the king's name, to march to Elven near Rochfort; he obeyed, hoping still to be able to execute Puisaye's orders by the 16th. The Blues defended Elven, and were beaten. Tinténiac then received orders to repair to a certain chateau beyond Josselin to receive instructions. He still obeyed, and was stopped by the enemy at that town. He drove them out of the place, but he lost five hours in effecting it. He was afterwards attacked by a third column before he reached the appointed rendezvous. It was then the 15th, and the next day he was to be at Baud. While he sat at table with the emissaries of the agency, the Blues attacked his advanced posts; he rushed to the field, and was shot by a republican in the act of giving him quarter. "So died," says Puisaye, "the most loyal, and the bravest man I ever knew." After his death, a creature of Bronier's took the command of the troops, and marched off to St. Briene.

Immediately after his debarcation, Jean Jan received orders, in the name of the king, diametrically opposed to those sent him by Puisaye; and his Chouans, already disgusted with the chicanery, as it seemed to them, of the various generals, forthwith dispersed.

Thus the plots of the agency succeeded. The *émigrés*, shut up in Quiberon, could undertake nothing in Brittany, and began to re-embark to seek another landing-place. The credit of Puisaye was destroyed. The Chouans returned home to their cottages or their retreats in the forests; and the republicans, whom accident had placed under the white flag, and who might possibly have remained faithful to it if victory had crowned their arms, deserted in numbers. And yet, strange to say, the troops in garrison at the fort, which was the key of the peninsula, and for whose fidelity he had no guarantee, Puisaye neglected to exchange for more trustworthy men. His infatuation cost the army its very existence.

Such was Puisaye's position when, on the 20th of July, Hoche determined to make his long-meditated attack. On that day he left his camp at eleven o'clock at night. The weather was in his favour.

Chapter XIII

The tramp of men and the clang of arms were drowned in the noise of wind and rain and thunder. General Humbert was in command of the advanced guard. By a pass through the rocks, along which they were conducted by a deserter, the soldiers marched rapidly and noiselessly to turn the fort and leap the palisades. The adjutant-general Ménage was to scale the walls, and put to the point of the bayonet all who should make the slightest opposition. No shot was on any account to be fired. These orders were executed with promptitude, energy, and success. At two o'clock in the morning, Ménage, whose soldiers had marched up to their middles in water, scaled the fort, with the assistance of a hundred conspirators belonging to D'Hervilly's division. At the same time the outworks were carried by another column; and now, for the first time, the royalist camp was made aware of the presence of the enemy by the roll of musketry. The advancing republicans were thrown into a momentary disorder by a storm of artillery; but the dawning light revealed, to the amazement of the royalists, the tricolor flag waving over the fort, and the assailants recovered from their panic. Their ranks were swelled by all their old companions in arms, who had been madly left to oppose them. Count d'Atilly, a lieutenant-colonel of the Royal Louis, was slain by the very men he was leading to battle. As to the royalists in the heart of the peninsula, they were rather a mob than an army; women, children, old men, and unarmed peasants being mixed indiscriminately with the combatants. Hoche now advanced along the peninsula, driving before him the herd of terrified royalists, who saw no alternative before them but to embark in the English vessels or be lost in the sea. The onward movement of the republicans was, however, checked by Sombreuil, a young officer encamped with an effective company towards the extremity of the peninsula, in a position to defend the embarcation; and Puisaye hastened to Commodore Warren, the commanding officer of the English squadron, to urge him to send boats to carry the people off.

Sombreuil might have done much more than merely cover the embarcation, but he appeared to lose his presence of mind. Always in the thickest of the fight and in the most perilous position, he exhibited no cowardice; yet he fell back before a force three or four times smaller than his own. The main body of the republican army halted near Fort Penthièvre, and Humbert alone pushed forward to encounter Sombreuil; for Hoche seemed willing that the embarcation should proceed, and forbore from crushing the royalists under the force of his seventeen thousand men. Several sloops now approached the shore, and an English corvette opened a lively fire on the republicans, under cover of which a crowd of fugitives rushed into the sea to gain the boats. Three or four hundred were drowned; and all the boats would have been swamped, if those who had contrived to get on board had not saved themselves by slashing the hands of the wretches who were trying to climb in out of the water. Sombreuil was entreated to take the offensive, and give time for the five thousand peasants who were crowded on the beach to save themselves in the ships. But the royalist chief hesitated, and at length seeing Humbert approach as if to parley, amid cries of "Surrender! surrender!" he marched forward to meet him. After several minutes' conversation, he returned to his soldiers, to say that he had made a capitulation, from which he had excepted himself. Some of the *émigrés* exclaimed against the act, and it was, indeed, in direct contradiction to the orders of Puisaye; but the majority approved it, and the corvette received orders to cease firing. Still many of the royalists, sword in hand, waited to see the result of the capitulation; and a body of seven hundred grenadiers charged them with the bayonet, and a great number were slain. The rest laid down their arms, and the battle was over. Immense quantities of stores and victuals fell into the power of the Blues, and four thousand prisoners. Among the prisoners was the Bishop of Dol. At the approach of the Blues, his brother, who was one of his vicars-general, cast himself upon

Chapter XIII

his knees before him, saying: "Now is the moment for offering to God the sacrifice of our life." "My sacrifice is made," said the holy bishop.

Puisaye himself escaped in the English convoy. He had been the first to leave the shore to communicate with Commodore Warren. His whole life, and the confidence reposed in him by the bravest Chouans, place him far beyond the reproach of cowardice. Still, it is the duty of a commander to stay with his army to the last. Puisaye might have sent an officer upon that errand; and the act of desertion will for ever cloud the memory of his long and brilliant struggle with the republicans.

The prisoners were divided into two columns, and conducted to Auray. They were placed under a very feeble escort, who were all drunk, and exercised but little surveillance over them. The road, too, afforded many opportunities for escape; but very few of the royalists would avail themselves of them. "We have nothing to fear," said they; "it is a capitulation." Unfortunately the Republic had so often violated its promises, that it had now no honour to sustain; and a massacre of all the prisoners was determined upon. Immediately after the battle, two commissioners of the Convention departed for Paris, and on their report the bloody order was given. "The waves," cried they, "have thrown back the hirelings of Pitt under the sword of the law. Their chastisement must be proportioned to the heinousness of their crimes." They had the audacious wickedness to say that the poniards found on the "accomplices" of England were all poisoned. Upon this Lemoine was commanded to shoot all the *émigrés*, and he hastened to execute his orders.

Lemoine, however, made a show of going through the forms of justice, and appointed military commissions to sit on the accused. Sombreuil was first put to the bar; and being examined, he said to the judges: "I die as I have lived, a royalist; and I swear, knowing that I must shortly appear before God, that there was a capitulation; an engagement was made to treat the *émigrés* as prisoners of war. I appeal to some of these soldiers here present." A few movements were made in corroboration of his assertion; but they were instantly repressed. At the same time the Bishop of Dol was condemned. "Weep not for me," said the pious bishop to the peasants, on his road to execution, "I have come only to absolve you and to die." Fourteen prisoners were shot that day. Afterwards the tribunal became more expeditious. At the end of a week the executions had numbered five hundred. But presently the commissioners who had presided over the butchery began to be tired, and threatened to acquit the survivors. They were dismissed, but it was impossible to find a single officer to replace them. The number of the slain reached seven hundred and thirteen, and four hundred more died of their wounds in the hospitals. The peasants who had not held any command were then set at liberty, on condition that the communes to which they belonged would lay down their arms, or pay a ransom in wheat or forage.

Many of the officers who had been taken at Quiberon were men who had long neglected the duties of the religion for which they fought; but at the approach of death they exhibited as much faith as ever they had displayed courage on the field of battle. Scenes occurred in the prisons of Auray and Vannes worthy of the first ages of the Church. The walls resounded with the voice of prayer; the priests confessed their fellow-prisoners; and all recited in common the office for the dead, and prayed for their executioners. Among them was Sir Henri de Valude, a knight of Malta. He was very young; but he appeared younger than he was. Some one recommended him to understate his age a year or two, in order to escape death. "Uncle," said he to M. de Kergarion, an old captain in the navy, "do you think life worth the price of truth?" "No," was the answer; "I consider it better to die than purchase life with a lie." "So do I," said the young knight; and he gave in his true age, and was executed. The uncle, when his own turn came, said to those who were to form the same *fournée*, or batch with himself, "I propose

Chapter XIII

we should walk barefoot, in imitation of the Passion of our Saviour." Pages might be filled with anecdotes of this kind. The people of Auray called the place of execution "the field of martyrs," and the name exists to this day.

The causes of this disaster require no long investigation. The first and greatest blunder was undoubtedly that of remaining shut up in Quiberon instead of vigorously pushing on to Rennes. Yet, but for the intrigues of the agency, this error was not irretrievable. After the defeat of the 16th July owing to the absence of Tinténiac the expedition failed for all purposes of the insurrection; but if Fort Penthièvre had been defended by royalists instead of republicans, the retreat of the insurgents would at least have been protected. And even after the taking of that fort, if Sombreuil had acted with as much decision as courage, and Puisaye had continued at the head of his troops, the embarcation would have been successfully effected. All of these errors were due to the want of unity between the commanders and the Abbé Bronier, a defect which the presence of one of the royal princes would have supplied. If the Count d'Artois had personally accompanied the expedition, instead of deputing to Puisaye, Charette, and others the defence of his rights, neither the royal agency in Paris nor local jealousies could have frustrated an attempt so well supported by regular troops, English ammunition, and native enthusiasm.

Chapter XIV

Georges Cadoudal—Puisaye after Quiberon—Frotté in Normandy—Fresh dissensions between Charette and Stofflet—The Count d'Artois at the Ile-Dieu—His vacillation—Dispositions on both sides towards peace—Death of Stofflet—Last combat, capture, trial, and death of Charette—Submission of Brittany in 1796—After three years' dubious peace the Chouannerie breaks forth again—Bonaparte becomes first consul, and treats with Bernier—His vigorous measures, and their success.

THE INSURGENTS of Morbihan, in which department Quiberon is situated, scarcely suffered less from the ill-fated expedition of Puisaye than the *émigrés* themselves. They had been nearly a month under arms, during which they had lost many of their men, and had made great sacrifices for the ransom of the prisoners who were liberated at Auray; and yet, by the energy of Georges Cadoudal, that department soon assumed so formidable an appearance, as to inspire the republicans with the greatest alarm. Georges Cadoudal, the chief of the Morbihan, was then twenty-four years of age, a native of Kerleans, a village near Auray. His father was a man in easy circumstances, farming his own land, and able to give his children a good education. In 1793, Georges had just concluded his studies, having been designed for the ecclesiastical state; but anxious to fight for his Church and country, he joined the insurrection in La Vendée upon the pacification of Brittany, and took part in the whole of that great struggle which resulted in the disastrous passage of the Loire. On the concentration of the grand army, he easily found followers in his own province, where his fame as a soldier had spread far and wide, although his qualities as an able general were yet to

Chapter XIV

be developed; and after the defeat at Quiberon, he contrived to organise a system of defence for his own department which the republicans were never able to overcome.

Puisaye escaped from Quiberon, as we have seen, on board the English squadron, and took refuge in the isle of Houat; but after six weeks he landed again, and penetrated into the interior. Cadoudal received him without displeasure, but it was soon apparent that the two chiefs could never agree. Puisaye still claimed the supreme authority, and opposed the designs of Cadoudal. Cadoudal and the officers decided that Puisaye had forfeited the confidence of the royalists, and the fallen chief was compelled to seek a command in the department of Ille and Vilaine.

The Chouannerie continued to progress; and in Bas Normandy, a man named Frotté organised a body of three thousand insurgents, with whom he gained many victories over the Blues. In the north of Brittany, also, there were several large companies of Chouans; but these forces were all isolated. Each chief contented himself with defending his own territory. Not even Cadoudal, whose energy and military spirit fitted him for the greatest enterprises, thought of leaving Morbihan. He was satisfied with beating the republicans, seizing their baggage, and driving them back to the towns, and then retiring into his own retreat.

In La Vendée, the division between Charette and Stofflet broke out with renewed violence. The former, now completely under the influence of the royal agency at Paris, wrote to the Committee of Public Safety an open defiance,—"I swear never to lay down my arms till the presumptive heir to the crown of France is on the throne of his fathers." On the other hand, Stofflet appeared anxious to maintain the peace. Thus the two chiefs had exchanged the sentiments which they had previously professed. When Charette arranged the treaty with Ruelle, it was Stofflet who held out; now Stofflet would maintain the present state of affairs, and Charette is strenuous for the resumption of hostilities. The cause of this is evident. Charette had received from the king the most flattering testimonies of his regard, he had named him his lieutenant-general, given him the red ribbon, conferred on him the command of the royal armies, and styled him the second founder of the monarchy. Poor Stofflet, who was a simple gamekeeper, was rewarded with no such testimonies; he obtained only the title of field-marshal, with the cross of St. Louis. "As for the red ribbon, that," said the agency, "he could not of course aspire to, not being a gentleman."

Things were in this state, when suddenly news came of the arrival of the Count d'Artois upon the coast. Instantly all disunion ceased. The Chouans recovered all their enthusiasm; the chiefs thought only of the great cause in which they were embarked, and on all sides volunteers armed for the approaching struggle. The prince came with an armament far greater than had accompanied Puisaye, and the hopes of the west were raised to the highest pitch. It was agreed to effect a landing on the coast of Poitou, according to the plans of the agency. This was a grave error; La Vendée, wasted with fire and sword, had no resources comparable to those which Brittany could have furnished; yet the choice of the prince was justified by the disastrous result of Puisaye's expedition. After wasting twelve days in Quiberon Bay, the fleet sailed on; and on the 27th September summoned the garrison of Noirmoutiers to surrender. The summons being rejected, they cast anchor off the Ile-Dieu, a rock four miles in length and about nine miles from the mainland. Here the prince landed with his staff, and fortified himself with cannon; and on the 5th October wrote to Charette to name a spot for the debarcation on any point between Bourgneuf and Aiguillon.

Charette, overjoyed with this good news, and knowing how much precious time had been lost in Quiberon Bay, immediately collected his men and advanced towards the coast. His army, fortified with Sapinaud's division and a great number of peasants, amounted to fifteen thousand men; and all marched with the

Chapter XIV

greatest enthusiasm, chanting royalist and Catholic songs, and beating several republican columns which attempted to arrest their progress. They were already within sight of the ocean, when Count Grignon, one of the prince's officers, met them, and informed them that the debarcation was deferred. Charette, stupefied with indignation, answered,—"Tell the prince that he sends me my death-warrant. Today I have fifteen thousand men, tomorrow I shall not have fifteen hundred; nothing remains for me but to fly, or to seek a glorious death. My choice is made, I will perish." Grignon tried to calm him, and gave him from the prince a sabre, with the following inappropriate device—"*Je ne cède jamais*." But Charette was inconsolable; and it is impossible to acquit the prince of the basest ingratitude to the noble man who had shown such generous devotion to his cause.

This event was only the preliminary to a still more distressing one. On the 17th November, the count commanded the delegates from Puisaye, Stofflet, and Charette, to inform the chiefs of the west that he was summoned back to England by the British government. The announcement was made with tears and with every demonstration of sorrow; but the prince did not hesitate to obey the summons, and he departed, leaving the insurgents to their fate. The most contradictory opinions have been held upon the whole subject. Some writers have laid the blame on the British government; others, on the contrary, said that Warren, the officer in command of the English expedition, several times offered to land the prince on the coast. The insurgents also accused some the prince, and some the English ministers. In all probability the failure was owing to the prince's indecision; from first to last the royal family showed themselves unworthy of the loyalty of the insurgents. The war lasted seven years, and the princes were the whole time promising their presence; yet they never approached the scene of insurrection. At any moment in the earlier years of the struggle, they might have averted many of the disasters which the country endured for their sake, even if success

His vacillation—Dispositions towards peace

had not crowned their efforts by the subversion of the Republic and the restoration of the monarchy. But they preferred to live in foreign capitals in gaiety and excess, while their brave subjects were devoting their lives to set them again upon the throne. And when at length, after many years, the allied forces restored the Bourbons to their rights, as little trouble was taken to reward the efforts of the Vendean royalists as there had been to second them at the time.

The vacillation and cowardice of the Count d'Artois conduced more to the termination of hostilities than all the efforts of the Republic; especially as the generals intrusted with the subjugation of the insurgent provinces had adopted a conciliatory tone in the matter of religion. It has already been frequently said, that the insurrection was a religious one, and only political by accident. The priests embraced the royal cause as believing it identified with the liberty of the Church. But the despicable conduct of the royal princes disabused them of that conviction; and when Hoche, who had been despatched to La Vendée after his successful dispersion of the *émigrés* at Quiberon, began to proclaim the free exercise of the Catholic worship as an integral part of his policy, many of the most devoted clergy preached to their flocks submission to the Republic. Charette obstinately held out; but the vast majority of the peasants refused to serve under him, and maintained a strict neutrality in the very presence of the republican army.

In return for this peaceable disposition, Hoche exerted himself to prevent all acts of pillage and violence on the part of his soldiers, and showed himself uniformly friendly towards the population. The burden of all his proclamations was simply this: "Build again your cottages, worship God as you think fit, and till your land." The consequence of which was, that mutual goodwill grew up between the Blues and the insurgents; and but for Charette, the army of Hoche would have been nothing more than an army of occupation.

Stofflet and the Abbé Bernier shared the general feeling, and without positively submitting to the Republic, exerted themselves

Chapter XIV

to maintain peace. The royal princes, notwithstanding their own cowardice, continually excited their chiefs to arms, and at length raised Stofflet to the rank of Charette, and created him their lieutenant-general. But it was long before he would assume a hostile attitude towards the Republic; and when he did, he found himself unable to assemble a company of more than three hundred men. Hoche, hearing of the new movement, regarded it with the most contemptuous indifference. "The Stoffleian war," said he, "will last just a fortnight;" and he was right. The chief of Anjou succeeded in taking Argenton-le-Chateau, but from lack of men was compelled to fly before his foes; and on the night of the 23d February 1796, he was surprised and captured by a party of republicans. He was taken to Angers, and brought before a court-martial. Without hope, as without fear, he replied briefly to the questions of his judges, and was shot on the 26th, exhibiting in his last moments the courage of which he had given so many proofs on the field of battle. After his death D'Autichamp called himself commander-in-chief of Anjou and Haut Poitou; but it was an empty title,—he had no army to command.

Charette alone remained to be overcome. It is said that the Directory (for the form of the revolutionary government had been changed) offered to the chief of Bas Poitou a sum of a million francs to retire to England and abandon the struggle; but the brave man refused the bribe with indignation. Now followed by about four hundred men, he tired out for three months all the divisions sent against him. Hoche, however, pursued him with unremitting perseverance; and gradually, though surely, drove him further and further towards the sea, hemming him in as he proceeded, and cutting off all chances of escape. Still the republican general seemed disposed to make honourable terms with his gallant enemy, and such of his chiefs as would submit. Many of them thought the moment had arrived when farther resistance was useless; but Charette said that each was free to follow his own opinion, he, however,

Death of Stofflet—Last combat of Charette

would die with his arms in his hand. A few encounters took place subsequently, and then many of his officers surrendered. By an infamous violation of the rights of war, most of them were put to death.

Abandoned thus by all his friends, Charette was still an object of terror to the government, and Hoche again endeavoured to treat with him. He offered him permission to retire to England, with all who chose to accompany him, or to Switzerland, by a route avoiding Paris; and to receive the revenue of his estates for the last three months. The Vendean general hesitated, but at length replied,—"I can perish sword in hand: but fly?—abandon my brave comrades?—never. All the vessels of the Republic would not suffice to transport them all to England. Far from being alarmed by your threats, I am on the very point of attacking your camp."

But his time was drawing nigh. On the 21st February his troop, now reduced to less than two hundred men, was attacked by General Travot, one of the ablest of the officers of Hoche. The Vendeans behaved with the greatest courage, but they were overwhelmed with numbers. The eldest brother of the general, Charette la Colinière, and several officers fell; and he himself escaped with difficulty, followed by only fourteen men. The next day all the surviving chiefs of the insurgent army gave in their submission, and nothing remained but to capture Charette himself. The republican generals, well informed by their spies, were in hot pursuit; and yet he contrived to carry on the campaign for a whole month longer. On the 23d March, he was surrounded by four columns. "This, then," cried the hero of Poitou, "this is the spot where I must fight and die." The adjutant-general, Valentine, was the first to charge. Charette, conspicuous by his white plume, was the mark for every bullet; yet, as if he had borne a charmed life, he long escaped unhurt. At length one of the German deserters seized his cap, and putting it on his own head, said, "Save yourself, my general; they will take me for you." This generous devotion cost the man his life, without saving his leader. He was soon slain; but Travot prevented

Chapter XIV

the escape of Charette. The Vendean chief, wounded in the hand and in the head, attempted to leap a ditch; but, held by a branch which had become entangled in his dress, he was thrown upon his face. Two of his soldiers were killed in the attempt to set him free, and Charette at length fell into the hands of his enemies. By Travot's orders, the last representative of the Vendean insurrection was treated with respect. With so great joy was his capture received by the republicans, that a general, writing from Paris, said,—"We have gone mad at the good news you have sent us; we have been beside ourselves ever since."

Dragged from town to town, Charette was sent to Angers, in order to be conducted to Paris. But Hoche thought it more politic to judge and execute him at Nantes. To that city he was accordingly sent,—that Nantes which he had entered but a short year before in the glory of a veritable triumph. Under what altered circumstances did he now approach his native city! At that great entry the sun shone brightly, and the people, wild with joy, came forth to meet the hero of La Vendée. Now it was dark midnight, and the garrison was under arms; and instead of royalist cries, the shouts of the victorious Blues resounded through the streets.

On arriving at his prison, the general of the Catholic and royal armies found an officer with fifty chasseurs and four grenadiers, charged with the duty of mounting guard over him. General Duthill, who commanded the garrison, indulged his hatred to the royalists by heaping upon his prisoner the grossest insults. Far from imitating Travot, who thought himself sufficiently happy to have obtained possession of his great enemy, without sullying his success with indecent manifestations, he paraded him through the streets of Nantes to the sound of martial music, and accompanied by a procession of republican generals in their most splendid uniform. Charette, pale, exhausted, and suffering agonies from his wounds, fainted in the midst of that barbarous triumph. A charitable person brought him a glass of water from a neighbouring shop. Unhappily, his name has not been recorded, but it was a courageous act; for to appear humane was in those days a crime. When he had recovered from his swoon, the illustrious prisoner continued his march, which lasted for two hours longer. And when at length he reached the Castle de Bouffay, which had been selected as his prison, he could not refrain from saying to General Duthill, "If you had fallen into my power, I should have had you shot on the spot."

In prison his demeanour was calm and dignified, and worthy of his great name. He asked to be allowed to see his sister, who had already applied in vain several times for the sad pleasure of embracing her brother. At last she was admitted, along with two of her relations. He rose to meet her, and flung his arms round her neck. The heart of the poor lady was ready to break with grief. He who had been her pride, who had been the hope of the royalists and the terror of their foes, was about to pass from prison to death. As she wept, and her companions with her, he said, with a trembling voice, "Do not weep thus. Do not shake my courage. I have fought for God and for the king, and it is for them that I am going to die. I have need of all my firmness. I implore you, restrain your tears. Sister, have you not often said, that in heaven we shall meet again?"

The trial took place on the 28th of March. After five hours of examination, during which the Vendean belied not for a single instant the firmness of his character and the nobility of his cause, his judges pronounced upon him sentence of death. He heard it without emotion, and requested only, that as he had fought, so he might die, a Christian, and that he might enjoy the consolations of religion. They sent him the Abbé Guibert, a priest who had taken the oath to the constitution. Before entering his cell, the ecclesiastic begged that the prisoner might be searched. Charette was indignant at the man's alarm. "Does he think," cried he, "that the general of the Catholic and royal armies is an assassin? Let him come without fear."

Chapter XIV

The Abbé then entered, and said, in a trembling voice, "I am come, monsieur, to offer you the consolations of religion in your unhappy strait."

"It is for that purpose I sent for you," replied the Christian hero. "I abhor your principles, I do not regard you as a legitimate minister; but I know that in the hour of death you have power to absolve me. Come, listen to my confession. I do not want your exhortations, I desire absolution." So saying, he fell on his knees, and, notwithstanding his wounds, remained in that posture for two hours. Then he arose, pardoned, and ready to appear before his God.

At last the fatal moment arrived; the gate of the prison opened, and Charette was led forth to the place of execution. By his side walked the priest, and together they recited the *Miserere* psalm. On the way a furious republican assailed him with threats and insults; but Charette, unmoved, raised his eyes to heaven, and continued his prayer. By his calm attitude and noble and resigned bearing, he attracted more attention than all the magnificence and pomp with which his enemies sought to adorn their triumph. As he passed by a certain house in a street indicated by his sister, he humbly bowed his head. An old man clad in black, and holding a white handkerchief, was at a window; it was a Catholic priest, whom the piety of Mademoiselle de Charette had stationed there to give to the warrior, who was going to die for God and the king, the benediction of heaven. None but a few Vendeans who were hidden in the crowd knew why Charette had thus inclined his head; but they blessed God for the grace He had accorded to His faithful soldier.

After a long slow march through the town, the victim at length arrived at the Place de Viarmes, the spot selected for the execution. A vast crowd thronged the *place* and the adjoining streets, and more than five thousand men were drawn up in a large square with the officers on horseback in the centre, their brilliant uniforms and tricolored plumes conspicuous above the triple row of bayonets. In the hour of death Charette first knew how great he had been in life.

Death of Charette

Himself on foot, calm, impassible, he disdained to address a single word in self-defence; but he raised his voice in behalf of an enemy, a republican general named Jacob, who had been incarcerated with him as a traitor. The priest, before retiring, was about to comfort him; but he said, "I have gone to death a hundred times without fear, and today I go for the last time." He refused the handkerchief with which they were about to bandage his eyes; and advancing towards the picket who were to shoot him, he let fall his wounded hand, and putting the other upon his heart, he said to the soldiers,

"Soldiers, aim true! It is here that you must strike a brave man. *Vive le Roi!*" and as his lips were formed to utter the cry of his whole life, he fell pierced with seven balls. So perished Charette. The royalists bewailed him, and even the Blues did homage to his courage. No cry of joy or triumph burst from the crowd as he fell beneath the fire of the soldiers; a mournful silence reigned on the place of execution, and a sort of stupor spread itself over Nantes. Lest the relics of the dead hero should animate the vengeance of the Vendeans, and in death Charette should be more terrible than in life, his body was taken to a quarry on the Rennes road, and thrown among a heap of other corpses.

Of Charette it may be said with truth, that his death was the utter ruin of the cause. Few are the leaders who can boast so great a panegyric. It was said of Larochejacquelein, yet the insurrection long survived the fall of that chivalrous young chief; but when Charette died, Hoche withdrew his troops from La Vendée. Royalty had no longer any partisans in the province to excite the alarm of the Republic. The insurgents had secured liberty of conscience, and no more blood was to flow for an ungrateful and irresolute prince.

The strife, thus concluded in La Vendée, was, however, still raging beyond the Loire. Cadoudal was in insurrection in Morbihan, Scepaux in Upper Brittany, and Guyon in Lower Brittany and Maine. On the appearance of Hoche, the two latter submitted.

Chapter XIV

The news of the executions of Charette and Stofflet struck terror into the hearts of the Chouans under their command; and on the 14th of May the general-in-chief of the republican army announced that the Chouans of the departments of Mayenne, of Maine and Loire, and of Loire Inférieure, had given up their arms to the Republic, and promised to live under the laws.

In Morbihan, where Cadoudal exerted absolute authority, nearly fifteen thousand insurgents, upon the whole well provided with all military equipments, were under arms. By its maritime position, this department could readily be supplied with ammunition from England. The peasants had also acquired considerable knowledge of war in many engagements, and were bold enough to attack even strong divisions of the enemy in open field. The strength of the insurrection evidently lay in this quarter, and there Hoche determined in person to prosecute the war. He made Vannes his head-quarters; and commenced his operations with so much vigour, that even Cadoudal began to feel that he must shortly follow the example of Scepaux. Puisaye, who had repaired to the camp of the Chouan chief on the failure of the insurrection in La Vendée, advised him to apply to Hoche for a suspension of hostilities, with a view of gaining time. The republican general was not to be so checked in his career of success. His answer was prompt and decided. "You wish for peace: so do I, monsieur; and I mean to obtain it. The suspension of arms which you desire cannot be granted. Give us your submission to the laws of the Republic, and that instant our movements cease." Seven days after this, that is to say, June 15th, 1796, Hoche reported to the Directory the submission of the Chouan chiefs in Morbihan. Cadoudal, however, remained in the country, with unabated influence over the population.

In Normandy, where Frotté, whose influence had been rapidly extending, had been engaged in a successful struggle with the republican troops, the insurrection was suppressed by reinforcements sent forward by Hoche; and about the same time that Cadoudal

Submission of Brittany—The Chouannerie breaks forth

submitted, Frotté set sail for England. Puisaye alone remained to be overcome. In Ille and Vilaine his influence was still paramount; and he obstinately refused to enter into any negotiations. La Vieuville, Boisguy, and Chalus, his principal officers, were of the same mind; and all resolved to attempt a hopeless resistance. Surrounded by numerous troops, well provisioned and sure of victory, they sustained defeat after defeat, and their soldiers fell away. La Vieuville was killed early in July. Boisguy made his submission. Chalus, who alone remained, at length followed the general example; and the struggle was at an end. Puisaye refused even now to believe that all was lost, and remained in hiding in the woods till he could escape to England. Hoche received from the Directory the thanks of the Republic, and the most magnificent presents, upon the successful termination of the civil war.

But France had not yet seen the last of the Chouannerie. La Vendée, exhausted by its dreadful sufferings, sincerely desired the maintenance of peace. But Brittany had suffered less; its resources were still very great, and the chiefs held themselves in readiness to renew the war, satisfied that at the very first summons their old soldiers would all be eager to raise the flag of insurrection. There were many *émigrés* in hiding in the heart of the country; and wherever they were found, the spirit of hostility to the Republic was sure to be violent. Morbihan, where Cadoudal still maintained his military organisation, was the mainstay of the hopes of the insurgents; and notwithstanding the external air of peace which the country wore, the republicans regarded the state of the province with the greatest anxiety.

Under these circumstances, Puisaye, in concert with Frotté and many other Chouan chiefs, made, in December 1797, great efforts to induce the Count d'Artois to head a fresh insurrection in Brittany. This the prince absolutely refused to do; and Puisaye, disgusted that the representative of the royal family should be the only man to show apathy in the royal cause, abandoned the object

Chapter XIV

of his life, and sailed to end his days in Canada. The other refugees in London equally resigned all hope of a successful struggle with the Republic, and Georges Cadoudal remained the sole chief of influence in the Chouannerie. He alone did not despair. Hoche, after conquering La Vendée and Brittany, had attempted that disastrous expedition against Ireland which resulted in the destruction of his army and the loss of his *prestige*. Napoleon was in Egypt—a continental war was raging which demanded from the Republic its greatest efforts—the nations of Europe were leagued against the government of France. What more favourable moment could be selected for the renewal of hostilities? The chief of Morbihan seized upon it to address a vigorous proclamation to the "brave Chouans and the generous Vendeans," which was responded to with great ardour, not only in Brittany, but on the other side of the Loire also; for there religious persecution had recommenced, and with it the spirit of insurrection. The Count d'Artois signified his intention to appear shortly at the seat of war,—an intention never carried out, if it ever existed; and a general rising of the whole west was arranged to take place from the 15th to the 20th of October 1799.

Partial movements had, however, taken place before that period. The Chouans had opened the campaign by a series of successes. At Nantes, at Mans, at St. Briene, at Breton, and many other places, Cadoudal and other chiefs had conquered the Blues in hard-fought battles. England had, moreover, seconded the efforts of the insurgents by the most munificent supplies of money, artillery, and ammunition. La Vendée did not exhibit the same ardour. Forestier and D'Autichamp were the chief leaders; but the people were not enthusiastic, and obeyed the call to arms in small numbers. The Abbé Bernier, with his usual acuteness, saw from the first that the insurrection would not be general, and held himself aloof from it.

The Directory supplied its army in the west with such reinforcements as could be spared for the emergency. But Cadoudal and his colleagues still remained on the offensive; and things were in this

Bonaparte becomes first consul, and treats with Bernier

state when Bonaparte assumed the head of affairs as First Consul. His first act of power was to institute negotiations towards the permanent pacification of the west. With that object he entered into communication with the Abbé Bernier, to whom he caused it to be intimated that he depended on his influence to establish a durable peace. Bernier replied, that he could only treat with the first consul on the assurance first given, not that the Catholic worship should be barely tolerated, but that he should leave it completely free, and extend to its ministers the protection of the laws. Barré, who was Napoleon's agent, received full powers to concede whatever Bernier should demand; and Bernier, on the other hand, promised to labour for the immediate establishment of peace. The majority of the Chouan chiefs, and among them Cadoudal, inveighed against the act of the Abbé, and insisted on the necessity for the continuance of hostilities; the Count d'Artois, who repeated his old promise of an immediate descent into Brittany, and even those royalists who were on the side of Bernier, endeavoured to protract the negotiations. When Napoleon perceived this, he instantly gave orders for the active prosecution of the war; and issued two proclamations—the one to the insurgents, the other to his own soldiers. To the first he said, "Religious liberty is guaranteed; there are unjust laws, they shall be repealed. The government will pardon all who surrender, and strike those who dare to resist." To the soldiers he addressed himself as follows: "Let me hear shortly of the defeat of the rebels. Exterminate the wretches: they are the disgrace of the French name. Make a short and good campaign."

It was evident now that the time for hesitation was gone: the chiefs must either fight or tender their submission. They had to do with a man with whom to design was to execute. By Bernier's advice, La Vendée kept separate from Brittany; and a general meeting was convened at Monsançon on the 18th Jan. 1800. There the great majority declared for peace. Upon this most of the Breton chiefs laid down their arms; Cadoudal, Frotté, and Bourmont, were the

Chapter XIV

only men who held out. Brumé, the general-in-chief of the republicans, immediately marched against the former with twenty thousand men; and on the 2d February the Chouan chief laid down his arms. Two days later Bourmont also submitted. Frotté was the last to surrender, and was shot by order of Bonaparte, who owed the chief of Normandy a personal grudge. Peace was again established in the west, and at length on a permanent basis. The man who was able to obtain it by a judicious combination of concession and intimidation, knew also how to preserve it by a just observance of the conditions on which it existed.

Thus at length La Vendée desisted from opposition to the Republic. After seven years of strife, during which her best blood had been poured out like water, and no work of social life, of husbandry or building, of commerce or manufacture, could be commenced with any prospect of a successful termination; years of civil war, in which kindred fought on opposite sides, and the nearest ties of blood were regarded as nothing in comparison with the bonds of party; years of brutality, in which the defenceless had no protection, and innocence no safety; when the maiden durst not walk the highway, and the old man and the child feared to be left alone in the cottage; years, during which the Holy Sacrifice had not been offered but in desolate places, and the churches had fallen into ruin, and the young had grown up in ignorance of their faith;—after seven such years La Vendée had succeeded in wringing from the nation the poor boon of liberty to worship God according to her conscience: poor, indeed, in the estimation of those who conceded it, but of priceless value to the Catholic children of the west. The issue of this insurrection may teach the military student the utter hopelessness of the struggle of undisciplined peasants with regular troops; its history may furnish an example of the inevitable dissensions which will arise among men devoted to the same cause, but subject to no supreme authority; moreover, it may be taken as an illustration of the truth, that the holiness of a cause is no guarantee for the virtues of its supporters; for Stofflet could murder his colleagues, Joly could execute his own son, and Charette's camp in the Marais was the scene of rioting and excess. These, and many other reflections, may arise out of the war in La Vendée; but the considerations most to our purpose are, that God will never forsake His Church, and that the blood of martyrs is never shed in vain. When were the prospects of religion so dark as during the French revolution? What more wasteful to human eyes, than the deaths of Cathelineau, and D'Elbée, and Lescure? Yet to tell the tale of the revival of the faith in France would occupy more space than this passage in its decline and fall. The soil on which these men fought and bled is now bringing up Christians purer in their lives, more devoted to the Church, more humble children of the Holy See, than were known in the days of Bourbon sway. The nation is making reparation for its own crimes. Beneath the flag under which Turreau directed his infernal columns, and Carrier his noyades, new churches are rising, and the faith is protected, and the Cross is set up before all eyes. The harrowing details of the past but suggest the augury of a glorious future; and if, as is possible, other countries may have to endure the same searching trial—if unjust governments should seek to destroy that which can never be destroyed, and their Catholic subjects should be subjected to ruin and persecution—the looker-on may call to mind the dealings of Almighty God with France, and the sufferings of La Vendée; and, instead of despairing of the ultimate victory of the Church, gather from the very danger matter of rejoicing.

Chapter XV

Intrigues in Paris—Fouché—Moreau—Conspiracy of Pichegru, Moreau, and Cadoudal—Death of Cadoudal—The infernal machine—The Concordat—The Little Church—The Abbé Bernier Bishop of Orleans—Royalism in the west under the Empire—Rejoicings at the Restoration—Ingratitude of the Bourbons—Insurrection in 1815—Crafty conduct of Fouché—Death of Louis de Larochejacquelein—Defeat at La Roche Servière—Pacification after the battle of Waterloo.

WE ARE NOT writing a general history of the revolution in France, and are therefore only so far concerned with the intrigues which were incessantly carried on against the government of Napoleon by disaffected republicans on the one side, and royalists on the other, as they bear upon the history of the west. Although the pacification of 1800, because based upon religious liberty, was permanent and complete, there yet remained, especially in Brittany, several influential leaders who refused to give in their adhesion to it. Compelled to desist from open opposition, these men still maintained a secret correspondence with the partisans of Louis in the capital. Their chief was Georges Cadoudal, or as he is more commonly called, Georges. The last to succumb before superior force, this great Chouan steadily refused the overtures which the first consul made to him. That unfailing sagacity which Napoleon displayed in the discrimination of genius had at once detected the talents of the Chouan general; and on the termination of hostilities, Cadoudal was offered the rank of lieutenant-general in the republican armies. He replied, that he had sworn allegiance to the house of Bourbon. Upon this, Napoleon offered him a pension of a hundred thousand francs to remain neutral; but this proposition he also rejected. And Georges, who had taken refuge in England, continued to foment in France the spirit of insurrection against the consular government.

At the time of Napoleon's accession to the consulate there existed a ministry of police, at the head of which was a most able, but ambitious and unscrupulous man, of the name of Fouché. He had been implicated in the reign of terror at Nantes, and was the leader of the Jacobite party at this period. To him, in a great measure, the military despot owed his elevation. But Napoleon was not slow to perceive, that the unbounded influence which the minister enjoyed might as well be directed one day against himself as it had been exerted in his favour. In order, therefore, to check the power of his dangerous friend, Napoleon established a secret police, acting independently of the public and recognised department, and watching its movements. But Fouché had many bitter enemies at the Tuileries, the most powerful of whom was Talleyrand himself, who were not content with espionage, and did not cease from devising the ruin of their hated rival. For a long time the influence which the police minister exercised over Napoleon secured him from disgrace; but the fears of the first consul at length overcame his gratitude, and he adopted the decisive resolution of ridding himself of the danger by suppressing the office. In announcing this act of authority to the senate, Napoleon alleged that the change of circumstances had rendered a police ministry no longer necessary; but that should the same combination recur which had originated that bureau, the talents and energy of Fouché pointed him out as the fittest person to preside over its administration. The fallen minister perfectly understood the motives of his master's conduct, and submitted with the greatest apparent cordiality to the honours which were heaped upon him in the less influential sphere of the

Chapter XV

senate to which he was transferred. But inwardly he resolved, that it should be through no fault of his, if, from an absence of intrigues, the consul should sit so securely in his chair as to feel no need of a ministry of police.

From the moment that he had seized the supreme power, Napoleon fixed his mind on attaining the name and dignity, as well as the substance of royalty, and founding a dynasty which should survive his own life. His measures towards this end were taken with a wisdom which now excites our astonishment, and did not fail at the moment to rouse the suspicions of many men who had attached themselves to the revolution from the beginning, and could not endure the thought, that they had been but the puppets of an ambitious soldier; or that they had but dethroned one king to make way for another, and him their own leader. Of these far-sighted republicans, Moreau, the conqueror of Austria and the hero of Hohenlinden, was the chief. This brave soldier did not hesitate openly to protest against the course which Napoleon was pursuing. When, in imitation of the ancient system, more splendid uniforms were introduced into the *salons* of Paris; when a more rigid etiquette was practised than was consistent with the rude simplicity of republican manners; when decorations were worn as in the days of the old *noblesse*,—Moreau moved through the splendid throng in the plain dress of a citizen.

In public he assumed a marked coldness towards his old general; and when, upon the occasion of celebrating the concordat, High Mass was again publicly solemnised at Notre Dame, he obstinately refused to sanction with his presence what he considered a retrograde movement. By this conduct Moreau became unconsciously regarded as the leader of the disaffected republicans, and his assistance was confidently expected by all who looked for a rebellion against the government.

These things did not escape the vigilant observation of Fouché; and as there still existed among the royalist party men ready for any attempt against the first consul, he determined to unite the discordant factions of which Moreau and Georges were respectively at the head in one conspiracy against Napoleon, which should be ruinous to both, and demonstrate the necessity of re-establishing the suppressed ministry of police. This design was not less ably carried out than it had been craftily conceived.

Pichegru was in London, whither also Cadoudal had retired; and there the two royalists, the general of the old army and the Chouan chief, consulted measures for the re-establishment of the Bourbons. Fouché first endeavoured to promote a reconciliation between these men and Moreau by means of mutual friends; and contrived the landing of Georges and Pichegru, with other royalists, on the coast of Normandy, from which they cautiously, and thanks to the ex-minister's measures safely, found their way to Paris, where Moreau had a conference with Pichegru. The agents of Fouché had represented to either party the anxiety of the other for a coalition; but the result of their conferences was to show the impossibility of any such event. For Moreau, though jealous of the government of the first consul, had no one in view to substitute in his place; while the royalists would only treat for the restoration of the ancient family. In consequence of this disagreement, the conspirators separated, determined to undertake nothing in concert; and were on the point of leaving Paris, when Fouché, who judged the proper moment to have arrived for the explosion of his mine, and had been privy to every step in the conspiracy, caused them all to be arrested.

Georges himself escaped the agents of the police for some time; but the avenues from Paris were strictly watched, and he was at length seized in the street; not, however, without a struggle, which cost the life of more than one of his captors. He was then cast into prison, and treated with the greatest indignity. All this he bore with the utmost indifference, and exhibited the same behaviour on his trial, when he boldly proclaimed his intention to have attacked

Chapter XV

the first consul. With a clemency to which it is impossible to assign the cause, whether from an admiration of the conduct of a noble enemy or from motives of policy, Napoleon offered the condemned man his pardon on condition that he would abandon the Bourbon cause. But the Chouan disdained to be beholden for his life to the man against whom he had plotted, and preferred to die for the king. Before leaving his prison, he exhorted his fellow-prisoners to fortitude in terms worthy of his whole history. "If," said he, "in the trials which are before us, you should lose your firmness, cast your eyes on me, and remember that your fate will be mine also. Yes, in death we cannot be separated; that should be our consolation.... Think no more of the past. Here we are by the will of God; and in the hour of our death, let us pray that one day our country, freed from the yoke which oppresses it now, may be happy under the sway of the Bourbons. Never forget, it was from these walls that Louis XVI. went forth to the scaffold. Be his example your model and your guide!" He was executed on the 25th June 1804, on the Place de Grève. He insisted on being the first to die, that his companions, who knew that he had received the offer of a pardon, might have the satisfaction of feeling that they had not been deserted by their chief.

The Chouan party were unhappily disgraced by the complicity of some of their members in the atrocious attempt upon the life of the first consul by means of the infernal machine. On the 24th December 1800, as Napoleon was driving at a rapid rate from the Tuileries to the theatre, a terrible fire burst from one of the houses in the Rue St. Nicaire, which shattered the windows of his carriage, killed eight persons, and wounded twenty-eight. He owed his own life to the address with which the coachman passed a cart which had been purposely overturned in that narrow thoroughfare. The Jacobins were at first supposed to be the guilty parties; but Fouché soon discovered that certain of the agents of Cadoudal were the real criminals. Georges was himself accused of the crime; but there

Death of Cadoudal—The infernal machine—Concordat

exists satisfactory evidence to show, that the diabolical act was not only without his knowledge, but that it excited his utmost indignation; that it had frustrated his whole plans, and, in his opinion, had put a stop to all hopes of continuing the insurrection. There is little doubt that the pacification of the west was secured by the very means by which, in their misguided zeal, a few of the Chouans sought to disturb it. Throughout the departments of La Vendée and Brittany, a revulsion of feeling in favour of the first consul, through whom the wearied people were enjoying peace and liberty of conscience, followed the attempt at his assassination.

The tranquillity of the provinces so long insurgent was further secured by the formal restoration of the Catholic faith as the religion of the nation. By the concordat which Napoleon concluded with the Pope, although the liberties of the French Church were assailed by the terms on which Napoleon insisted, the people at length enjoyed undisturbed repose. The churches were again opened for public worship, and the priests not only permitted to say Mass, but paid by the state. And in La Vendée, which had suffered more from the revolution than any other province of France, vast sums were expended in the restoration of the ruined churches, and the building of the priests' houses.

Napoleon was guided by no love for religion in this act of justice, but by the most selfish considerations. He knew that no government could be raised on a permanent footing without a national religion; and as France was Catholic at heart, he must needs treat with the Head of the Church for the establishment of the popular faith. He took care to pare down the supremacy of the Pope to the lowest limit consistent with its integrity; but he admitted it as essential to the being of the Church which he had resolved to restore. The suggestions which were made to him by those who had failed in diverting him altogether from his purpose, that he should frame a Church upon the model of the English Establishment, of which he should be himself the supreme head, and over which the Pope

Chapter XV

should have no control, he treated with the utmost contempt; no such institution could be permanent, or meet the requirements of the nation. As he had been a Mahometan in Egypt, so he would become a Catholic in France for the good of his people.

Many republicans, who had not the same interest as Napoleon in the policy he was pursuing, violently inveighed against the concordat; but the people rejoiced at the revival of religion, and the first consul was indifferent to the arguments of his more consistent friends. Opposition, however, arose in a quarter from which it was little expected. Some of the parishes of La Vendée, which had most energetically resisted the constitutional schism, separated from the Holy See upon this occasion. They accused the Head of the Church of having outstepped his powers in superseding their own bishop and appointing a nominee of the government, and they refused to submit to an authority which they regarded as illegitimate. This body was called the Little Church. Some traces of its existence continue to this day; but after beginning in an excess of zeal, it soon lost itself, according to an invariable rule, in disorder and ignorance. It was productive of much evil at the period of its origin. The faithful priests, who well knew how to oppose the republican government when in arms against the Holy See, and to submit to its authority when the Pope sanctioned its acts, were much impeded in their arduous labours to restore religion among their distracted flocks by the attitude of the Little Church. Its partisans were not numerous; but they were obstinate, enthusiastic, and most bitter against all who treated them as schismatics, or threatened them with excommunication.

The evil, however, soon bred its own cure. The enthusiasm in which the Little Church had originated impelled its members to the perpetration of acts of violence, which, as in the affair of the infernal machine, so far from eliciting the sympathies of the people in its favour, brought down upon it general reprobation. The new Bishop of La Rochelle, M. de Pancemont, upon the strength of the

The Little Church

submission of the great majority of his clergy, was guilty of some imprudences which the schismatics could not pardon. He superseded old pastors for no other fault than that they were held in no great veneration by their parishioners; and in his pastoral instructions he spoke somewhat too submissively of Napoleon, his august patron. In revenge for these offences, a party of the insubordinate Chouans stopped the poor bishop in the middle of a *lande*, tore off his episcopal habit, and dressed him as a miller; they then exacted from him a ransom of thirty thousand francs, and at length sent him away so terrified with his adventure, that he fell ill and died. The inhabitants showed but little pity for the fate of the perpetrators of this outrage; and the priests were unanimous in their condemnation of it. A circular from the vicars-general was read at the Prone, in which those who had laid their sacrilegious hands on the Lord's anointed were stigmatised as "brigands, wretches, and monsters." The Little Church daily acquired a better right to its name. The old Chouans, not to be confounded with the authors of the unpopular deed, stoutly disavowed it; and at length, so manifest was the general reaction of feeling, that even the military conscriptions, which had always met with the most vehement opposition among the Armorican population, were effected with comparative ease.

Napoleon knew how to conciliate the insurgents, and attach them to himself. Afterwards, when they were thoroughly subjected, he cared but little either for his own promises or their good-will. He enforced upon them a more rigorous conscription than they had ever suffered under the Republic, and declared open war against the Supreme Pontiff. These things he did when he was once firmly seated on his throne. But while his power was as yet limited, and he was only half-way up the ladder of glory, he neglected no opportunity of winning to his side the noble hearts which had conducted to a successful termination that struggle which he himself termed "a war of giants." After the conclusion of the Concordat with the Pope, Napoleon appointed to the see of Orleans the man

Chapter XV

of all others who had exercised the greatest influence over the insurgents, the Abbé Bernier. By this single act the first consul made reparation for a host of injuries.

Invested with his new dignity, the Abbé himself presided at the restoration of the Catholic faith, to which his own councils had contributed so much. As soon as he touched Vendean soil, the whole population came forth to meet him. His journey was one magnificent triumph. In vain some of the royalists, more fanatical than wise, or more political than religious, inveighed against the new bishop for a traitor and a turncoat. The peasants saw in him the representative of Catholic Vendée, and rejoiced in his elevation, as the symbol of victory; and the plaudits with which the old chaplain of the Catholic army was greeted redounded to the popularity of the first consul.

The subsequent conduct of the bishop justified his appointment. He had many enemies. The revolutionists of his old parish in Angers regarded him with a hatred only equalled by the love borne towards him by his Catholic flock; and while the latter knelt to receive his benediction, the former sent him bottles filled with blood. Bernier knew how to treat such insults. He devoted himself to his episcopal duties with the same energy that he had displayed in conducting the affairs of the insurrection, and with a humility and fervour which made him a saint in the eyes of his friends, and a hypocrite in those of his foes. The reader of this history will not question his sincerity; he will regard him as a truly great and good man, whose actions may not be always free from the charge of ambition, but who had the glory of God and the salvation of souls always before him. He was at first a hearty and a fervent royalist. But intensely disgusted with the meanness of the royal family, and profoundly convinced that the nation had for ever rejected them from the throne, he consulted the true interests of the people, in supporting the policy of Napoleon, and promoting the pacification of the West. He lived but a few years as bishop; but he contributed greatly to the restoration of true religion. He died in 1806.

The Abbé Bernier—Rejoicings at the Restoration

His people were not all so far-seeing as himself. Like him they submitted to the republican government; but they still entertained a distant hope of witnessing the restoration. Their submission to Napoleon indicated no diminution in loyalty to the house of Bourbon. In the enjoyment of their religion, and hopeless of successfully contending with the armies which had defied Europe, they lived in quiet obedience to the laws of the Empire; and not even the incessant conscriptions, which were so many years enforced to feed the ambition of Napoleon, could rekindle the spark of insurrection. But they lived still in the hope of seeing the ancient family restored; and when that event actually took place in 1814, the accession of Louis XVIII. was hailed with every demonstration of joy. The aggressions of the Emperor against the Pope had indeed increased the numbers of the disaffected, and the disasters of the Russian campaign had raised the hopes of those who would have resented that insult to the highest pitch; but the West had taken no hostile steps against the imperial government, when the tricolor flag was suddenly removed, and the white banner of the Bourbons was suspended from the steeple of every parish.

Much as the family whose fortunes were thus unexpectedly restored owed to La Vendée, they made but a poor return to her for all her blood. Louis feared to offend the liberals by the least exhibition of gratitude; and the Vendeans believed that their king had forgotten the very existence of his most devoted province, till the hour of trial returned; and then the man who could not remember his benefactors in his prosperity, had recourse to them when the flatterers by whom he was surrounded deserted to the enemy. On the 1st March 1815, Napoleon landed on the coast of Provence; and the marshals of the Empire, notwithstanding that they had sworn allegiance to the king, flocked over to his standard. Then Louis appealed to La Vendée; and the Prince de Condé repaired to Angers, where Charles D'Autichamp was already in command of a body of insurgents throughout the country.

Chapter XV

The Prince de Condé was personally unknown to the people; and after a few days, being unable to form any definite arrangement, he left La Vendée without a leader; a few bands of insurgents were under arms, who acknowledged the authority of D'Autichamp, Suzannet, and Sapinaud, under the old names of the armies of Anjou, Basse-Vendée, and the Centre; and about the same time Louis de Larochejacquelein landed on the coasts, which Charette had rendered for ever famous, with a convoy of arms and ammunition. Auguste de Larochejacquelein undertook also to organise the insurrection in the Haut Poitou. But in consequence of the intrigues of Fouché, these generals were unable to arrive at a mutual understanding; nor could they succeed in rousing the people, as in the old days of Cathelineau and D'Elbée.

On the arrival of Napoleon at Paris, his attempt to form an administration had commenced with the appointment of Fouché to his old post of Minister of Police. That astute statesman accepted the office, although he clearly foresaw a second restoration impending; and set himself, with his accustomed duplicity, so to discharge his present functions as to stand well with the king, when that event should take place. When the insurrection assumed shape in La Vendée, the emperor despatched two of his generals, Travot and Lamarque, with twenty thousand men to crush the royalists. To military force Fouché added intrigue; and with the greatest address insinuated into the counsels of the insurgent chiefs such elements of discord as effectually paralysed their operations. Louis de Larochejacquelein, penetrated with the memory of his brother's achievements, and inflamed with the same chivalrous fire, insisted upon an instant and vigorous appeal to arms, and claimed the supreme command. To this his high birth, the prestige of his great name, and his influence with the British government, clearly entitled him. But his colleagues, at the same time that they were jealous of his authority, had allowed themselves to be impressed with the arguments of Fouché, which were to this effect—that the Empire could not long stand; that a great European war was about to burst forth in Belgium, on the issue of which the future must depend, and not on a trifling contest maintained in an obscure corner of France; and, above all, that no appeal ought to be made by men who loved their country to foreign assistance. The English would only help them for their own profit; the Vendeans should, therefore, conclude a truce till the inevitable restoration occurred. So great weight had these reflections on the minds of D'Autichamp and Sapinaud, that while Louis de Larochejacquelein, with all the followers he could muster, advanced to meet Travot, they disbanded their volunteers, and retired to watch the issue of events. By this advice, Fouché hoped to ingratiate himself both with Napoleon and with Louis, should he be restored; with Napoleon, as paralysing the efforts of the royalists, by sowing division among them; with Louis, as having given the best advice, and saved the blood of his most devoted followers.

There was yet another cause for the inaction of these men. They had been all engaged in the former war, and remembered the times when the insurgents had flocked in thousands to the appointed rendezvous. Now from the whole country but a few volunteers presented themselves. The contrast was to them a proof of the altered state of feeling in the country; and satisfied that they should meet with insufficient support, they held themselves aloof. The true cause of this backwardness of the population was not any want of loyalty, but their reluctance to plunge their province in blood for political considerations. So long as they could practise their religion in peace, they were content to abide in patience the issue of the struggle.

Louis and Auguste de Larochejacquelein, on the contrary, with Ludovic de Charette, the nephew of the hero of Bas Poitou, and some other generals, who fought for the first time in La Vendée, entered on the struggle with the greatest ardour. But the event proved D'Autichamp and Sapinaud right in their anticipations. Only a

Chapter XV

very few thousand men followed the white banner. Charette and Louis de Larochejacquelein soon found a soldier's grave. They fell nobly fighting at the head of a handful of insurgents; worthy of their great names, worthy of their cause, and to the intense sorrow of their whole country.

Upon the death of Louis de Larochejacquelein, Sapinaud was elected to the chief command. Abandoning his retirement, he appeared at the head of fresh troops, with D'Autichamp and others. Lamarque, who had assembled six thousand men at Nantes, entered La Vendée, proclaiming death to all insurgents who should persist in their opposition; but guaranteeing protection to the lives and property of such as should submit to the emperor. The insurgents upon this resolved to stop the Buonapartist general at La Roche Servière. On the 19th June an affair took place between the advanced guards, in which the Vendeans had the advantage; but on the next day their main body, after a sharp battle, was repulsed in disorder; their ammunition having failed at a critical moment of the combat. D'Autichamp endeavoured, with a reserve of six thousand men, to arrest the conquerors; but he, too, was defeated. Lamarque crossed the river above and below the village of La Roche Servière, and the royalist army retreated in confusion.

This affair, badly planned and worse executed, gave the death-blow to the insurrection at its first onset, by deterring the mass of the people from joining it. Lamarque proceeded farther, making the same propositions of peace to those who would submit; of confiscation and death to all others; and the superior officers of the royalist army, in a council of war, decided by a majority of twenty to twelve to enter into a treaty of peace. This negotiation was concluded on the 26th June, although the news had already arrived of the utter defeat of Napoleon at the battle of Waterloo.

On the other side of the Loire a similar agitation occurred, with a very similar result; a brief strife was terminated by a pacification after the news of the fall of the emperor. The chief general

Defeat at La Roche Servière—Pacification after Waterloo.

on the royalist side was the old Chouan, Sol de Grisolles. Morbihan was the theatre of the most active operations, and the strength of the insurgents was there increased by the gallant co-operation of the pupils of the College of Vannes. The narrative of their brave conduct forms one of the most interesting episodes in the history of the campaign of 1815; and we shall hereafter present it to our readers, as affording an insight into the state of the Breton people at that period.

Chapter XVI

Insensibility of the Bourbons to the services of La Vendée—Charles X. appeals again to the loyalty of the West—The Duchess de Berri in La Vendée—Brave conduct of the peasants at the Chateau of Penissière-de-la-Cour—Death of the son of Jacques Cathelineau and of Mademoiselle de Roberie—Departure of the Duchess de Berri—Cause of her failure—The end.

TWICE THE BOURBONS had appealed to the loyalty and patriotism of the Vendeans; twice the Vendeans had responded to their sovereign's summons by the most generous devotion of life and property in his service; and twice had all their sacrifices been forgotten or ignored. Had they consulted but their own interest, they might well have regretted the triumph of the very cause for which they had suffered so much. The Count d'Artois and the Duchess d'Angoulême did indeed sometimes assist the necessities of those whom the civil war had rendered destitute of all things. But it was not alms that La Vendée required; she asked for nothing more than the bare acknowledgment of her services. But while honours were heaped on the party that had been foremost in the usurpation and most faithless to royalty, she was neglected and despised. Napoleon had granted Madame de Bonchamps a pension of twelve thousand francs; Louis XVIII. reduced it one-half. The widow of Lescure and of Louis de Larochejacquelein, who had twice lost a husband in the royal cause, was treated as a suspected person. The king would not pay honour even to the dead. If a column is raised on the field of Torfou,

Charles X. appeals again to the loyalty of the West

where the Vendeans defied the noted soldiers of Mayence, it was the Marquis de la Bretesche who defrayed the expense; if an obelisk at Maulevrier commemorates the heroism of Stofflet, it is due to the family Colbert; if in the church of Chanzeau a chapel is devoted to the gallant band which that parish furnished, they owe the suffrages that are offered to the Count de Quatrebarbes; and when at length Louis consented to admit to his gallery the portraits of the Vendean generals, it was objected that Cathelineau and Stofflet were of peasant origin, and must be excluded. Not even the memory of Saumur and Laval could ennoble the blood of a pedlar and a game-keeper. When the Count d'Artois succeeded by the title of Charles X., he repaired the injury which his brother had inflicted on the two heroes of La Vendée; but he displayed towards that province scarcely more gratitude in power than he had shown courage in adversity. And when the revolution of July 1830 broke out, and for the third time Paris expelled her king, he blushed not to appeal again to the devotion of the West.

La Vendée received the abdication of Charles X. with anxiety and sorrow; but at length even the royalists of the West had yielded to the conviction that the cause for which they had hitherto fought was desperate, and no answer was made to the royal exile's summons. Nevertheless the authorities of the new government, mindful of the past, suspected some secret insurrection to be hatching; and by harsh and severe measures rendered the dangers real which only existed in their imagination. In the Bocage, in Brittany, and elsewhere, numerous conflicts took place between the national guards and independent bodies of insurgents, and the antipathies which arose out of these insignicant quarrels originated the more determined resistance on both sides of the Loire. In La Vendée, one Diot, and in Morbihan, Mathurin Mandar, were the chief leaders of the royalist party. But no important results took place, and the strife ceased to excite the alarm of the partisans of Louis Philippe.

Chapter XVI

It was, however, well known to the legitimists that the Duchess de Berri, mother of the Duke de Bordeaux, grandson of the late king, and in whose favour Charles X. had abdicated, was anxious for an appeal to arms; and towards the close of 1830 the question was seriously mooted. After that time two years were spent in intrigues, discussions, and adjournments; but at length a rising was arranged for the 2d of May 1832. The South was represented as ripe for revolt, and La Vendée engaged to arm in the royal cause, should the attempt there be successful.

On the 29th April the Duchess de Berri landed at Marseilles, and received a notice that the town would rise the next day. Shortly afterwards she was informed that the insurrection had miscarried, and that she must quit France. This she refused to do; but in the dress of a man, and under the name of Petit-Pierre, and accompanied by another lady, Mademoiselle Eulalie de Kersabuc, in a similar disguise, and calling herself Petit-Paul, she proceeded to La Vendée. Compelled to fly from chateau to hovel, and undergoing imminent danger of discovery, she led a life romantic and novel, the privations of which she supported with heroic spirit. But her unexpected arrival in La Vendée distressed rather than pleased the insurgent chiefs; for their promise of support had been conditional on the success of the rising in the South; and while a few agreed to support the duchess in whatever attempt she might make, others declared that, willing as they were to make any personal sacrifice for the crown, they could not in conscience drag the peasantry into an undertaking of which there was no chance of success. These latter were stigmatised by the advocates for war by the nickname of *Paucalliers*, from a sort of vegetable which makes rapid growth and then suddenly perishes away.

Marshal Baumont had been appointed commander-in-chief of the royal armies, and had been at Nantes since the 19th May; but the duchess, impatient of delay, gave the signal for insurrection without asking his advice. The marshal hesitated to countermand

The Duchess de Berri—Brave conduct of the peasants

her order; but disapproving of so great precipitancy, resolved to wait for further instructions from the royalist committee then sitting in Paris. M. de Chateaubriand, one of the members of that committee, sent her a letter conjuring her to depart at once from France, and strongly deprecating the insurrection. Acting on that opinion, the marshal enjoined his officers to do nothing without further orders, and persuaded the duchess to leave the country. She consented, but retracted her determination; and at length a general taking of arms was arranged for the night of the 3d and 4th of June. In the interim an important seizure of documents relating to the insurrection was made at the Chateau of La Chasliere, the residence of M. de L'Aubessin; but this mischance did not prevent the execution of the plan; and on the 4th, at two in the morning, the tocsin sounded in a vast number of towns and villages. The Chouans, however (for in 1832 all the insurgents were so named), assembled in very small numbers. Here five hundred, there six hundred peasants, in another place four hundred, were the largest bodies engaged with the soldiery; and in other places smaller numbers still were all that could be mustered. The struggle was insignificant from the beginning, and can hardly be said to have commenced, when it was altogether extinguished. But although the numbers were so small, the bravery of the few was worthy of the reputation they had inherited from their fathers. To terminate the history of this campaign, it remains but to relate the details of one combat that would not have disgraced the heroes of the old wars.

The ancient chateau of La Penissière-de-la-Cour, near Clisson, was chosen as the rallying point for all the insurgents in the neighbouring communes. On the 6th June, 42 men assembled there; and Pinson, adjutant-major of the 29th regiment, obtaining information of their rendezvous, hoped to take the whole number prisoners. With this view he surrounded the chateau, and gave the signal for attack. The insurgents permitted the enemy to approach within twenty yards, firing at random upon the windows; they

Chapter XVI

then received them with a brisk and well-directed fire. The soldiers staggered and fell back; but they advanced to the attack a second time, when they were again repulsed. They still, however, kept up a wild sort of fusillade, while Pinson formed a corps of picked men, and attempted to set the chateau on fire. The gable end, having no apertures, could not be defended; and there the besieging party contrived to raise a ladder and mount the roof. They then burst through the tiles and set fire to the garrets. In a few moments all the upper part of the building was in a blaze; and the soldiers without, taking courage from the flames, commenced a fresh assault. Nothing daunted by their horrible position, the Chouans maintained a steady fire on the enemy; they cared not for the burning house, and thought of nothing but fighting. One of them who had a trumpet kept blowing martial airs to encourage his comrades; the best marksmen of whom quietly picked off the besiegers, while the others loaded their muskets. In this way a perpetual fire was kept up, and the soldiers fell back to avoid certain death.

It was now five o'clock in the evening, and the battle had lasted for some hours, when the chief of battalion, Georges, who was a very able and energetic officer, arrived and assumed the command. He gave orders to force the ground-floor, and set the house on fire from the bottom. The soldiers accordingly, preceded by a few sappers, marched up to the doors, and after the sappers had beaten down the panels with their hatchets, rushed into the interior. The Chouans had now retired to the first story, and having made holes in the floor, they fired down upon the heads of the besiegers with murderous precision. The Blues rushed out immediately from their unseen foes, pursued by the gallant Chouans, shouting, *Vive Henri V!* and the trumpeter blowing blasts of triumph. However, they quickly rally and dash again into the house, armed with burning torches of pitch and dry wood. Now the hapless Vendeans find themselves enveloped in flame—it is beneath their feet—it is above their heads! Yet they slack not in their fire, and the trumpet is as

Brave conduct of the peasants at Penissière-de-la-Cour

shrill as ever. But the Blues now stand to their arms. They are content to wait. They are satisfied that there is no escape for the men whose dauntless courage has so long kept them at bay. However, the besieged are far from thinking their position so desperate, and resolve on a sally. Thirty-four of them rush out by the garden-door, and all, except six who are slain, contrive to get off. Eight remain in the chateau, and there continue their fire with the same coolness, though they are in momentary danger of a horrible death. The soldiers now enter the building, in order to be on equal terms with them; but they take refuge in a sort of loft, the staircase to which is still standing, and the entry to it they defend with such fury, that the commandant, Georges, withdrew his men, that he might not expose the *élite* of his battalion to inevitable death. And now the flames enveloped the whole building from pavement to roof-tree, the timbers fell in, and the Blues, hearing no cry, concluded that the Chouans were buried in the burning mass, and retired at nine in the evening with their dead and wounded. At midnight those brave men, half-suffocated with smoke and exhausted with the heat of the chateau and the fatigues of their fight, left the ruins. They had found a shelter beneath a niche in the massive wall, and the blazing embers had spared them in their hiding-place. The number of men under the command of Georges amounted to twelve or fifteen hundred, two hundred and fifty of whom are said to have been killed; while the forty-two Chouans, who had been originally attacked in the chateau, only lost the six men who were slain in the garden. This immense disproportion is owing to the excellence of the Chouan marksmen and the cover behind which they were posted.

If the bravery of the insurgents of 1832 recalls the memory of the old Vendeans, the cruelty of the republicans was not unworthy of their revolutionary predecessors. On the 2d June, General Dermoncourt wrote to the military authorities throughout the country *to take no prisoners*. The order was nowhere rigorously

Chapter XVI

obeyed, yet the laws of war were sometimes shamefully violated. Jacques Cathelineau, son of the general-in-chief of the grand army, had been chosen to command the insurgents of Anjou, under the orders of D'Autichamp. Forgetting that the Bourbons, for whom he had fought in 1815, had remembered neither his own services nor the glory of his father, he agreed, against his better judgment, to second the insurrection. But, as a marked man, he was compelled to remain in hiding till the moment for commencing hostilities. However, his retreat was discovered by the enemy. Concealed with two friends under a trap-door, he heard the soldiers beating furiously at the gate of the house; and fearing to be discovered and murdered, he resolved to give himself up. The Marquis of Curac, who was one of the three, would have shown himself first; but Cathelineau insisted on taking the honour and peril. Then raising the trap-door, he said, "We are unarmed—do not fire—we surrender!" "Fire!" cried Regnier, the commanding officer; and when the men hesitated to obey the bloody order, he seized a musket and executed it himself. Cathelineau fell mortally wounded. A few days afterwards, a lady, Mademoiselle de Roberie, the daughter of one of the insurgent chiefs, took refuge from the soldiers in her father's chateau; they placed the muzzle of a musket at her head and shot her dead on the spot. A more ruthless murder was not committed in the worst days of the infernal columns.

On the failure of the insurrection, the Duchess de Berri attempted to fly the country. Again assuming the disguise of a peasant, she proceeded to Nantes, from which she hoped to escape to England. Her faithful companion through all these vicissitudes was Mademoiselle Eulalie de Kersabuc. The royal lady, unable to bear the fatigue of the thick shoes worn by the common people, was compelled to walk barefoot, and to smear her ancles with the black mud, in order to hide the whiteness of her skin, which might have betrayed her. She gained Nantes in safety; but the details of her life there, her arrest and captivity, do not belong to this history.

Death of the son of Cathelineau—The end

She was the victim of an error of which nothing could ever disabuse the royalists. The writers, orators, and politicians of that party never could see the true character of the Vendean wars. For nearly forty years they had transformed the Vendean and Breton peasants into mere defenders of the divine right of kings. Without denying the profoundly religious spirit of the West, they had refused to view its volunteers as leagued in the Church's cause; and the duchess naturally believed that her simple presence would be sufficient to raise an army. From the very first her error became apparent. The peasants refused to rise. They were more occupied with the interests of the altar than of the throne, and religion did not appear to them to be endangered. "Our greatest obstacle," cried one of the most ardent partisans of royalty, in a moment of anger, "is those priests, who will not put themselves at our head. If the soldiers of Louis Philippe do not rip up a dozen of them, we shall never make these obstinate Vendeans move a step." The clergy considered it their duty to remain neuter; and the people, satisfied as to the safety of the Church while their pastors deemed it unnecessary to strike a blow in its defence, and somewhat weaned of their attachment to the monarchy by their experience of its ingratitude, kept to the labours of the field, and abstained from participation in the attempt of the duchess. The experience of the years that have passed since that time has given them no reason to regret their choice. They are in the full enjoyment of their religion; the representative of the illustrious family of Larochejacquelein has formally attached himself to the government of the present emperor; and the Vendeans are happy in the liberty of the Church under the judicious rule of the third Napoleon.

THE LITTLE CHOUANNERIE

Chapter I

The College of Vannes.

THE WAR WHICH the Vendeans so heroically sustained, in defence of their faith, against all the forces of republican and infidel France, whatever success may have attended their efforts, was most disastrous as respected the religious state of the insurgent provinces. The priests were faithful to the Church, and refused the constitutional oath, but it was at the cost of banishment or death; and the people were deprived of the ministry of their pastors in consequence of that very fidelity. But for the presence of a few of the clergy, who preferred the dangers of the army to the safety of a foreign shore, the population must have grown up without the sacraments, and with no more of religion than the parents might have been able to impart in the uncertain intervals of peace. As it was, there were to be found in many parishes young men and women who had scarcely seen their church used except as a barrack or a storehouse, who had never heard Mass except on the moor or in the forest, who had been familiar with scenes of blood and violence from their earliest years; and who, although taught that all this fighting was in defence of their religion, must have little understood what it was for which their fathers were contending.

The College of Vannes

When, therefore, upon the accession of Napoleon to the consulate, the Catholic religion was re-established, the Vendeans looked forward to the return of the priests with a twofold joy. They exulted in the prospect that they should see their ruined churches rebuilt and the old rites restored; they exulted also in the hope that their children would be brought up as Christians, and instructed in the faith for which they had all suffered so much.

Yet, when their priests began to return, with what bitter disappointment was their cup of joy mixed! How many places were vacant in that faithful band! Many who had been driven away in the hour of persecution had died in foreign lands, weighed down with sorrow and shame at the ruin of God's heritage. And of those who were living to enjoy their recal, and hallow the triumph which their flocks had won, there were few who were not feeble and decrepit. Grown old in banishment, they had come back but to die. Thus many parishes looked in vain for their pastor; others saw him return unfit for his duties. And notwithstanding the nominal restoration of the Church, the most sanguine of the friends of religion were in despair at its prospects. For the immediate exigencies of the time were by no means the whole, or even the worst part of the evil. The fate of the next generation could not be viewed but with the gravest apprehension. Where was the nursery from which the ranks of the priesthood could be recruited? Was the First Consul a man on whom the Church could rely in a matter of such vital importance? The whole resources of the province had been exhausted by the civil war. There were neither funds for the erection of seminaries, nor professors to fill the chairs of public instruction; and it was to be feared that there would be a lack of candidates for the ministry.

Happily this latter fear proved groundless. The wisest men predicted another and not distant day of trial, when fresh palms might be gathered by the servants of the altar; and the very mothers, notwithstanding their bloody experience of the past, were ambitious

Chapter I

of the perilous distinction for their children. Candidates flocked in; in default of regular seminaries, each parsonage became a college, and each priest a professor; and in 1804 the famous college at Vannes, the capital of Morbihan in Brittany, which had been dissolved in 1791, was reopened for the education of the future clergy, and in a very short time numbered five or six hundred pupils.

In that college many of the greatest sufferers of the revolution had been trained, and it was now established again with all its old traditions unimpaired. The professors who had departed returned to resume their former functions, and even some of the former scholars came back to complete their course. Twelve Chouan chiefs, four of them chiefs of battalion, whose studies had been broken off by the dissolution of the college, presented themselves after ten years of civil war, during which their original vocation had only been suspended, humbly to finish their apprenticeship, that they might at length serve God peacefully at the altar, whom they had served so valiantly on the field. By their thick beards and wrinkled brows they might have been taken for the fathers of their fellow-students, who looked up to them with the reverence of sons, not for their greater age, but for their heroic actions. They did not, indeed, remain long in the college; the life of sacrifice and devotion which they had led for so many years had trained them for their vocation, and their novitiate was abridged as much out of respect for their character as by the necessity of providing for the wants of the diocese. But before going, they had inspired the boys with their own enthusiasm; each new-comer caught the infection; the whole college espoused the cause of the Chouannerie, and preserved its spirit from generation to generation by an unfailing tradition; so that eleven years afterwards, when our story commences, it was found flourishing in all its original earnestness.

At first the principles thus propagated found their only expression in the collection of annals of the Chouannerie. The lads fed their love of the cause by hunting up every scrap of history, every anecdote and legend, every story of personal prowess and miraculous escape, which the villages of Morbihan could furnish; and as there was scarcely a parish which was not represented at the college, a great mass of local tradition was brought together, and again distributed over the country as the boys dispersed at the vacations. This was, perhaps, of little or no public consequence, so long as merely narratives of the past were so circulated; but when military despotism had put itself into open hostility to religion, the part which the scholars were enabled to play as publishers of intelligence in their several parishes acquired a great importance. Through them the old priests conveyed their warning to the people; and upon the suppression of the newspapers by the imperial police, the network formed by the scholars supplied the means of communication between different parts of the country. In this way the Bretons became acquainted with the aggression of the government upon the Sovereign Pontiff, and of the bull of excommunication which the Pope had launched against the emperor and his abettors,—facts which the authorities would gladly have concealed from the western provinces. And thus it was, indirectly, that all the resistance to the laws of the emperor which distinguished the period between 1808 and 1814 originated. The scholars of Vannes became famous throughout the country, as at once reflecting and fomenting the general exasperation.

Nor were there wanting private and personal grounds for the animosity of the boys against the government; for an imperial catechism was imposed upon all teachers of youth, in which obedience to the emperor and his dynasty was made almost a matter of salvation. This catechism, although it received the cardinal-legate's approbation, caused great dissatisfaction among the royalists of the west. But this was not the only grievance of which the scholars had to complain. Their vacations had become positive times of mourning. In the sea-side parishes the women were for the most part widows, the children orphans; for their husbands and fathers

Chapter I

were in the blockaded squadrons, or languishing in the prisons of England. In the country parishes things were still worse, on account of the severity of the conscription; so that the scholars had to return to homes wasted by the unpopular wars in which the emperor was engaged.

The government, always jealous of Catholic education, further incurred their indignation by the abolition of two festivals, which from time immemorial had been kept in every school and seminary in France: one, the feast of St. Catherine, the 25th November, for the pupils of philosophy; the other, the feast of St. Nicholas, the 6th December, for all scholars. In lieu of these time-honoured holidays, Napoleon appointed a day in honour of Charlemagne, founder of the university system as well as of the empire. The pupils of Vannes repudiated the name of the great emperor; as often as the 25th November came round, the class of philosophy played truant, in defiance of the threats and reproaches which were certain to be launched against them on the morrow. The annual protest against the suppression of the feast of St. Nicholas was not made with the same spirit or the same unanimity: first, because the children of the lower classes were hardly bold enough to brave their masters; and secondly, because the tragic death of a scholar on the 6th December 1809, who had been surprised alone by his enemies near the cemetery of St. Patern, a church in the suburbs, had made the day rather one of sorrow than of rejoicing.

These enemies, of whom no mention has as yet been made, belonged to the revolutionary *bourgeoisie* of the town, who regarded with bitter hatred the Catholic demonstrations of the college. In Vannes was a large tobacco manufactory, in which a number of strangers were employed as workmen; and these made common cause with the partisans of government in the town. Between them and the scholars,—the "town" and the "gown,"—occurred very serious collisions. The slightest insult offered by a republican to the youngest scholar was regarded by the rest as a declaration of war, and the next morning hostilities took place which sometimes called for the interference of the gendarmes. As early as the year 1805, while the old Chouans were yet at the college, this feud had become alarming. A boy was attacked on the quay during the night, and about to be thrown into the river, when some soldiers, attracted by his cries, came up very opportunely and rescued him. No search, however, was made for the cowardly miscreants who had perpetrated the outrage, although the poor lad was at first supposed to be mortally wounded; but not the less deep were the vows of vengeance uttered by his companions. The police were immediately on the alert to prevent an encounter; but a pitched battle was fought, and the belligerent parties were only separated by a picket of gendarmes whom the principal, unable himself to exercise any control over the heated passions of his pupils, had apprised of the disturbance. From that time forward continual and often bloody affrays took place, in spite of the opposition of the principal and the threats of the municipal authorities; and on the 6th December 1809, a lad was brutally murdered by the workmen. On this account St. Nicholas' Day was thenceforward an anniversary of mourning. But St. Catherine's Day was always kept by the young rebels. She was held in veneration by the class of philosophy, because through her four-and-twenty philosophers had received the grace of conversion, and eventually the crown of martyrdom.

The majority of the pupils who attended the lectures of the college were lodged in quiet houses in the suburbs, kept chiefly by pious women, who took as much care of the souls as of the bodies of their young charges, and exercised as much influence through their example as their words. Based entirely on moral persuasion, their authority always sufficed to restrain the unruly, and was often delegated to one of the senior boys. He arranged the times of study and recreation of the others, read the morning and evening prayers aloud, took them to Mass, and kept order in the dormitory and refectory. The habit of monthly confession rendered stricter

Chapter I

surveillance than this unnecessary. Unseemly acts and words were unknown among the lads, who always kept in mind the holy profession for which they were intended.

The school which had thus espoused so warmly the Royalist and Catholic cause received the news of the restoration of Louis XVIII. in 1814 with the enthusiasm that might have been expected. In the year 1813 the students had shared the general gloom that pervaded the whole of France; and in Easter 1814 they went home for the vacation, not knowing whether on their return they should not find their college and their country passed into the hands of strangers.

Eight days afterwards, a group of scholars from the neighbourhood of Lorient were walking early in the morning along the road from Port Louis to Marlévenez, and singing aloud to attract the attention of their schoolfellows, some of whom had promised to join them on their way, when all at once they saw approaching a horseman at full gallop with a white cockade in his hat, and crying *Vive le Roi!* It may be imagined with what surprise they heard the magic words; instantly they formed themselves in double file, and marched forward bearing aloft a white handkerchief on a pole. As they advanced they found that the news had spread like wildfire through the country. The inhabitants of Auray seemed mad with joy, and received them with acclamations as they entered the town. At their head walked a boy of the name of Le Tiec, an untiring singer, one of those extraordinary *improvisateurs* who are so common among the villages of Brittany. He burst forth into wild and picturesque songs; and at the end of each stanza the whole school joined in the chorus, and announced their coming to the imperialists of Vannes long before they were in sight. At length they entered the town, and marched up the *grande place*. Their old enemies watched the procession with sinister looks, but durst no longer give vent to their anger; and without pausing, the boys entered the cathedral to take part in the *Domine salvum fac Regem* that was to be sung after Benediction, and to protect the service from a threatened interruption of the Blues.

It was then that the scholars conceived for the first time the idea of military organisation, in order to figure with more effect in the fêtes and rejoicings which were to follow. Each class formed itself into a company, the officers of which were elected by the soldiers, and constituted a kind of council, which held its sittings in public. There was something intensely ludicrous in the gravity with which all this was conducted. When the important affair of the election of a commander-in-chief came on, the whole school split into two factions. One party declared for Aliz, a little fellow who could talk like a military proclamation, but had little dignity of manner, the other for the great Nicholas, who was a tall youth, and would, as they said, give an air of majesty to the troops, though he had not the fluent eloquence of his rival. At last, after a hard poll, Nicholas was elected. He owed his elevation to the expected visit of a prince of the blood, who, it was determined, should take away with him an impression of a manly regiment of scholars. The prince came—the Duke d'Angoulême—and fêtes were held; but the scholars were neglected, their harangue was not delivered, their music was not heard, their evolutions were not performed.

This disappointment was soon forgotten, and a more profound impression than any fêtes could produce was made in their hearts by two solemn religious ceremonies which were celebrated in the Cathedral of Vannes; one a funeral service performed on the occasion of the interment in consecrated ground of the victims of Quiberon, whose remains had lain for twenty years barely covered by a little earth on the sea-shore; the other a requiem for the repose of the soul of Louis XVI., sung upon the 21st January 1815, the twenty-second anniversary of the royal martyr's death. Then first were they made acquainted with all the details of that affecting tragedy; for the history of the revolution and its crimes was but imperfectly known to the scholars. Any works that would have

Chapter I

supplied them with such information had been carefully excluded from the library at Vannes, and it was not till the restoration that they knew all that the murdered king had suffered. They assisted at the Mass for his soul, as at the canonisation of a saint. Their old enemies, who had joined in the massacre at Quiberon, and had exulted over the murder of the king, viewed these exhibitions of Catholic loyalty with ill-disguised anger; and when the event of the 20th March placed them again in the ascendant, they were not slow to retaliate upon the boys for the fresh insults they had received.

Upon the first news of the landing of Napoleon from Elba, the scholars, calling to mind their military pretensions, assembled tumultuously in the quadrangle; and after a short debate, decided upon drawing up a petition to the minister of war demanding to be supplied with arms and led against the invader. Count Floriac, then prefect of the department, was intrusted to deliver the petition,—a commission which he received with a respectful admiration and a significant movement of the head that the boys were at a loss to interpret. Their innocent hearts could not conceive the possibility of the defection of the marshals and generals who had sworn allegiance to the new monarch, and concluded the Count to mean that the invader would be repulsed before their application could arrive. Rejoiced at the prospect of his easy overthrow, they nevertheless went home for the Easter vacation not a little chagrined at having missed so good an opportunity of winning their spurs.

Chapter II

Insubordination of the scholars—They arm, and join the insurgents.

UNDETERRED by the significant events of the last ten years of the eighteenth century, the new government ventured to brave the spirit of the western provinces by decrees which were certain to elicit a hostile movement. A conscription was set on foot, an oath of fidelity imposed, from which the priests were not exempted, and the tricolor was ordered to be substituted for the white flag on the parish steeples. Of the general consternation which followed these decrees, the scholars were witnesses during the vacation; and they returned to Vannes boiling with indignation, and eager to distinguish themselves by some desperate achievement.

The professor of mathematics at the college, who was in very bad odour with the boys on account of his imperialist predilections, first lit the spark of actual insurrection. One day, after goading his scholars to madness by his insufferable air of triumph, he had the audacity to walk across the court before the very eyes of the young royalists parading an enormous tricolor cockade. They resented the insult by rushing with loud cries upon the enemy, and rolling his hat with its offensive appendage in the mud. Complaints were made to the local authorities; but the poor principal, anxious to compromise the matter, drew up a sort of lame apology, which he prevailed upon one of the boys to read to the prefect in the name of the college.

The professors of the school, afraid of incurring the anger of the imperialists, yet anxious to conciliate their pupils, endeavoured

Chapter II

to steer a middle course between the two parties. This produced a constant controversy between the upper boys and their masters; and protestations were perpetually being made against some fresh act of concession to the usurping power. When any such protestation had to be made, some boy was chosen for spokesman who was at the head of the class, and who wore in token of that priority a little cross of silver with *fleurs-de-lis*. This symbol, at once Catholic and royal, the prefect of the department ordered to be changed for the imperial eagle. The poor principal, although he knew what an effect this order would produce upon the boys, durst not refuse to enforce it, as such an act would be considered tantamount to rebellion. He endeavoured, therefore, to effect the change by a stratagem. He began by being extremely bland and affectionate; and then said to a little boy of the name of Rio,* who wore the decoration, and who owed to that circumstance the important part which he subsequently played, "My good friend, give me that cross; I will return it to you in a few days." At these words every eye was fixed upon the lad upon whom had devolved the duty of expressing the general feeling. The little fellow well knew that all his companions dreaded to see him submit; and he said, proudly, "Sir, I have to tell you, in the name of all my companions, that you had better keep your eagles to yourself, unless you wish us to tread them under our feet. We will not change our decoration as often as some people change their cockades (this was in allusion to the professor's having worn a very tiny tricolor cockade); and our breasts are not made to be soiled by what we consider an emblem of apostasy." The school was silent at this audacious reply; but the little orator could read in all faces an applause more flattering than any cheers would have been. The poor principal stammered out a few words of menace, and then drew from his pocket a lecture ready written on the inevitable ruin which their obstinacy would bring upon the college.

* Since favourably known to the world as the author of *La Poésie de l'Art Chrétienne*, and of other interesting works.

Insubordination of the scholars

These events were not unknown out of doors; and many of the townsmen secretly approved of the resistance of the boys, without, however, giving them any encouragement. But their old enemies were infuriated, and loudly demanded vengeance. They required of the prefect of the department the immediate expulsion of one hundred scholars; and at any rate insisted on an *amende honorable* to the imperial symbol. The prefect, who was unwilling to drive matters to extremities, passed over the first demand; but was compelled to concede the last,—the only difficulty being as to the mode of making the said reparation. No one supposed that the scholars would ever do homage to the eagle, or wear it on their breasts; how, then, extort from them the semblance of a submission they could never be induced really to pay? Their ingenuity devised a notable expedient.

In the dead of night, armed with ladders and paint-pots, cunning artists were despatched to paint over the college gateway a colossal eagle—an eagle worthy of the empire—an eagle whose outspread wings should extend as far as the wall would allow. The next morning the scholars who lodged in the town assembled as the bell rang, and the first object which met their eyes was this gigantic bird staring at them from its inaccessible height; while streets and windows were filled with spectators curious to see the young royalists pass under the yoke, and rejoicing in the prospect of a laugh at their expense.

But instead of entering the college, they all stood outside discussing the state of affairs, and at length formed into a series of semicircles round the object of their wrath, the townsmen wondering the while what was coming next. It had rained hard in the night, and the feet of some hundreds of scholars soon worked up the road into a thick paste. At a given signal all threw down their books and their dinners, and gathering the mud in their hands, discharged a heavy battery on the bird. Gradually it disappeared from the light of day, in five minutes not a feather was to be seen;

Chapter II

and then, with triumph in their faces, and *non indecoro pulvere sordidi*,* they went to their classes, where the masters were awaiting them, trembling with terror at the audacity of the young rebels for whose good conduct they were responsible.

The indignation of the Blues may be conceived; they would have put the whole school to the sword, if General Rousseau, who commanded the forces in the department, had not restrained their intolerance; and the most that they could obtain from him was that an expedition half-civil half-military should be despatched, part with sponges and hot water, to wash the bird, and a little varnish with which to touch him up again as good as new, and the rest with muskets and bayonets, to defend their comrades while they were engaged in this interesting operation. Furthermore two sentinels were left to mount guard night and day over the eagle so renovated.

But the next morning the noble bird, the object of all this care, appeared with a black band round its neck, as it were to be hanged, and its body in divers places blotched with ink. A ladder was immediately raised to remove the stains; but the marks were indelible, and the disfigurement was only increased. It appears that a scholar, whose name was never discovered, had approached the sentinels at night in the guise of an apothecary's lad. On being seized, there was found upon his person what they at first mistook for a horse-pistol; but on examination it proved to be a syringe of a particular sort, with which, he said, he had been sent to a sick person next door; and while the guards were laughing at their mistake, he discharged the squirt at the luckless bird and made off.

After this the townspeople left their eagle to its fate. It still expanded its scored wings across the gateway, still stretched out its inky neck; but the scholars rather regarded it as a trophy of victory, and began to consider their cause victorious. But in the height of their fancied security, an event occurred of a far more serious

---

* "Soiled with no dishonourable dust."

nature. It was early spring, when the fields were full of white blossoms, and white ones only. Three of the boys were returning home from a ramble, with their hats adorned, according to an immemorial custom, with white sprigs, and without the least idea of giving offence. However, as they passed through the streets the townspeople regarded it as a royalist manifestation, and a crowd collected around them; while some of their foes endeavoured to rouse the officers of the garrison, by pointing with fierce gesticulations from the unhappy eagle on the other side of the road to the white flowers in the lads' hats. In the crowd was a young rascal, who had been lately expelled from the college for theft, and a year afterwards was put into the pillory on that very spot before being sent to the galleys. As soon as he saw the flowers, he thought a favourable time was come for taking his revenge. Crying *A bas les brigands*, he set a number of idle and vicious lads upon the three scholars. Two of the three immediately ran away; but the third, a brave fellow named Lamenach, disdaining to fly, manfully stood his ground, and began by laying three or four of his assailants in the mud. A mob immediately collected; and Lamenach was fighting his way through, when a picket of gendarmes came up and led him off to the mayor's prison.

The scholars, hearing what had befallen Lamenach, rushed into the town; and were met by the women, who told them with tears and lamentations that the least the poor prisoner could expect was to be tried overnight and shot on the Garenne in the morning. With General Rousseau in the town such a catastrophe could not occur; but it was reported that groans and blows had been heard to proceed from the guard-room; and the scholars were frantic at the thought that their companion should be subjected to ill-treatment without a trial. Some of the most eager would have rushed upon the bayonets of the guard, and carried the prison with their sticks. However, a little boy with blue eyes and light hair, not appearing a very formidable "brigand," had contrived to obtain a sight of the

Chapter II

prisoner, and perceived him lying quietly on a camp-bed conversing with his sentinel. This intelligence, which was true, pacified the boys for a time; but a horrible scene had already taken place.

The officers who had arrested Lamenach, to magnify the importance of the service, had represented the offence of the prisoner as a conspiracy against government; and orders were received from the minister of war to compel him by all possible means to reveal the names of his accomplices who had escaped. Upon the strength of these instructions, the poor boy was tortured and maltreated by the brutal gendarmes till the blood gushed from his mouth from some internal rupture; and still, with a heroism that would have done credit to a maturer age, he refused to divulge the names of his companions. Even when he was threatened with immediate death,—and they made a show of conducting him to execution,—still he adhered to his refusal. After some days' confinement and ill-usage in the Petit Couvent he was taken to the college, where all the scholars were drawn up for the ceremony; and then the principal read out his sentence, which was that he should be expelled the college, prevented for ever from entering the university, and ordered to leave the town within twenty-four hours.

Lamenach, restored to liberty, threw himself into the arms of his companions, and then set off for his native village, where other trials awaited him as severe as those from which he had escaped. The news of his disgrace had preceded him, and the curé of the parish, being one of those who had taken the constitutional oath, had denounced him from the altar. On entering the village, therefore, he met only sullen looks. At a farm-house where he asked for a drop of milk, the woman threatened to set the dog at him. His father received him with silence and in consternation. Still, after two or three days at home, he thought the worst over, when a picket of gendarmes came to summon him before the mayor of the commune. The mayor offered him a choice of three things: either to return to Vannes, on condition of crying *Vive l'Empereur!* in the court before all his companions; or to go to the Lycée at Pontivy, where he would have to make a profession of political faith in the government; or to be enrolled as a common soldier in the emperor's service. "Well," said Lamenach, "if there be no alternative but conscription or dishonour, a conscript I will be; but from this moment count me a deserter." With that he rushed out by a back-door; and before the gendarmes knew where he was, he had gained the neighbouring forest.

In his state of health this action was tantamount to voluntary death; and if his adventure had not that tragical termination, it was owing to the humanity of the gendarmes, who gave him secret information that if he liked to return home, and merely absent himself once a week, they would make their domiciliary visit on that day, and continue their connivance till his health was restored. And this was done.

In the college this event made a profound impression, and the scholars came to resolutions which may appear too romantic to belong to the region of fact. But the details we are narrating are from the mouth of an eye-witness and participator in the whole affair; and be it remembered the scholars were of an age when the warm blood laughs at difficulty and danger, and has little sense of the ridiculous. Outside the college they formed a little republic, with its own laws and traditions. The authority of the professors, paramount as it was in the chair, vanished when they descended from it; and the parents were too distant to exercise over their children any control, and had too much confidence in them to be afraid that they would abuse their liberty. Thus abandoned to themselves in all that did not immediately concern their studies, the boys were subject to none of those rules by which experience restrains enthusiasm; they had only a consciousness of the justice of their cause and a strong sense of right and wrong.

Any stranger who had mingled with them on the night of the outrage on Lamenach, would have been speechless with

Chapter II

astonishment at all he saw and heard;—a knot of beardless boys, with teeth set and visages pale with rage, speaking seriously of an armed insurrection, and deliberately weighing the relative dangers of remaining quiet and taking up arms against the government. "Lamenach," it was thus they argued, "had been condemned in defiance of all law. His case might any day be theirs; there was not one of them but was equally liable to blows and imprisonment: why not, therefore, openly rebel? They could scarcely be in greater danger as declared insurgents than as disaffected scholars; they could only secure safety by abandonment of principle, which was not to be thought of." It was decided, therefore, that from that day forward they would assume an air of outward resignation, as if they had been cowed by the example of Lamenach, and remain in college two or three weeks while they were organising their conspiracy; for which purpose a provisional committee was immediately named, consisting of Rio and three or four others of the head boys.

Quixotic as their project seems, the young conspirators proceeded to put it in force with the utmost despatch. They selected their committee, chose their captain, and proceeded to the discussion of ways and means. In all these transactions the greatest secrecy was observed; and although every boy in the school knew that something was going on, not a hint of the conspiracy reached either the professors within or the authorities without.

Their great difficulty lay in procuring arms and ammunition. At first they thought that their united pocket-money for the quarter, together with the produce of the sale of whatever they could dispose of, would suffice for the equipment of three hundred "men." But they soon discovered their mistake: and they had considerable trouble in disposing of their property; for their financial operations being necessarily clandestine, not to arouse the suspicions of their foes, were retarded by the scruples of the purchasers, who could not divine the meaning of such a number of mysterious transactions, and were fearful of becoming receivers of stolen goods.

They arm, and join the insurgents

Not less difficulty had they in the secret purchase of weapons. Some of the boys were bold enough to tempt the probity, or rather the sobriety of the garrison; and others were clever enough to effect an exchange of a glass of brandy for a packet of cartridges; for they reckoned among their number some who were quite up in the diplomacy of the café. But all that they could obtain of any value was five or six muskets; and the committee were compelled to put up with fowling-pieces, pistols, and any other sort of weapon which could be procured, upon the understanding that they were to be substituted for more warlike arms after the first victory.

By little and little stores were collected, though not so rapidly as their ardour would have desired; and as they were obtained, were carefully secreted in a hiding-place outside the town. They then set about their drill. "Every thing," they said, "depends upon drill; without drill our weapons are useless." Accordingly they diligently watched the exercises of the conscripts, and at daybreak rose to imitate them. When the garrison-troops paraded, they were there to look on; nor were they above taking a lesson from the clumsy movements of the national guard. They got on very well; but they were sadly in want of a sergeant. A regular drill-sergeant would have been worth his weight in muskets. But how to procure one? how apply without giving rise to inconvenient inquiries? Evidently the advantages were outbalanced by the danger.

There was among the officers of the garrison a good-natured Gascon, an imperialist heart and soul; but very kind to the boys, whose spirit he admired, and whose sufferings he pitied. This brave servant of the empire became the instructor of the scholars, only they received his lessons at second-hand. The youngest of the executive committee, the little Rio, went to him, and told him that he had been ordered by the medical man to practise the broadsword exercise every day as hard as a recruit. Would monsieur have the goodness to be his master? The lad looked ill: it was not uncommon for doctors to order their pupils a course of gymnastics. With all

Chapter II

his heart; they would begin tomorrow; and at break of day master and pupil met in the Salle d'Armes, for a good hour's lesson before the subaltern's parade. And this went on for some weeks. About dusk the pupil turned master, and in some vault or corridor assembled a dozen champions, armed with sticks for muskets, and taught them as he had been taught himself; and all with a serious face which it was impossible to look at without laughing. When the first dozen were perfect, another advanced; and so on, till the troops had all practised, by which time the young sergeant was thoroughly exhausted.

The next question which suggested itself, and which perhaps has occurred to the reader, was how to begin: what was to be the first step? The plan of hanging out a white flag, and declaring themselves in insurrection in a country full of troops, had been proposed in the first heat of enthusiasm, but was too absurd to be seriously entertained. And to do them justice, the committee proceeded with a discretion really incomprehensible in such mere youths. They rarely held their sittings twice in the same place; they had succeeded in obtaining arms for a great portion of their body; and they had ascertained that arms were to be had in the neighbouring villages for the asking, as soon as they were in open revolt. They now determined to wait for the departure from the town of the troops who had been ordered to join the main army against Wellington. This took place towards the end of April. But even when these were gone, there remained enough to crush them at a single blow; and they were sharp enough to see that their success depended on the immediate co-operation of the rural population. To secure this, some glorious achievement must first be performed by themselves.

After a long deliberation, they determined to scale Fort Penthièvre, which was only defended by a feeble garrison of veterans. A rapid march across country at night would bring them there in six hours; and they might perhaps carry the place before the astonished garrison discovered by daylight that there was scarcely a

They arm, and join the insurgents

musket in the hands, or a beard on the chin of one of their assailants. Ladders and victuals were to be procured in the neighbouring villages. The successful execution of this design would, they were certain, act like magic on the inflammable peasantry, and produce a general rising.

When all was ready for the expedition, no one could be found to undertake the command in whom they had any confidence. They felt that more was required to scale a fortified place than mere enthusiasm, and none of the lads possessed the requisite qualifications. At length, in the simplicity of his heart, Rio, the young drill-sergeant, bethought him of his friend the Gascon, and gravely proposed to confide their secret to him, and offer him the command. The other scholars, with equal *naïveté*, considered this a very luminous idea, and the incredible negotiation was intrusted to its proposer. The astonishment of the imperial officer may be conceived, on receiving an invitation from three hundred schoolboys to head an attempt against a garrison of his own troops. Happily he was not the man to betray them; although he told them, that by concealing their conspiracy he became their accomplice, and exposed himself to be shot at the head of his regiment; and with tears he entreated them to abandon their insane attempt. When the lad returned, and reported the result of his interview, his friends shuddered at the escape they had had, and perceived that unless a leader could be found in their own ranks they had but a small selection to choose from.

The chateau of the Chevalier de Margadel was in sight,—a brave man, who had distinguished himself greatly in the Chouannerie. They resolved to offer the command to him, assured that they were at least in no danger in admitting him into their confidence. The chevalier embraced them with joy, informed them that the whole country was on the point of rising, and promised that the scholars of Vannes should take part in the general insurrection. But he impressed upon them the necessity of patience; for a premature blow would compromise the cause.

Chapter II

The scholars returned intoxicated with delight, and readily consented to wait till the proper moment had arrived. But after three tedious weeks, some of them became anxious to ascertain the real state of the peasantry, and for that purpose made a circuit of the neighbouring parishes. By day they found the population all engaged, as usual, in the labours of the field; and a superficial observer might have supposed the people the most peaceful in the world. But no sooner had the *Angelus* sounded, than every man turned over his musket, and began to burnish the rusty weapon; while the women repaired to some chapel dedicated to the holy Virgin or the patron saint of the parish, to pray for a blessing on the arms of their husbands, their lovers, or their sons.

Joyful as the tidings were which the exploring party brought home, they were less gladdening than the intelligence which awaited them on their return—that the day of departure was fixed at last. Through the kindness of an officer in the prefecture it was known that fifty of the ringleaders in the school were going to be seized, carried off to Belle-Isle, and enrolled in the colonial army. The list of proscription had already been drawn up, and would be published before long. Under an imperial government this was not a menace to be trifled with, and the Wednesday following was accordingly named for the declaration of hostilities.

If the republicans had been in the habit of attending church, they must have suspected that something was going on by the way in which the confessionals were thronged. The boys all crowded to the holy tribunal as to a first communion, although not with the same angelic serenity in their faces. To their great astonishment, and even scandal, some of the priests discountenanced the undertaking. Nevertheless, they left them free to follow their own conscience, dreading the consequence, but not forbidding the attempt; for most of them in the old Chouannerie had borne the crucifix on the battle-field.

Nor was confession their only act of preparation for the solemn duty, as they regarded it, upon which they were entering. They

They arm, and join the insurgents

bound themselves to each other by a solemn oath never to make peace with the usurper, and to die, if need were, sooner than desert a comrade. This oath was taken with all accessories that could render it more imposing. In a private chamber an altar was erected, upon which they set a crucifix and candles: they swore upon the holy Gospel; and the pupil who administered the oath was a seminarist, named Bainvel, who had already received the tonsure, and by his ecclesiastical habit gave a sort of religious character to the ceremony.

At length the long-expected day arrived. For the last forty-eight hours all the pupils had been in the secret; for it was necessary to select the three hundred who were to compose the expedition. The very youngest children were anxious to join, and stoutly avowed their perfect ability to endure the fatigues of a campaign. Some of them, indeed, announced their intention of following, if they were not permitted to accompany the rest; and they kept their word.

All assisted with great devotion at the first Mass. After which they proceeded to the classes as usual, as they were not to start till the evening. At length the college clock struck four, and closed the studies for the day. During the next two hours the young soldiers were making the last arrangements for their departure. They then left the town in different directions, pretending to be playing at some childish game in order to divert the attention of the sentinels at the gates. By seven o'clock almost all were outside the walls; and so little was their absence suspected, that the housekeepers got ready their supper as usual.

Thursday came, and passed without any tidings of the absentees; and still no importance was attached to the circumstance by the authorities of the town, nor did the professors feel any great uneasiness, as Thursday was generally spent by the scholars in the fields. The bell on Friday morning rung forth the regular summons just as the boys, who should have obeyed its call, were engaged in their first encounter with the Blues. The professors, on entering

Chapter II

the court, were stupefied at the mournful silence which reigned around. No pupils were to be seen but a few children and invalids. But at length they ascertained what had happened; for presently arrived the remains of the column which the boys had helped to rout, who reported that the Chouans had risen with all their old obstinate bravery, and had been joined by the scholars of Vannes; and that the latter had performed prodigies of valour. This news spread consternation among the imperialists of the town; and the arrival of the scholars to take vengeance upon them for the outrage on Lamenach was imminently expected. The authorities revenged themselves upon the Little Chouannerie by confiscating the revenues of their college and turning the building into a barrack.

Chapter III

Battles of St. Anne's, Redon, and Muzillac—Debarcation of arms and defeat at Auray—Victory at Plescop.

THROUGH the management of the Chevalier de Margadel the first movements of the scholars were combined with those of the principal corps, placed under the orders of General De Sol de Grisolles, who was to manœuvre about Auray and rally the several Chouan chiefs. But it was necessary that a demonstration should be made on the Nantes or Rennes road, to draw off the attention of the garrison of Vannes; and the scholars, who were not yet armed, were ordered to join the Count of Francheville, who was under arms at the head of a battalion of coastmen capable of encountering an equal number of the best troops which could be sent against them. This detachment was placed under the command of Le Quellec, a fine courageous young fellow, in spite of his feeble health. Thus for a short time the scholars were separated.

On leaving the college on Wednesday night, they marched directly to the chateau of the Chevalier de Margadel, whose eldest daughter served out to the boys white cockades and cartridges which she and her sisters had made with their own hands, thus giving an air of chivalry to the expedition that was not lost upon the young hearts of their champions. Towards midnight they arrived at the chateau of Pontsale, where they found a good supper waiting for them. But in the middle of their repast arrived an express to report the advance of a column of Blues from Baud to intercept their reinforcements. Two of the youngest scholars were instantly

Chapter III

despatched to mount guard a musket-shot from the chateau, on the edge of a little wood, with strict orders to fire on the head of the advancing column. They set off full of confidence, and proud of the trust committed to them; but it was not till the morning that the Blues passed by; and as it was not Margadel's intention to provoke an encounter, the boys were posted in a thick copse, where they could only be attacked at great disadvantage.

Besides this column from Baud, two others were reported, one from Lorient, the other from Pontivy, which sought to effect a junction about Auray, in order to suppress the incipient insurrection. The advance of these several detachments might have been checked by an unexpected attack from the scholars; but it was of more consequence not to miss the general rendezvous, and Margadel would not suffer time and ammunition to be wasted in a skirmish. He therefore pushed on across country to join the insurgent forces.

It is needless to speak of the joy with which the young heroes met the old Chouans, with whose names and story they had been so long familiar. It was the realisation of their brightest hopes, the consolidation of all their castles in the air; and when, upon the sounding of the *Angelus*, they witnessed the whole army on their knees, and the camp in a moment changed into a place of prayer, it seemed to them as if heaven had come down upon earth, and they had been transported into the midst of an army of angels.

That day, Thursday, passed without alarm. About sunset they got under arms, and at midnight came upon the track of the enemy. They followed him as far as St. Anne's, where they halted for food and rest. But they were roused from their repose by the approach of the Blues, under the guidance of a man evidently perfectly acquainted with the ground. The peasants immediately ranged themselves under their leaders. At the head was Gamber, a glorious old Chouan of tried valour, and much dreaded by the Blues. After Gamber came La Thiesse with the celebrated men of Bigrar, and last in the order of march were the coastmen of Auray, commanded by Joseph Cadoudal, brother of Georges.

The last column had not started when the advanced guard, under the command of a scholar, was already engaged. The lad conducted himself with wonderful nerve. Though wounded, and seeing men fall on all sides, he gave his orders with as much coolness as if he had been conducting a sham-fight at Vannes. The scholars occupied the centre, under Margadel; while Gamber on the left and La Thiesse endeavoured to place the enemy between two fires. But the latter failed in his movement, and a number of cowards turned and fled. The day was going badly, when Cadoudal came up, and joining the brave fellows who were still fighting firmly by the side of La Thiesse, by the impetuosity of his courage in twenty minutes changed the face of the battle.

But the ammunition of the Chouans was beginning to fail; the best-provided had only twelve or fifteen cartridges left, which would not last above half-an-hour. Unless, therefore, they could carry the day by a sudden blow, they must lose it. They accordingly dispersed themselves among the trees and ditches, to take a particular aim, so as to kill an enemy at each shot; for the Chouans were all good marksmen. This movement was rewarded with complete success. A cry of victory rose from the insurgents, the drums of the Blues ceased to beat, and their rout became general, the Chouans following in full pursuit. And bloody the retreat would have been, but that the ill-armed conquerors were more intent upon picking up weapons and ammunition dropped by their flying foes than in impeding their escape; although some followed even to the gates of Vannes. However, a few muskets were the only spoils.

Their most valuable prize, on account of the judicious use made of it, was the prisoners who fell into their power, and who were the flower of the enemy's army—old soldiers and *fédérés*, who would have sold the victory very dear if they had been better supported. As it was, they continued fighting long after the rest had run away;

Chapter III

and when they were captured, the barrels of their muskets were too hot to be touched. These men, being marched off to head-quarters, evidently supposed they were going to execution; and such an act, however brutal, would have been but a retaliation in kind for many similar atrocities perpetrated by the republicans,—nay, these very men had richly deserved it, for they had threatened to make a triumphal entry into Auray, each with a head upon his bayonet. But the Chouans were careful not to tarnish their first victory by cowardly reprisals. "Had you been the conquerors," said Cadoudal to the commanding officer of the Blues, who was one of the prisoners, "would you have done the same?" "It would have been my wish," he said, lowering his eyes; "I cannot say it would have been in my power."

This victory, doubly glorious to the Chouans for the valour with which it was won, and the mercy with which it was crowned, must be ascribed in a great measure to the religious character of the place. In choosing, or rather in accepting the village of St. Anne for the field of battle, they had more than doubled their chance of success. It is the national sanctuary of the province, to which many thousand pilgrims annually resort. On such a spot there was not one of the peasants who did not see an invisible arm fighting by his side. To the modest little chapel, at the risk of having to fight fasting, the scholars, and many of the old Chouans, had paid a visit early in the morning; and indeed were still at prayer when the cry of alarm was raised. And after the battle the concourse thither was greater still, when the peasants, stained with blood and dust, came to pay the vows they had made to St. Anne in the heat of the fight, and return their thanks for her assistance.

No time was to be lost in securing the good results which the battle of St. Anne promised. In spite of the briefness of the combat, almost all their ammunition was expended; and if the column which hung about Baud for several days had attacked them the same evening, a dispersion could alone have saved them from destruction. The danger would have been still greater if the garrison of Vannes, which was within three hours' march, had had courage to pursue them; but they were deterred by the exaggerated accounts of the strength of the new Chouannerie given by the runaways. They had thus a little respite, during which the insurrection spread over the whole country. The news of the victory was transmitted from village to village with the rapidity of a telegraph; and every where the ringing of church-bells, the distribution of white cockades, public dances, with royalist songs, defacing imperial eagles, and above all, the substitution of white flags for the tricolor on all the steeples on the Feast of Corpus Christi, bore witness to the popular excitement and sympathy with the insurgents. On that day the procession of the Blessed Sacrament took place with more than ordinary pomp and splendour; and the altars were all covered with lilies.

On the morning after the victory, the scholars who had shared it set off to join the detachment of their comrades under Le Quellec, who had encamped at Kercohan, eager to report the glorious news of their first engagement and victory. On their route the whole population turned out to greet them. The news of their spirited attempt had preceded them; and wherever they went they received the most enthusiastic applause, to the no small delight of the young soldiers. The country through which they passed seemed to be abandoned by the Blues. The gendarmes on duty had forsaken their quarters, and the excise officers had fled; so that the hateful impost on salt was no longer enforced,—a circumstance of itself sufficient to make the Little Chouannerie popular. Nevertheless, with so much to cheer them, they approached Kercohan with somewhat heavy hearts; for in dressing the wounded after the battle, they had found a young bourgeois bleeding to death from a shot in the crural artery, who could scarcely summon strength to ask whether his brother who was in the college at Vannes, had formed part of the troop against which he had fought. In spite of

Chapter III

reiterated assurances to the contrary, the dread of having, perhaps, been wounded by a brother's hand, embittered his last moments. His brother was at Kercohan and was, therefore, spared this terrible blow; but as he could not but regard every one of those who had shared the action as possibly the poor lad's murderer, they dreaded to meet him. Happily he was not at the camp. Of all the scholars, he only had gone to the work with a faint heart; and after the first nocturnal alarm, had fairly deserted.

On arriving at Kercohan, a treble voice called *"Qui vive?"* It belonged to the youthful sentinel, who was mounting guard with a very fierce expression of countenance and a cocked pistol. He was, however, scarcely impressed with all the importance of a sentinel's office; for he deserted his post in his eagerness to hear the news, and accompanied his old friends into the camp. Oh, the embraces, the long stories, the showing of wounds, and gabbling of tongues,— the all speaking at once and no one listening! If the enemy had come up at that moment, what more should we have had to say of the Little Chouannerie?

The departure of the whole party for the general rendezvous was fixed for the next evening, up to which time detached parties of Chouans came dropping in. All the newcomers had heard of the brave young scholars, and were eager to make their acquaintance. Their appearance, at first sight, not being very imposing, some equivocal compliments were passed upon their prowess. The coastmen of Rhuys, under Count Francheville, who were all very fine men, surveyed their pigmy comrades with immense contempt, and asked whether the requisite number of nurses had been engaged. The boys assumed a look of offended dignity, and wished to know whether courage was to be measured by height.

That evening they started, and marched all night and all the next day, by cross-roads, towards Ploermel, where they had heard that, after a short fusillade, a few Chouans had established themselves. But on arriving, the town was found evacuated, in consequence of intelligence that a column of the enemy, four thousand strong, had left Rennes with cavalry and cannon enough to cut them to pieces. All exhausted as they were with hunger and a twenty-four hours' march, there was nothing to be done but to press on to Josselin, where, notwithstanding the late hour of the night, they received a very hearty welcome. Fortunately they were not disturbed that night; the Blues continued to keep a respectful distance, and the Chouan leaders took advantage of the respite to organise the new recruits which poured in every day. Thanks to the continued and laborious efforts of the chiefs, the insurgents soon presented a compact and orderly force, capable of sustaining a contest with troops of the line even in the open field. The interval of ten days which elapsed between the affair of St. Anne's and their next battle, gave them leisure to take possession of a number of small towns, such as Muzillac, Josselin, Ploermel, &c. &c.; also to complete the supplies of ammunition. In some places the royalists pushed their generosity so far as to melt down their pewter plate for bullets. Whether it was with the consent of the proprietor that the roof of the feudal castle of the princes of Rohan at Josselin was stripped of its lead, no one knows; but the fact is, that it supplied the whole army with bullets. Ingots of gold would have gladdened less the eyes of the insurgents than those loads of lead; and at the moment of the adventurous expedition into the department of Ille-et-Vilaine, the forces had acquired a consistency which astonished the old Chouans.

At the head of the old school was the general-in-chief, De Sol de Grisolles, who had signalised himself in the wars of the Chouannerie, and, except Rohu, was the only surviving contemporary of Georges. But he had now lost all his energy. He was a feeble listless old man, worn out by suffering, and quite unfit for the post which courtesy alone assigned him. Happily La Boissière, who was over the staff, a man of indefatigable vigilance, and very popular, made up for his chief's deficiency. His intelligent sympathy with the

Chapter III

Breton peasantry had given him a more real power over them than his title of commissary-extraordinary to the king. The other chiefs were Rohu, an old Chouan of great vigour, but rugged, and fiercely anti-aristocratic; La Thiesse, whose division had nearly doubled since the victory at St. Anne's; Langourla, and Gamber. Langourla was especially popular for his sad history. He was about to be united, under the happiest auspices, to one whom he tenderly loved, when his bride sickened and died; since which time he had sought death under every form, and seemed to bear a charmed life. The troop of Gamber was remarkable for its religious character. When he had first taken arms, the army was called *L'Armée Catholique*; but its present name was *L'Armée Royale*; and it was his ambition to animate his troops with the old spirit. Often after the exercises of the evening the men might be seen at prayer; and during the march they strode on reciting their rosary, as in the old days of the Chouans. The order and discipline of Gamber's men excited the admiration of the scholars; and they requested their own captain, the Chevalier de Margadel, to give them a drill-sergeant, promising, if he would, to obey like conscripts and fight like veterans. Margadel gave them an old sergeant, who had been wounded at Leipsic, named Bertaud. He was a rough uncouth man, who could not utter a reproof or a word of praise without many unnecessary and unbecoming expletives. But they forgave him every thing when they saw him at work. At the first rattle of the fusillade he rubbed his hair in an ecstasy; his eyes gleamed, his voice deepened, he was all on fire. But notwithstanding their respect for him, the scholars reserved the post of honour for their comrades Nicholas and Bainvel, who, having received the tonsure, were regarded by them as the Lord's anointed.

At every town the inhabitants disputed among themselves who should entertain the boys. The women, especially, fêted them, wept over them, and petted them. Maids and mistresses alike gave up their beds, and mended the garments torn upon the march, while

Battles of St. Anne's, Redon, and Muzillac

the little soldiers slept; and high-born ladies thought it an honour to wait upon their own true knights. On one occasion they had lain down exhausted with hunger and fatigue on the turf of a courtyard, while supper was being prepared. Presently they heard a sweet voice exclaim, "It's the scholars!" The next moment all the windows, which had been hermetically sealed at the approach of the Chouans, were thrown open, and there appeared a number of girls, laughing and looking particularly gracious. It was a boarding-school of young ladies quite as enthusiastic in the cause as themselves. To testify their sympathy, they threw out handfuls of ribbons, white cockades, and flowers; and the most sensible of them abstracted from the larder of the community cakes and other delicacies, which they conveyed to the scholars furtively in their bonnets. Wherever there were women the lads were welcome; and at many inns the good-wife would not accept of payment. "Do you sell wine here?" "O yes, to strangers, but not to you," was the common reply: but sometimes they reckoned upon it too hastily. "Do you sell wine, my good woman?" said a lad, who had not a sou in his pocket; "Yes, my child," was the unexpected answer. "O, then," stammered the disconcerted little fellow, "please to give me some water."

It was at length resolved no longer to wait for the attack of the Blues; but to take the offensive, by falling unawares upon Redon, the small garrison of which were expected to lay down their arms on the approach of so large a body of men. The intention of this movement was to second the general operations of the insurrection, by connecting the Chouans of the Bas Maine with those of La Vendée. To effect this object two preliminary conditions were essential: the first, a decisive victory in La Vendée; the second, a debarcation of arms on the coast of Brittany; and no position was more advantageous than Redon for awaiting these two events.

The day chosen for the expedition marked the great difference between the present insurrection and the old Chouannerie. The army that took Rochfort in 1793 established every where religious

Chapter III

services, the present army did just the reverse; for they selected the octave of Corpus Christi for the attack on Redon, at the imminent risk of interrupting the procession, and causing the Blessed Sacrament to fly as before an army of pagans. But De Sol was not a man to be stopped by such considerations. The chaplains he had provided for the army always carried a bottle of brandy in one pocket to balance the breviary that never came out of the other; and he selected the octave of Corpus Christi for the expedition without scruple.

The secret of their march on Redon had been kept so well, that their appearance on the heights above the town was the first intimation the inhabitants received of their approach. The first object which the army perceived was an altar resplendent with flowers and lights, towards which, with their backs towards the soldiers, a long procession wound, preceded by a cross and banners. Suddenly, as they were looking on, the whole crowd turned round, and the canopy which covered the Blessed Sacrament was seen to retreat with dignity, although in haste. Nothing could be more ill-omened for the royalist troops, who reproached themselves and their leaders for the insult they had offered to their Saviour. They seemed like the Philistines, before whom the ark of God retreated. But the next moment the bells rung out their warning, and the Chouans learned that the garrison, contrary to expectation, intended to contest the day.

An hour before the battle the scholars sent a deputation to the general, to solicit the perilous honour of forming the advanced guard. They were on the point of obtaining their petition, when it was represented that they were the flower of the Armorican youth, and that on them mainly depended the future of the Church in Brittany. Their request was accordingly refused. They were ordered to march in the second rank, to the great indignation of Bertaud their sergeant, who at the first shot disobeyed his orders, and rushed forward to join the fighting in the front. The post coveted by the scholars was assigned to Langourla's troop. The unhappy man here met with the death he had so long and vainly sought. Advancing alone in front of his men, he fell pierced with many balls.

The plan of attack as laid down by the chiefs consisted in investing the town on all sides, and so rendering the flight of the garrison impossible. It had been arranged beforehand that the scholars should take the right, and force their way in face of all obstacles to the *grande rue*; from which they were to turn rapidly, and put the enemy between two fires. When the word "forward" was given, Le Tiec as usual began with one of his martial strains; but he was sternly reproved by Margadel, and bid hold his peace in the ranks. They proceeded silently till they came to a convent, from which the nuns, in their white habits, looked down on the battle, waving their white handkerchiefs, and crying, *Vive le Roi!* and *Vivent les écoliers!* and then they could not suppress a cheer; but presently the balls of the enemy began to whistle in their ears, and they had something else to do.

These shots proceeded from gendarmes who were in ambush in the vines, and caused some disorder in the ranks of the scholars; but the mass of them continued their way in a steady and soldier-like manner, under a fusillade from right and left, till at length they debouched in the *grande rue*. The Chouans, who had preceded them, were held in check by musketry from the windows of the market-stalls, within which the little troop of brave fellows who composed the garrison had retreated. But when the scholars came up they abandoned that position, and shut themselves up in the church-tower.

General de Sol had already failed against this very tower in the year 1799, and now received only insulting answers to his summons to capitulate. In vain the besiegers threatened to burn the building, and under their very eyes proceeded to heap up combustible materials against the wall; the Blues were not to be duped into a surrender by such demonstrations. They knew that the royalists

Chapter III

would never expose a town to conflagration which numbered so many partisans; and the higher the Chouans piled their faggots outside, the keener grew the sarcasms of the soldiers within.

At length night fell, and the tower still held out; and at intervals the fighting continued. Though the Chouans kept carefully out of harm's way, the garrison fired on every spot where the least light or noise indicated the presence of an enemy. From time to time, in the darkness of the night, the tower would be suddenly illumined like a furnace; and the besiegers, thinking this the prelude to a sally, would cry, "To arms!" The cry, repeated by the patrols, was carried from point to point, disturbing every one from food, or sleep, or prayer, as the case might be. So that when morning came, the royalist army were completely exhausted, with the exception of Gamber's company—who had slept back to back in the street, and had set sentinels that they might not be roused from sleep by any false alarm—and the scholars, who had been too tired over-night to be awoke by any alarm at all. They lay all night in the market-stalls, exposed to the first attack in the event of a sally; but they rose in the morning refreshed, and with Gamber's soldiers occupied the attention of the Blues while the rest of the army beat a retreat from the town. If the siege had been maintained but a few hours longer, the garrison must have surrendered from thirst. They had pierced a thick wall to get into the church for the holy water, and on hearing of the departure of the Chouans they ran and cast themselves all black and gasping into the stream.

The loss of the Blues was insignificant, while the Chouans had many killed and wounded, and were in evil case. Their spirits were depressed—they had been beaten. Their ammunition, too, was all but exhausted; and yet they were liable to attack at any moment, and had to protect the embarcation, upon which all the success of the insurrection depended, and which might take place from day to day. To add to their discouragement, they received at this time very painful intelligence from La Vendée. Instead of the great victory

Battles of St. Anne's, Redon, and Muzillac

upon which they had counted, they learned of the death of Louis de Larochejacquelein; and what was worse, of the misunderstanding that had sprung up between the Vendean chiefs.

Under these distressing circumstances, their looks were impatiently turned towards the sea for the promised arms and ammunition. Meanwhile they were in a very precarious state; and instead of encamping boldly in some of the villages on the coast, from which the signal of the convoy could be seen, they were compelled to hide themselves where they could, and prowl about night and day to conceal their position from the Blues. For more than a week they endured great hardships; but the scholars bore up manfully, and put to shame many a desponding old soldier.

On the 8th June they learned that a transport detached from the convoy off Ile-Dieu had come to an anchor in the mouth of the Vilaine, and had brought from four to five thousand muskets and ammunition in abundance. This joyful news inspired the whole army with fresh vigour. They lay down to rest, rejoicing that the next night they should sleep without fear, each with a musket by his side; and they started the next morning to possess themselves of the prize.

On the 9th they slept at Muzillac; and at five o'clock the next morning, while they were all dispersed about among the houses and barns, they were awakened by firing from the advanced guard of the enemy, and in a few minutes the whole army might be seen hurrying down to the bridge which formed the entrance to the town. This bridge would have been surprised but for the vigilance of Cadoudal, who was on the spot to occupy it with five or six of the brave men of Auray till Rohu could come up with his coastmen; and thus defended, it could not possibly be forced. But it might, nevertheless, be turned by a mill-bridge about a quarter of a mile below the town; and there the scholars were ordered to take up their position. As they proceeded to the spot indicated, they soon perceived the enemy across the stream; his van engaged with

Chapter III

Cadoudal and Rohu, his rear concealed by a turn in the road. Some pickets of cavalry occupied the centre; and certain preparations which they perceived in progress among the bushes gave them reason to suspect they should soon hear for the first time the roar of artillery.

And indeed two minutes had scarcely elapsed before they heard a tremendous report and the hoarse whistling of cannon-balls over their heads. Instinctively they bowed to the passing strangers,—an act of courtesy which called down upon them a volley of oaths and sarcasms from their old sergeant. They proceeded, laughing at their own weakness, and inwardly resolved to be more discreet for the future; when poor Le Tiec broke out with one of his chants—

> "If e'er in the heat of the combat I chance
> To be struck to the ground by the point of a lance,
> I will sing;—"

and there his song ended. A ball struck off his head; and his horrified comrades were covered with his blood and brains. Alas, for the credit of the Little Chouannerie! The young lads had not around their hearts the triple panoply of battle, and their ranks were thrown into complete disorder by the sad catastrophe. Some stood still gaping with horror, others ran and embraced the corpse. It was not that they had never looked upon death; but Le Tiec was the favourite of all. This, however, did not last long. The old sergeant called out in a voice of thunder, "Is this the way we have learned war? Have we come here to indulge our feelings, and go into hysterics? What will it be when we are being mowed down by dozens? Right about face!" Conscious of their error, the brave fellows turned, and steeled their hearts for the rest of the day.

They continued their course along the river toward the mill-bridge, while the sharpshooters of the enemy, running parallel with them on the other side, kept up against them a well-directed fire, which the lads unfortunately could not return till they had reached their post, on account of their scarcity of ammunition. At last they took up their position on a rocky knoll which commanded the whole field of battle, forming the extreme right of the line. Between them and Cadoudal, on the extreme left, detachments were drawn up *en echelon* at short intervals and in excellent positions; and the best marksmen were interspersed among the rocks and bushes all along the river. They had some hopes, therefore, of avoiding a defeat, but very little of routing the enemy; for, besides their want of ammunition, a third part of their troops were absent. Gamber had slept at some leagues distance, and had not arrived; yet his battalion were of all others the best suited for a conflict with troops of the line. Secillon's yet more numerous division was also absent, besides the coastmen commanded by Francheville. Thus, with forces reduced one third, and with very little ammunition, they had to engage regular troops, who had all the advantages of cannon, cavalry, and cartridges in abundance.

The firing across the river continued for some time; when General Rousseau, who commanded the Blues in person, was seen to reconnoitre the position in front of the line in order to effect a crossing. The scholars imagined that he was selecting their post for the attempt, and were nerving themselves to contest with their lives every inch of the ground, when suddenly the attack burst upon Cadoudal and his coastmen. The impetuosity of the enemy was so great, that for a moment they seemed to have forced the bridge; but the instant afterwards they were driven back. Then a fresh company of light infantry charged the Chouans; but with less effect. At each repulse of the enemy the boys cheered as only boys can cheer, and felt a thrill of delight as they saw General Rousseau preparing for an attack on their own position.

If the general thought that he could easily cross by the millbridge, and ascend the hill as only defended by a troop of boys, he was woefully mistaken, and must have been astonished at the resistance he encountered. All seemed over at the first shock; but

Chapter III

when the enemy had climbed half-way up the hill, the struggle became more exciting. "Do as I do, my lads," cried Margadel; and rushing forward, he took aim at a Blue who was in advance of the others, and killed him. Nicholas, their captain, not less brave, was about to do the same, when he was shot through the heart, and fell into the arms of his brother, who immediately afterwards was himself killed. By this time the scholars were proof against their feelings, and passed on without so much as knitting their brows. The noise of the discharges, the smoke that blinded their eyes and impeded their breathing, the dizziness of a confused *mêlée*, and the strangeness of fighting,—all conspired to throw them into a state of excitement impossible to describe. The combatants fired upon each other from so short a distance as to burn their clothes, and had at every instant to extinguish the smoking wadding, lest the cartridges should explode in their boxes. At last the cloud cleared away, and the Blues were seen rushing headlong down the field, leaving behind them their dead and wounded; the enthusiastic bravery of the Little Chouans had beaten off the best troops of the line.

This double check appeared to disconcert General Rousseau, and for half an hour there was a pause. It was a golden half-hour for the royalists; for if the Blues had maintained their attack at that point they must have won the day, for the scholars had not two rounds a-piece left, and the rest of the army were scarcely better provided. How anxiously, then, they all looked for some cloud of dust which should betoken the advance of Gamber. But in vain; no cloud was to be seen, although the battle had now lasted four hours. Assistance, however, came from a quarter whence no one expected it. On the border of the *lande* appeared a group of women in white caps and aprons, advancing rapidly towards the army. All supposed that they were coming to share the dangers of the field, in performing works of mercy for the wounded. But they brought neither food nor lint in their aprons, but cartridges with bullets made out of pewter vessels. Without this timely relief, the insurgents must have laid down their arms, instead of returning to the conflict with greater vigour than ever.

The enemy during the respite had dragged their artillery on to a hill on the other side of the valley, opposite that on which the scholars were posted; and had laid out their infantry *en echelon* parallel to the royalist line, with the evident intention of forcing a passage under cover of the battery. The cannon were pointed full on the little clump of scholars, who, without protection, seemed set up as a target for practice. For a moment or two there was an ominous silence maintained, as by mutual consent, in both armies; then came the roar of the cannon-balls whistling over their heads, and crashing among the rocks. To offer the less mark, the lads lay down on their faces at a given signal, and then, when the balls had passed, jumped up and waved their hats and shouted; while the Blues, furious at having to do with a troop of children, as they knew by their treble voices, took the more time to point their pieces, and so allowed the lads to fire at a few sharpshooters who were climbing the hill at their feet.

The gunners had just found the range, and the sharpshooters were increasing in number, when suddenly the firing ceased, and a bustle in the enemy's camp announced that something of importance had occurred in favour of the Chouans. In an instant Rohu, who had mounted to the roof of a shed, as a sailor climbs a mast, cried out to his men, "Gamber! Gamber!" and the cry, repeated from one to another, was passed along the ranks to Cadoudal. It was soon seen that the Blues were in full retreat, and were leaving the royalists masters of the field.

But Gamber and his disciplined Chouans had no idea of arriving merely to see the enemy beat a retreat. He followed them instantly with his single battalion of only four hundred men, and took his measures with so much precision and energy, that even General Rousseau could not withhold his admiration. The

Chapter III

fusillade only lasted five minutes; but it was more murderous to the Blues than the whole of the preceding battle. The scholars would have joined in the pursuit; but Margadel, fearing to see them cut to pieces by the cavalry, who were still in good order, restrained their impetuosity. After a short time the cavalry began to give way under the fusillade; and then the word of command was given, and the lads rushed down the hill pell-mell. But they were stopped by an obstacle which they could not pass. Some of the wounded had dragged themselves out of the way close to the mill-bridge by which the boys were about to cross the river in pursuit, and a few unworthy Chouans were plundering the unfortunate men,—some wounded, some dying, some dead. Indignant at the sight of brutality so unworthy of the holy cause in which they had fought, the generous young lads stopped short to drive off the robbers and mount guard over their wounded foes. It was an affecting sight, to see children, almost suffocated with grief at the death of their companions, guarding the very soldiers from insult who had slain them. An old grenadier, whose hairs had grown grey in battle, lay weltering in a sea of his own blood, with his fists clenched in impotent rage, and cursing the savages who had rifled him of all he possessed; among whom he at first reckoned the scholar who was engaged in defending him. But when he observed his sweet and feminine countenance, the rugged soldier began to weep; and blubbering out some words, certainly not of malediction, fumbled in his pockets for a watch or a purse to give his deliverer. "Those thieves have left me nothing," he said sadly; "but here is a gourd," he added, smiling,—"after five hours' fighting you must be thirsty. Go, my child, drink to my health, and that will do you good and me too." The hero of this little scene was himself doomed to swell the number of the victims of that campaign; it was the young Candal, the weakest and the youngest of all the scholars, but at the same time one of the ablest and the most lamented.

Battles of St. Anne's, Redon, and Muzillac

In order to reap as soon as possible the fruits of their victory, the army received orders to march that same evening for the debarcation as soon as they had taken necessary refreshment. The little town of Muzillac now re-echoed with shouts of joy,—men, women, and children sharing in the general delight. The scholars alone were sad; and before they would consent to recruit their strength with food or rest, they hastened to perform the last duties towards their dead comrades. They took the road to the cemetery of Bourg-Paul; and here, in a common grave, the bodies were laid, amid the sobs and tears even of the villagers who attended the service. It was in these exhibitions of feeling alone that the scholars failed to profit by the lessons of the old sergeant. Whether it was that the passive stoicism which he inculcated was above their years, or that they were animated by a higher courage, certainly they never rose, or they never descended, to his level. When little Leray sat down to cry in the battle from the pain of his wound, which of his comrades thought the less of his courage? Without exactly reasoning upon it, the lads felt that their bravery and the bravery of veteran soldiers were different in kind.

Some days afterwards the *Journal de l'Empire* published a report from General Bigarré on the situation of the department comprised in the thirteenth division, of which he had the command, which contained the following words:

"The Chouans appeared disposed to lay down their arms; with the exception, however, of the pupils of the College of Vannes, who exhibit an obstinacy culpable indeed, but happily not very dangerous."

The undesigned coincidence of this eulogy with their brilliant exploit at Muzillac, which at once justified the praise and contradicted the qualification, had all the effect of an apotheosis among their countrymen. Their name was uttered, not from mouth to mouth, but by all mouths at once. They were proclaimed the *compagnie d'élite*, with all the privileges attached to that designation,

Chapter III

including a double ration; and all the glory of the day was conceded to them, though Cadoudal's coastmen and Gamber's troop had at least an equal claim to it. From that day they became the acknowledged heroes, and the darling favourites of the whole army. To receive a shake of the hand from a scholar was an event to be talked about; the soldiers gave way to them on all occasions, made room for them in the crowded inn, appealed to them in all disputes; and more than once the mere sight of one of their officers quelled a mutiny which the other chiefs could not subdue.

These tokens of sympathy and admiration touched the hearts and perhaps turned the heads of the young scholars; but could not console them for the companions they had lost, especially the brothers Nicholas and Le Tiec. Poor Le Tiec! who could supply thy place? Thy fire and thy voice were buried with thee, and only thy memory now lived in the hearts of thy old comrades. When they set off from Muzillac, instead of the inspiring strains which had hitherto been wont to beguile the road, they now marched silently and with watery eyes. Allio, their corporal, yielded to their entreaties to chant forth one of their favourite marches; but when he attempted to sing, his voice failed in the first stanza. After a while he controlled his emotion, and he continued to be their regimental musician; but he never had the gift of electrifying his hearers as Le Tiec had used to do. He was only a mortal singer—Le Tiec was inspired.

Allio, when he had done singing and fighting, returned to his studies as if nothing had happened. After two or three years he became a priest. But he was a Chouan to his last breath. He lived, poor fellow, a few months too long. He saw the flag he had fought against flying from his own church-tower; and the sight recalling the days of the Little Chouannerie, he had his musket brightened from the rust which had grown on it since 1815; and then, after gazing upon it with affection, he had it laid by his side, and died like a Knight-Templar, holding his weapon in one hand and his crucifix in the other.

Debarcation of arms and defeat at Auray

With a farewell discharge over the remains of their comrade, the scholars followed the main body of the royalist army to Foleu, a town on the Vilaine, which they reached the next morning. Here they found that the fishing-boats of the parish of Billiers, which had been put in requisition for that purpose, had brought up the river five thousand new muskets, with the proper accoutrements, and a good supply of ammunition; these were brought ashore in large chests like coffins, and then followed the artillery, which, although it only consisted of two field-pieces and two howitzers, filled the whole army with transports of joy, as if the bare possession of them rendered their cause invincible. An old *émigré*, named Coissin, who was reported to have served against the Turks as colonel of artillery, was appointed to organise the new service. Unhappily he did not acquit himself with any great skill. The Chouans, however, had full confidence in him, or rather in the guns, which they probably expected would work of themselves; and they boldly made the dust of the high-roads fly under the cannon-wheels, instead of scrambling over fields and stealing along lanes and bye-paths.

The Blues, after their repulse at Muzillac, shrunk from an encounter with the foes who had beaten them half-armed and were now fully equipped. The Chouans, on the other hand, were eager to use their new weapons; and on the fourth or fifth day the two armies met and exchanged a few shots. But General Rousseau declined an engagement, and De Sol would not suffer a pursuit. "It will endanger the convoy," he said. The convoy was to him a sort of palladium of far greater consequence than victory. "We shall easily beat them," said his officers. "Yes, but the convoy!" said De Sol. "If we destroy this column, as we may now, they will never recover the blow!" "Never mind; think of the convoy!" The next day they were warned by the villagers that the Blues would pass in an hour on their way to Ploermel. De Sol was immediately apprised of the fact, and the whole army prepared for the attack. Several chiefs, ambitious of the first onset, had posted themselves in front, when

Chapter III

orders came that they were to abandon their positions, and leave the high-road free to the enemy. Gamber's Chouans cried treason, many threw down their arms in disgust, and the officers all went to expostulate with their infatuated general; but two hours passed in useless recriminations and debate about the convoy before De Sol would give the order to advance; and by that time Rousseau was beyond the reach of pursuit. Some time afterwards De Sol had the mortification of hearing Rousseau say that he had concluded the day lost, and that nothing but the order he had received to effect a junction with General Bigarré at any cost, had induced him to subject his column to what he considered certain destruction.

The next morning numerous vacancies were to be seen in the camp. In the old Chouannerie it was rare for the men to remain for a fortnight together under colours; and although now, thanks to superior discipline, they had been retained for three weeks, it only required an act of folly in their general, like this, to send them away. However, enough remained to constitute a very formidable army, and a second debarcation was expected from day to day, which they considered themselves strong enough to effect at any spot they might choose between Vannes and Lorient. They took the road towards Auray,—a town dear to Breton hearts for its many heroic reminiscences of the old Chouannerie, and the various historical events with which it was connected. But in the height of their security they heard that the two generals Rousseau and Bigarré had effected a junction, and were now approaching at the head of five thousand men. At the same time it was announced that a column from Brest, another from Pontivy, cutting off the road to the forest of Camors, and a third, consisting of gendarmes, custom-officers, and national guards from Vannes, were on their road to hem them in on all sides, and drive them back into the sea.

De Sol was so little prepared for this combination, that he was paying a visit to Admiral Hotham on board his ship when an express summoned him to a council of war. He arrived at the camp

Debarcation of arms and defeat at Auray

on the evening of the 19th June, and found the chiefs in great anxiety. Some wished to evacuate the town for the sake of the inhabitants, upon whom would fall the responsibility of entertaining the army; others said it was necessary to fight on all sides at once, in order to give the Chouans, who were scattered about the country, time to form their respective corps. Poor De Sol, overcome with fatigue, slept during the whole debate, stormy as it was; and on awaking, proceeded to give orders which, from their nature, appeared to have been suggested in his dreams. He sent the weakest of his two battalions to strengthen the company of Baden and Plumergat, which guarded the bridge of St. Goustan, on the Vannes road; the other he directed on the town of Pluvigner, to engage the column from Pontivy; and Cadoudal himself, with the company of Auray, called that day to fight *pro aris et focis*, was posted at the causeway of Trech'-Auray, where he was soon joined by Gamber and Secillon.

At Auray, as at Muzillac, the Chouans were entrenched behind water; but with this difference, that they had six instead of two bridges to defend; that of Trech'-Rouse on the extreme left, defended by La Thiesse; three more below him, behind which several detachments lay in ambush; Trech'-Auray, the most threatened; and St. Goustan on the extreme right towards Vannes. No one appears to have thought of the plan of destroying the intermediate bridges; but such a measure would have certainly simplified the defence, and possibly affected the result of the battle.

A partial fusillade commenced in the afternoon between the sharpshooters on both sides; but General Bigarré would not hazard an engagement while his troops were fatigued by their long march; and he picketed his men in the cloister of St. Anne's, where the sanctity of the place would preserve them, as he knew, from the cannon of the enemy, and where they might procure five good hours of rest, while he kept the Chouans awake by false alarms. Gamber, who perceived Bigarré's design, urged on De Sol the advantage of frustrating it by a night attack upon the Blues, while

Chapter III

yet fatigued and unprepared; but the Chouan general rejected the proposition as too dangerous. Poor Gamber was that night found by the patrol weeping at his post; and on being asked what misfortune had occurred: "None as yet," he replied; "but I weep beforehand for that which *must* take place tomorrow."

At the first dawn Bigarré left his entrenchments, preceded by a detachment of dragoons; and avoiding the bridge at Trech'-Auray, which would have been hotly defended, charged the troops at Trech'-Rouse, carried the causeway by surprise, after a few shots, took possession of the little village of Brech, which was scarcely defended, and formed again on the Pluvigner road, by which he intended to enter Auray that day. The corps which had thus allowed itself to be surprised was the division of Bigrar, famous in the old wars under Guillemot, but, accustomed as it was to rely on its chief, worthless under La Thiesse. By an unpardonable neglect, the little *compagnie d'élite*, which formed the principal force of that division, was left idle in the market-place of Auray, and received no orders till the end of the battle.

Cadoudal, hearing the firing, divined what had taken place, and drew up his men in a *lande* which he had selected for the field of battle on account of the ditches by which it was surrounded on three sides, and behind which the Chouans might fire as behind entrenchments. The evening before he had sent a battalion towards Pluvigner, which he now calculated would take the Blues in the rear. He also expected that Coissin, with his cannon, would be ready to open upon them on their debouching in the *lande*.

Unhappily none of these calculations were verified, and misfortunes thickened upon the devoted army. First, a large part of Secillon's division, having never been under fire, pretended to take the order to retire from Trech'-Auray into the *lande* for a signal of retreat, and fairly turned round and ran away. Their noble chief, ready to tear his hair with indignation, went with the remainder of his men to station himself by Cadoudal, who, and not De Sol, that day really discharged the functions of general, and who was himself furious at a still more serious misfortune. He saw no signs of the cannon on which he had grounded his last hopes of victory. The Marquis de la Boissière galloped off to hasten the march of the artillery, when he was met by Rohu who, in his mad jealousy of the nobles, supposed the major-general to be running away; whereupon he seized hold of his horse's rein, and swore that he should not go a step further. This dispute between the two chiefs threw the whole army into disorder, and the intractable Rohu had only just been made to understand his mistake when the Blues appeared advancing rapidly to the attack.

The battle now commenced in good earnest. Bigarré came on steadily up to the middle of the *lande*, and was preparing to charge the Chouans before him with the bayonet, when Gamber opened upon them a murderous fire in flank, which Cadoudal and Secillon seconded by another not less destructive in front.

Three simultaneous discharges burst like thunder upon the women in Auray, more than three hundred of whom were assisting at the first Mass; and the priest had reached the elevation just as the fusillade began. At once sobs broke forth from all the nave: some old men who were kneeling by the screen of the choir rested their foreheads on the ground; none knew whether they were praying for the living or the dead. Overcome with emotion, the priest well-nigh staggered on the altar-steps, and his hands trembled as he raised the chalice; not only out of sympathy with the afflicted faithful, but at the thought of the bleeding sacrifice which each heart was offering to God in union with the Adorable Victim.

The Blues fell back in dismay at this double fire; and if the detachment from Pluvigner had then arrived, and the cannon had been at hand to support Gamber, Cadoudal, and Secillon, the action might have terminated in their favour; but neither were to be seen, and Bigarré, recovering from the first shock, perceived that, contrary to his expectation, he had the advantage in numbers. He

Chapter III

sent forward a cloud of sharpshooters on either side, which the Chouans could not face without exposing themselves to the fire of the main body. To this manœuvre was added a vigorous charge of cavalry on the fourth side of the *lande*, which was undefended by a ditch. The Chouans knew not which way to turn, or rather they turned their faces all one way, and fled in confusion, some hundreds of them being struck down as they were running; and the central column of the enemy began to march in good order upon Auray.

It is possible that, if the cannon had come up, the brave Chouans who yet stood their ground might have rallied their scattered forces. But the artillery manœuvred that day as if it had been served by Chinese cannoniers. At a great distance there was heard at last the report of one cannon; but Caisson was contented with that heroic achievement. Having been strictly enjoined not to expose his pieces, he judged that he should best fulfil that injunction by not using them at all, and he and his men hid them in a field of wheat as far removed as possible from the scene of action; and with a foresight worthy of their proceedings, left the horses harnessed to the carriages, by which the Blues the next morning not only discovered the cannon, but dragged them off to form the chief ornament of their triumphal entry into Vannes.

Although General Bigarré had thus twice conquered, Chouan obstinacy was not yet subdued, and the action was far from being over. The reserve under Margadel had not been engaged; the blood of the scholars was again to flow, though to less purpose than at Muzillac.

They had spent a joyous night on the *grande place*, dancing and singing, in blissful ignorance of the absurd measures taken by their chiefs, and rose in the morning secure of victory. But that illusion was of short duration; the fusillade which they heard approaching could indicate no success to the Chouans, and before long the multitude of runaways who passed through the town confirmed their fears. At the height of the panic a staff-officer galloped up with the order, "The scholars to the Field of Martyrs!" It was an ominous word for excited imaginations. There had been buried the victims of Quiberon, and the name could never be breathed but the tears would start from every scholar's eye. M. Margadel, who had been half-distracted at the folly with which the battle had been thrown away, at this order forgot every emotion but one of pity for the young victims devoted to slaughter; and dreading lest the impetuosity of the old sergeant should draw his pupils on too far, cried out, "My boys, I will be your chief this day; promise me you will keep by my side, and obey no commands but mine." With one united voice the promise was given, and then all marched to the Field of Martyrs.

The reserve, at the head of which were the company of scholars, had scarcely occupied the edge of a wood skirting the high-road when the Blues appeared at half a musket-shot distance. But as it was less intended to dispute the victory than to sell it as dearly as possible, they waited till the enemy were within pistol-shot, and then fired on the head of the column. The whole of the first rank fell, and the rest stopped short. General Bigarré received a wound which was long considered mortal, and his aide-de-camp fell by his side. But in a few minutes some sharpshooters appeared on the left; and then the boys were exposed to a double fire, which would have terribly thinned their ranks if it had been better directed. As it was, the balls only cut the trees in pieces over their heads, nearly blinding them with falling leaves. Presently the shots began to tell, and then it was that Margadel assumed the authority of a father, and gave the signal for retreat. Several who refused to obey it continued fighting to the last, and died gloriously.

Retreating, they found a second reserve drawn up in the cemetery at the entrance to Auray, consisting of a few brave men who had been hurried along in the general flight, and stopped short to expend their last cartridge. The Blues continued to advance steadily, and even majestically, under a fire from right and left. At the first

Chapter III

round, their sharpshooters scaled the wall of the cemetery; which, however, the lads held long enough to make it doubly a field of death. At the entry of the town a last effort, and the most gallant of all, was made by a gentleman of Auray. M. de Moëslien, putting himself at the head of a brave knot of Chouans, like himself animated with the courage of despair, barred the way against the enemy's column. Thrice he was run through by the bayonets of the grenadiers, thrice he raised his bleeding body to fight again; till, pierced with many wounds, he fell for dead on the pavement. He survived, however, and owed his life to the heroic devotion of his daughter.

The scholars, driven from the cemetery, separated into two parties; some retired to the suburb of St. Goustan, others took the road to Loc-Maria-ker. As these last were flying by the footpath to the lock, they were met by a woman of Spartan spirit: seizing the arm of the first who came up, she compelled him to turn back with his comrades, just at the moment when the imperial troops were about to occupy an important position commanding the suburb of St. Goustan, where the other scholars, and many Chouans, stood firm for three hours longer.

A bridge leads to the suburb; and the Blues, thinking the battle won, were about to cross this bridge, when they were astonished at finding themselves met by a vigorous resistance. In vain they occupied the surrounding eminences, and poured in their fire; the besieged were better marksmen, and replied with advantage. The scholars indemnified themselves during the last act of the bloody drama for their inaction during the two first, and especially Bertaud the sergeant. His retreat from the Field of Martyrs had been like that of a wild boar pursued by the hunters; and not satisfied with his murderous firing, he must now needs add insult to injury. Twice he stepped forward on to the bridge, under a shower of balls; and striking his hand upon his broad chest, offered himself as a mark to the first soldier who could shoot straight. In vain Margadel, in a voice heard above the roar of the battle, commanded him to return to his post,—the intoxication of the fight rendered him deaf to all authority.

All at once the officer at the head of the enemy's sharpshooters called to them to desist from firing, and shouted out the sergeant's name, "Bertaud!" He had recognised in the old Breton a comrade of the 150th, who had fought by his side at Lutzen, Baubzen, and Leipsic. The lion knew the voice of his old general, and the two, dropping their weapons upon the pavement, ran forward and embraced each other in the face of their astonished soldiers.

There was, however, but a brief pause, and the fusillade commenced again. But after three hours' fighting the Chouans were compelled to evacuate the suburb, to avoid being taken between two fires, as the approach of a column of fresh troops from Vannes, with artillery, was announced. Happily it stopped half-way; and as the victorious column was too feeble to pursue them, they effected their retreat on Plumergat as tranquilly as if they had gained the day.

But it was a melancholy tranquillity. Some battalions numbered scarcely enough to form a small company. The band of scholars had not suffered least; besides those who had been seen to fall on the Field of Martyrs, they had to bewail many brave lads who did not answer to their names, and whom nothing but a severe wound or imprisonment could have parted from their comrades. Inquiries were made after two especially, the tall Dagom and the little Lohé, the latter yet limping from a wound received at Redon. They were last seen fighting desperately at the entrance to the town; but a week passed before tidings were received of them. They had endeavoured to make their escape across the bay in a fishing-boat. Being pursued by a revenue cutter, they pointed their bayonets at their unlucky boatman, and compelled him to run before the wind. The cutter gained upon them, and fired; still, they would have been sunk sooner than give in but for the fisherman, who implored them to surrender for the sake of his wife and children,

Chapter III

who were weeping upon their knees on shore. The lads accordingly made a signal of surrender. "Give up your arms," cried the officer imperiously. "Come and take them," replied Lohé; and they threw them into the sea. The lads were taken to the Petit Couvent at Vannes, where Lamenach had been confined. As they were passing through the streets a *fédéré* observed the tall figure of Dagom, and said, "Well, there's a fellow worth powder and shot." "And why is the other worth less?" cried the little Lohé, indignantly. They heard sundry sinister speeches of this kind; but they kept their courage up, and at least their enemies had not the satisfaction of seeing them cowed.

The prisoners at Auray were set at liberty by General Rousseau, who was always distinguished by the generosity of his conduct. At the dinner of the officers, which took place after the battle, not an insulting word was uttered against the vanquished; on the contrary, every one spoke with admiration of the resistance they had met with at several points, as in the *lande* and the Field of Martyrs. One adjutant-major said he would have given his epaulettes for his foes in such a victory not to have been his fellow-citizens. General Bigarré himself, who was wounded, it was feared mortally, gave orders to the troops to respect the persons and property of the royalist party in the town. But for all that he could say and Rousseau could do, neither appeals to honour, nor threats, nor even blows could restrain the evil passions of a set of men better able to tarnish a victory than to gain one. Of these the custom-officers were the worst; they pillaged every house they could enter; and in the suburb of St. Goustan old men and even women were mercilessly slaughtered, whose only crime was that of being found in a house from which the Chouans had fired upon the Blues.

The Blues evacuated the town the next morning, leaving the wounded on both sides indiscriminately mixed together in the hospitals. They carried away their general on a hurdle of oak-branches. Then it was that the cannon of the Chouans were discovered,—a

Defeat at Auray—Victory at Plescop

capture which impressed the victors with the conviction that their foes had been utterly annihilated, as it was impossible to conceive an army who had any hope left, abandoning its artillery. Yet in forty-eight hours the Chouans appeared again in full force, with an heroic reaction of which the old Chouannerie supplies many examples. From cottage to hall the whole population turned out; and many gentlemen who had hitherto remained neutral, joined now at the eleventh hour.

General De Sol shared in the universal excitement; and after the disastrous day at Auray, appeared to have recovered all his former spirit. His lethargy and inertness were exchanged for vigour and impetuosity. He pressed on the new debarcations which had been promised by Admiral Hotham, and which were afterwards successfully effected on three different spots. The very morrow of the defeat at Auray, he sent off Guillemot to Finistère, to possess himself, as he could not fail to do in four or five days, of Guéméné, Gourin, and Cachaix. And when Rousseau resumed the field, not with any serious intention of taking the offensive, but to support the negotiations which General Lamarque had opened with De Sol through Bigarré, the royalist general replied to a summons to lay down his arms in terms as noble as they were laconic; they were as follows: "I shall follow the line of conduct which the king, your master and mine, has prescribed. I warn you only that you will have to answer before him for all the blood that is shed from this day forward." The news of the battle of Waterloo had reached Brittany when this reply was given.

This responsibility did not seem to weigh much with Bigarré, for he instantly prepared for a continuance of hostilities; and on the 5th July a girl, barefoot and dishevelled, ran from Plescop to announce the advance of a column of the enemy. Never since the campaign commenced had news been received with equal joy. The prospect of revenging the blood of their comrades at Auray animated every heart. The legion, at the head of which were the scholars, began the march, or rather the race; for they rushed on,

Chapter III

lest Gamber should beat the foe before they could arrive. But the lads outstripped the whole army, and gathered the first-fruits of the fusillade. In the smoke and confusion the rest of the Chouans shot at random, and their balls went closer to the *compagnie d'élite*, who were engaged in front, than to the Blues. But although the Blues suffered little from the fire, they suffered greatly from the reports, which, reverberating from a wood of willows near, struck terror into their craven hearts. They were drawn up clumsily upon a *lande*. Now then for a movement which the scholars had long and anxiously longed for an opportunity of practising, that is to say, a charge of bayonets. With their pieces levelled, and all ready for the word of command, they were waiting to rush upon the foe, when a derisive shout set up by the soldiers of Gamber at an unhappy Chouan gentleman from Gand, who, as soon as the balls began to whistle in his ears, lay down on his stomach for safety, rent the air; and the Blues, not understanding the cry, and anticipating a general charge of the whole line, turned round and scampered away; and a laughable rout it was. Away they went, tumbling and rolling about, casting away muskets, shakos, and cartridge-boxes, whatever could hinder their flight, raising their arms to heaven, and falling from sheer terror. The nimblest rushed towards the sea, and took refuge among the isles of Morbihan. Some gained the Isle of Monks, where they thought themselves so little in safety, that they confessed instantly to the curé of the parish, as if their last hour had arrived. Great was the joy of the Chouans at their victory; but they were intensely disgusted at finding their foes so unworthy of their arms. The mass of the cowards took the road to Vannes, whither the temptation was very great of following them; but happily it was not irresistible. To have shed blood in the capture of a place which would certainly be theirs in a few days without any such cost, would have been a wanton act of barbarity. A few scholars only indulged in two or three shots, for the sake of terrifying their old enemies, and after that harmless manifestation retired.

Chapter IV

Pacification—Triumphant entry into Vannes—The Cross of the Legion of Honour awarded to the most worthy.

FROM THE DATE of the victory at Plescop, the Blues abandoned the field, and left the whole country in the hands of the insurgents, with the exception of a few fortified towns, such as Vannes. Recruits poured into the Chouan camp, which was stationed at Muzillac, and the debarcations effected by Admiral Hotham proved insufficient for the numbers. General Rousseau then endeavoured to make terms with De Sol; but the demands, as coming from a conquered party, were too extravagant to be entertained for a moment. He threatened accordingly to join the army of the Loire, and organise a fresh campaign.

Meanwhile the demon of discord had flung a brand into the Chouan camp, which threatened to give the civil war a very unexpected turn.

It was reported, that among the arms landed by Admiral Hotham were some of a much lighter construction than the rest; and the boys, who were the darlings of all the old Chouans, were recommended to apply for these, because their shoulders were much galled by the heavy English muskets they had carried so long. They made the demand, with little expectation of being refused. But they were told rather dryly that those carbines had another destination, and that the English fleet had not been chartered to gratify the caprice of children. At these words the youngest of the petitioners pulled off his shirt, and showed his raw and bleeding

Chapter IV

shoulder. This argument, which they had reserved to the last as irresistible, had as little effect as their words; the officers only laughed, and they went away in a rage.

For some days they had known that another *compagnie d'élite*, consisting chiefly of obscure country gentlemen, who had only then joined the army, was in course of formation. To these were intrusted the weapons in dispute. With what bitterness did the poor scholars, who had sacrificed their all for the cause, and shed their blood on four fields in its defence, witness the promotion of this new troop—doubly their rivals, in name and weapon; although they had shared no dangers and won no laurels to entitle them to the distinction!

The next day, about noon, a courier arrived to announce that General Rousseau was on his road, determined to beat the Chouans or die in the attempt. By way of salve to their injured vanity, the scholars were allotted the post of honour as of danger at the head of the line. "And why does not the other *compagnie d'élite* march with us?" they asked; "we should like to see those fine gentlemen handle the weapons they have stolen from us." "Do your duty, and they will do theirs," said the aide-de-camp emphatically; "their post is inside the town, about the person of the general; and they have promised to make a rampart round him with their bodies."

This gave the finishing stroke to the sedition. Some of the boys cried, "We refuse to march;" others stormed against the staff, the general, and *his compagnie d'élite*. The tumult extended to the coastmen of Cadoudal and the peasants of Gamber, who, not less indignant, joined their clamours with those of the boys, and confirmed them in their mutinous determination. At last De Sol sent Margadel to exert his influence over the scholars, and they consented to fight as they were ordered; but they determined,—and in this determination they were confirmed by their hardy allies,— that if the other *compagnie d'élite* did not fight with the Blues, they would compel them to fight. Happily for all the battle never took

Pacification

place. General Rousseau was too humane and too able a man to attempt a stroke as useless as it would have been bloody; his only design, in this false alarm, had been to wring from the Chouans the dishonourable terms upon which he had insisted. But General De Sol adhered to his original resolution, and was careful to show that he was not to be frightened into submission. Whenever a parliamentary enemy paid a visit to the camp, he displayed before his astonished eyes the resources of the Chouan army—their six field-pieces, now served by Hanoverian cannoniers—their two howitzers, and their two twenty-four pounders—their well-armed troops and military organisation.

At last peace was concluded on somewhat regular terms. It was arranged that the Chouans should occupy the suburbs of Vannes; and that the Blues should remain masters of the town, where the tricolor flag should continue to float as heretofore. The good feeling which now existed between the two armies, the reciprocal esteem and desire to know more of each other, were the best guarantees for the preservation of peace. Above all, this chivalrous spirit was exhibited by the scholars, who looked forward with intense eagerness to the day when they should enter the walls in triumph from which, a few months before, they had fled as from a prison.

One ornament was wanting for their full triumph—the white satin flag which had figured in the fêtes of the preceding year, and on which the device GOD AND THE KING had been wrought in gold letters. Some little scholars, who came to see them at the town of Theix, when they made their final halt before the grand entry, informed them that the old principal had erased these words. A loud cry of indignation burst from them at an offence against both divine and human majesty. Some of the scholars proposed to seize the principal by night, and take him with his hands bound and a rope round his neck to do penance before the Calvary. Others,—and their counsel prevailed,—proposed to summon him, under pain of corporal chastisement, to deliver the flag, repaired, within

Chapter IV

four-and-twenty hours. Young Rio, who had returned the spirited reply to the principal when asked to surrender his cross, was commissioned to draw up a summons in terms sufficiently peremptory to act both as a warning and as a reproof. The letter succeeded; the flag arrived within the specified time.

Throughout the whole affair, Rio, although the youngest of the officers, had been the most distinguished, as well for his cleverness in managing the insurrection as his personal gallantry in battle. The next morning he was appointed to command the van on the entry into Vannes. But knowing it to be a mere ceremony of no military importance, he abandoned the post of honour in his eagerness to see his mother, who lived in the city. As soon as the officer had gone his rounds, he galloped off, assured that the Blues would not refuse to let him pass. To the *Qui vive* of the sentinel he answered, "*Officier des Ecoliers*;" and the words acted as a talisman on the lieutenant and soldiers who were stationed at the outposts. They belonged to the 75th of the line, and it was from their ranks that the balls had sped which laid low so many of his comrades at Muzillac. The lieutenant, moved by the recollection of that day, the glory of which he attributed chiefly to the scholars, was yet more affected when he heard that the young hero was bound on a pilgrimage of filial affection. "I, too, have a mother," he said, grasping his hand; "and I envy you your happiness in embracing yours."

On entering the suburb Rio met with a reception not less gracious; although the imprudent scholar had attached to his arm the badge of his degree, viz. a scarf of white silk fringed with gold. On his return from his mother's house at daybreak through the deserted streets, he saw an old man, pale and pensive, wandering alone like a ghost that had outstayed the dawn. It was the old principal, to whom he had just written that insulting summons. Overcome with shame, he would have passed by; but the generous old man clasped him in a warm embrace, only saying, "My dear friend, I recognised the hand well enough, but not the heart." Speechless with remorse, the lad answered not a word at the time; but he afterwards publicly made atonement for his fault.

When the day was fixed for the grand entry into Vannes, the question arose as to which corps should have the privilege of marching at the head of all the rest. The old Chouans settled it from the first in favour of the scholars; but the authorities would gladly have taken revenge upon them for their recent mutinous behaviour, by conferring the honour upon the other *compagnie d'élite*. At the first intimation of their design, the men of Gamber and Cadoudal expressed their indignation; and the battalion of Lainer declared that they would not swallow the dust of those fine gentlemen; and if they attempted to go first, they would fire upon them. Upon this the scholars' claim was admitted; and it was settled that, besides the privilege of marching in front, they should bear sprigs of oak in their muskets. The honour of bearing their flag was awarded to Le Quellec.

It requires no diviner's rod to conjure up the joyful faces and motley appearance of the scholars on this their golden day. We see them even now as they proudly march, their eyes glistening with delight and tears, their shoes and garments tattered and torn; we see the women sobbing as they pass, their mothers and sisters swelling with pride, the little boys cheering, and even their old foes, not a few of whom are turned to friends, unable to refuse the tribute of their admiration. Not the least part of their glory is the contrast between them and the rival company, whose elegant clothes are innocent of brambles—who have known no nightly bivouac, who bear arms that have never been discharged, and cartridge-boxes that have never been emptied.

The next morning the scholars repaired to the church of St. Patern, to sing a *Te Deum* in thanksgiving for the success granted to their arms, and all the population of the suburb accompanied them. The marks of kindness which were lavished upon them rendered their intercourse easy with all, even with those against whom

Chapter IV

they had just cause for resentment, as the persecutors of Lamenach. General Rousseau was so popular among them, that they offered to mount guard at his quarters; soldiers and scholars fraternised with each other, and those became intimate friends and associates who had known each other only as mortal and implacable foes at Muzillac or Auray.

When the capitulation had been completed, and the gates of the town were thrown open to the royalist army, these manifestations of friendship were redoubled. Before taking possession all assisted at a solemn Mass, which was celebrated by the Bishop on a spacious public parade, in order that the two armies, united at the foot of the same altar, might exhibit to the inhabitants the example of reconciliation. Most striking was the scene at the moment of the elevation—on one side the Blues, drawn up in line with one knee on the ground, on the other the peasants, some prostrate in adoration, some reciting the rosary, all praying with the utmost fervour. At the same instant the drums beat, and the cannon thundered forth. It was the culminating point of that solemn ceremony; the next moment the troops of the line unfurled the colours against which they had been so lately fighting. From that day forward there was but one army under one flag in Brittany, and Chouans with their chiefs acted under the orders of General Rousseau.

Two months elapsed between the capitulation of Vannes and the disbanding of the Chouans; but at the end of August the classes of the college opened again. Scarcely a scholar was missing except the glorious dead; all had returned to finish their studies. But of the professors there was more than one vacant place. Those who were most gravely compromised by their imperialist predilections had wisely resigned their appointments. Yet many of those who retained their chairs stood in need of considerable indulgence from their valorous pupils,—the poor principal himself not least of all; and then it was that Rio, who had written the insulting summons, repaired his fault by reconciling the master and the scholars.

Triumphant entry into Vannes

The college found itself possessed of a fame it had never enjoyed before. It became the chief lion of the department: every great personage paid it a public visit, and no stranger would leave the neighbourhood without first seeing the now celebrated spot.

The anniversaries of the Little Chouannerie became most important days in the calendar of the college. The taking of the oath, each comrade who had fallen, every battle that had been fought was commemorated in turn. But the victory at St. Anne's was the great feast of all. On the first return of this day, the whole school set off at sunrise in grand procession, bearing their famous flag. The Chevalier de Margadel accompanied the boys as a simple pilgrim. The command devolved on young Rio, in the absence of his elder comrades, Bainvel and Le Quellec. They arrived at St. Anne's amidst the ringing of the church-bells and the greetings and cheers of an immense multitude. After High Mass, they sang a *Te Deum*, which might have been heard at half-a-league's distance. The crowd was so great, that nine-tenths of the worshippers knelt outside on the grass of the churchyard. Afterwards there was a feast, given by the Jesuit Fathers, who had lately been established at St. Anne's; and then the little heroes returned to Vannes, exhausted less with fatigue than with the fervour of their emotions.

The story of the Little Chouannerie was made known to Louis XVIII. A detailed account, drawn up by a well-wisher of the college, was forwarded to his majesty, and drew tears from the royal family on its recital. Lainé, minister of the interior, caused it to be intimated to the boys that their services should be worthily rewarded. However, a long time elapsed before this pledge was redeemed. At length the royal decree appeared in the *Moniteur*. Its rewards were magnificent, far beyond the modest pretensions of the scholars. The devotion of the poor fellows who had been killed or wounded was recompensed by pensions to their families or themselves. Several exhibitions were founded in perpetuity in the college which the young warriors had rendered for ever illustrious; and finally,

Chapter IV

three officers, of whom Rio was the only one still a student of the College of Vannes, were named Chevaliers of the Legion of Honour. For him was reserved the highest distinction on the solemn occasion when the crosses were conferred.

During the brief and glorious campaign in which he had played so distinguished a part, Rio had had for his comrade one a little older than himself, who doubled his own watchings, fatigues, and privations, that he might lighten the burden for his friend; and in the evening, after the longest marches, made him pray before falling asleep that death might never come upon him unawares. When the auspicious day arrived which was to witness the decoration of the young heroes, Rio and his faithful friend knelt together to receive the cross of honour.

Here we may pause a moment to relate an incident which occurred long after the events just related. More than five-and-twenty years had gone by, when a priest and an eminent artist met in the saloons of Versailles. The former chanced to speak in tenderest terms of his own dear Brittany; on which the other remarked, that he also loved that country, although at the battle of Auray, in 1815, he had nearly lost his life there. With something of hesitation, the ecclesiastic asked under which flag he was fighting; to which the artist replied, that he was one of the young *fédérés* of Rennes, who had taken the field for the express purpose of acting against the scholars of Vannes. The priest's attention was excited, and he listened eagerly as his companion went on to relate how, at the attack on Auray, they had obtained from General Bigarré the favour of marching in the van in order that they might try their strength with the royalist students. "A few paces before me," he continued, "I saw the captain of the scholars—I think I see him still, in his black habit, musket in hand, with a white riband on his left arm. In the excitement of the moment, I led on my men to the charge; and when close upon him, I fired at my adversary, who at the same instant levelled his piece at me, and I fell to the ground pierced through by his ball."

The Cross of the Legion of Honour

It may be imagined with what feelings the good Abbé Bainvel, for he it was, listened to this recital of an incident in his life which he had never forgotten. He thought he had killed his opponent, and had never ceased to remember him in his prayers, and, since he had become a priest, to say Mass for the repose of the soul of his unknown victim on the 21st of June. Who can describe the joy he experienced when he discovered that all the *De Profundis* he had said had missed of their object! Knowing the generous character of the man with whom he was conversing, he told him at once who had been his antagonist on that memorable occasion. The two gazed for a moment in each other's faces, then, as the tears sprang into their eyes,—tears which were shared by the bystanders who had heard the touching narrative,—the once mortal foes cordially embraced.

But to return to the closing scene of our narrative. The altar was reared on the mournful field by the banks of the Garonne hallowed by the glorious deaths of the brave. Meet it was that the joyful ceremony should be ushered in by a requiem for the dead. The authorities, civil and military, assisted in full costume. The garrison was there with its music. The inhabitants of the town and suburbs, and a crowd of Chouans from all the neighbouring cantons, flocked to take part in the service. But not as to a funeral ceremony, or in mournful guise,—all came in gala dress, with their thoughts more on the living than the dead; for it was known that the honours of the day were designed for the scholars of the college, and for their sakes the beauties of Brittany appeared in their gayest attire.

A requiem Mass, and a chivalrous ceremony, in which fair dames took part as in the middle ages, appeared to no one an incongruous union. As soon as the celebrant had descended from the steps of the altar, two ladies splendidly dressed ascended in his place. She who, as the wife of the chief magistrate of the department, occupied the right, was a venerable matron of a gentle and noble presence. But her companion was the object of universal admiration, not only

Chapter IV

from her exceeding beauty, but also from the grace and charm of her whole bearing. When they were seated, the officer who presided at the ceremonial, after addressing a few words to the latter, went down the church to seek the chevaliers-elect. The joy of the young Rio may be imagined, who, from his youth and station, had anticipated no such mark of distinction, when he was informed that he was not only to receive his cross of the Legion of Honour from the hands of Mademoiselle d'Olonne, but also to have the privilege of saluting her on both her cheeks. He had to summon up all his Breton *naïveté* not to be a little bashful at this double kiss on the very steps of the altar, before so great a multitude; but the spectators were not in a disposition to be too critical. When the youths, at once friends, brothers-in-arms, and companions in study, advanced to receive the prize of valour, shouts of applause burst from every side; at the most interesting part of the ceremony the shouts redoubled, and they became absolutely deafening when Mademoiselle d'Olonne, herself an object of enthusiasm, graciously returned the salute she had received from her chevalier. As for the lad himself, so bewildered was he with delight, that the friendly arm of a comrade was needed to assist him down the steps. His head was fairly dizzy with the height of glory to which he had been raised.

Nor did his glory set with that day's sun. When he returned to Vannes with his cross of honour, to which he joined sometimes the cross of his class,—that cross he had once defended with so much spirit,—he became for several months a new attraction for visitors to the college. His comrades were proud of their hero, and the very townspeople also joined in the general enthusiasm in his honour. Twice a day, on his way to and from the college, he had to pass before a *corps de garde* which had been established within the precincts of the church, and twice a day a group collected on the *grande place* to see the sentinel render him military honours.

And all this took place in front of the very gate over which was once painted, for the discomfiture of the scholars, the unhappy bird whose fortunes have been already related, but whose effigy was now superseded by ingenious emblems, intended to transmit their triumph to posterity. Alas for the vanity of human expectations! A few years more, and the revolution of July treated the inscriptions and symbols of the boys, their *fleurs-de-lis*, and their white banners, as they had treated the imperial eagle. So passes away the glory of the world. On the portal of the College of Vannes now exists no memorial of the feats of the Little Chouannerie.

OTHER TITLES AVAILABLE FROM ST. AIDAN PRESS

View a sample chapter from each title at www.staidanpress.com.

CATHOLICISM AND SCOTLAND
by Compton Mackenzie

Much has been written about the desperate fight that English Catholics waged to keep the Faith, but Scotland's Catholic history is little known. Have you ever heard of David Beaton, Cardinal Archbishop of St. Andrews, and his struggles? Or of Fr. Ninian Winzet, who boldly challenged Calvinist champion John Knox to a public debate? Read this book and find out about the Scots who sought to defend their country and their Faith from the onslaught of Protestantism.

$12.00 — 138 pages. Available at amazon.com.

FICTION

THE QUEEN'S TRAGEDY
by Msgr. Robert Hugh Benson

"Upon the publication of former books of mine several kindly critics remarked that the reign of Mary Tudor told a very different story with regard to the Catholic character. It is that story which I am now attempting to set forth as honestly as I can."

$19.00 — 364 pages. Available at amazon.com.

THE NET
by Agnes Blundell

"Roger felt a freezing dew break out upon his forehead. The net was over him it seemed; in vain he told himself that he could establish his identity. His head was worth forty pounds to the vile creatures at the stair foot, and once in their clutches who knew if he could ever communicate with his friends?... Gaolers and pursuivants alike fattened on the traffic in human life and divided the spoils. Judges were as careless as callous."

$16.00 — 264 pages. Available at amazon.com.

THE ANCHORHOLD
by Enid Dinnis

Editha de Beauville had all that the world could offer: wealth, wit, and beauty. Yet a chaplain's sermon drove her to give up all this, and enter the religious life. But could a proud, strong-willed noblewoman accept and embrace the poverty and self-abnegation of the religious life, particularly that of full seclusion in an anchorhold? A difficult path lay before Editha. Read on to learn how she fared, and how her life affected those around her, including Sir Aleric, her erstwhile suitor, now a crusader knight; Fr. Nicholas, a young priest who was quite bright, and thought so too; and Fiddlemee, the witty yet wise court jester whose past held a surprising secret.

$14.00 — 194 pages. Available at amazon.com.

THE SHEPHERD OF WEEPINGWOLD
by Enid Dinnis

Sir Robert Luffkyn, rich grandson of a peasant, has purchased the manor of Weepingwold from the noble but impoverished de Lessels, intending to make the renamed Luffkynwold a busy center of his tanning trade. He sends Petronilla, last de Lessels, to Gracerood, intending her for its future Abbess, and plucks little Brother Kit from the cloister to become the new parson of the long-abandoned church. How will Father Kit fare with the parish and his own soul? What is Petronilla's true vocation? And is there really a witch in the parish?

$14.00 — 202 pages. Available at amazon.com.

SCOUTING FOR SECRET SERVICE
by Fr. Bernard F. J. Dooley

Frank and George are going to spend their summer vacation in the Adirondacks, thanks to Frank's uncle Ed. But once they get there, they realize something fishy is going on. Can they trust Pete, their Indian guide, or is he mixed up in it too? And is Frank's mysterious uncle really behind it all?

$14.00 — 188 pages. Available at amazon.com.

WILL MEN BE LIKE GODS? & THE SHADOW ON THE EARTH
by Fr. Owen Francis Dudley

Father Dudley's first two books on human happiness are published together here—his rare collection of essays together with a novel which illustrates the essays and introduces his most famous character, the Masterful Monk.

$15.00 — 216 pages. Available at amazon.com.

CANDLELIGHT ATTIC AND ODD JOB'S
by Cecily Hallack

Here are seven true stories in honour of the Seven Joys of Our Blessed Lady, and ten more invented ones about the delightful Barnabas Job, to make a comfortable book for those who are afraid of the dark.

$14.00 — 192 pages. Available at amazon.com.

THE HAPPINESS OF FATHER HAPPÉ
by Cecily Hallack

Shingle Bay did not know what to make of Fr. Savinius Happé. He was a cheerful, rotund Franciscan, a famous author of books on everything from Etruscan civilization to Alpine meadows to beetles, and someone who had never quite mastered the English language. His jovial demeanor concealed a wisdom that alternately bewildered, astonished, but ultimately won over the people of Shingle Bay.

$10.00 — 112 pages. Available at amazon.com.

CON OF MISTY MOUNTAIN
by Mary T. Waggaman

"It had been a long night for Con. Just what had happened to him he was at first too dazed to know. Dennis had flung him into the smoking-room with no very gentle hand, turned the key and left him to himself. And, sinking down dully upon a rug that felt very soft and warm after the hard flight over the mountain, Con was glad to rest his bruised, aching limbs, his dizzy head, without any thought of what was to come upon him next."

$14.00 — 190 pages. Available at amazon.com.

www.ingramcontent.com/pod-product-compliance
Lightning Source LLC
Chambersburg PA
CBHW022000100426
42738CB00042B/971